MEDIÆVAL ENGLAND

SIR GEOFFREY LOUTTREL ARMED BY HIS LADIES.

C. 1340.

Mediæval England

1066—1350

BY

MARY BATESON

BOOKS FOR LIBRARIES PRESS
FREEPORT, NEW YORK

First Published 1903
Reprinted 1971

DA175
B32

INTERNATIONAL STANDARD BOOK NUMBER:
0-8369-5725-3

LIBRARY OF CONGRESS CATALOG CARD NUMBER:
70-152973

PRINTED IN THE UNITED STATES OF AMERICA

PREFACE

INASMUCH as English and American readers are abundantly supplied with narrative political histories of England, I have chosen in telling the story of Mediæval England to treat the theme from a point of view which is not exactly that of the other volumes of the present Series. My object has been to keep social rather than political facts in view, and throughout to supply by illustration from contemporary accounts some of the characteristic detail which is apt to be crowded out in political histories. The story of social evolution may fairly be called the national story. The political story brings to view the procession of great events, the social story the procession of dead ancestors who acted, howsoever humbly, their part in shaping those events. In political history we see the trophies borne along in the triumphal cars, and in social history the groups of ordinary men, women, and children who fill the carriages or stream along on foot. There is not one way, but rather there are many ways of telling a nation's story: the growth of governmental institutions, fluctuations in territorial expansion, the spread of commerce, changes in foreign relations, the history of methods of thought, all make urgent claim to consideration. But not the least truthful measure of progress lies in those superficial indications of civilisation which are set aside as the province of social history. In the mediæval Englishman's domesticity there is an epitome of the life of the nation : English private life has its unity, its episodes and catastrophes, which reflect the shifting lights and shadows of the national story. The private history of kings and princes, nobility, clergy and commons, has become now, with the progress of historical study, a theme more easy of treatment than it was a while ago. Changes in the social relations of the classes of men can now be traced, changes that have had their part in shaping the story of a nation, no less than the evolution of the agencies of government, the historic series of victories and defeats, gains and losses of territory, the happy or the luckless political chance, the fateful power of the point of time. A history of mediæval civilisation that gives a hurried sequence of events is like a novel which never shows the characters save under the stress of conspiring fate, creatures not mortal because they never sleep or eat. It was certainly not rapidity in the movement of life which gives the English Middle Ages their peculiar colour.

In attempting to give a sense of the reality of the past, illustration in matters of historic detail seems in place, rather than a dogmatic teaching that is apt to

fill the sceptical with mistrust ; and it has seemed not
merely easier but wiser to handle only a few subjects,
and those the subjects of which most record has
been left. Undoubtedly it is hard to bring our
mediæval forefathers before the eye as they once
lived and moved and had their being. Contemporary pictures will not do the work for us ; the
monuments preserved in manuscripts and sculpture
often, for the earlier period at least, seem grotesque
by reason of the primitive character of mediæval
drawing and perspective. The men and women
appear misshapen, the houses and buildings are
ready to topple over at a touch. For reasons of a
somewhat similar kind we have lost the power of
conceiving much of their thought, and we are apt to
view with a half-pitying contempt the great folios of
their theologians, philosophers and legists, because for
very weariness of the flesh we cannot read them.
What seems grotesque in art or thought soon ceases
to charm. Yet surely there are living evidences
which bid us realise that in some respects our
ancestors were great where we are small. When
the list of their greatest conceptions is made out,
it may well seem that there were giants in the
land in those days, compared with whom we are
but pigmies. Much that they conceived and built
we can only admire and imitate. Though our
knowledge and much that we consider essential to
our world did not belong to them, yet our institutions are for the most part of their shaping. The
works of their hands and brains we have taken over
in their entirety, adapting them to modern needs.

It is no primitive or low civilisation that we have to describe in the England of 1066–1350 ; it differs from ours more in kind than in degree. In its own kind we cannot deny its majesty, for, though we may not always realise it, it still has dominion over us.

Further, it is to be remembered that the English Middle Ages are in their main character one with the continental Middle Ages : in certain aspects only have they a character peculiarly their own. In this volume the evidence must be strictly confined to England ; but to those who read the mediæval evidences it needs not to be said that much which is true of our country at that time is true also of others. Insularity was not in the Middle Ages a predominant English character. Our original oneness with the continent and the lines of our later divergence become most perceptible to us when we travel in Europe, for it is upon the continent that we most often come across some of the outward signs of mediæval life.

It may be that we stand nearest to the Middle Ages in churches, in market-places, at the toll-bar, in the courts of law, in the two old English universities, in pageants and processions ; but wherever we are, the past is never at any time far from us. The ghosts of our predecessors haunt us, whether we know it or not, whether we wish it or not : our speech, our thoughts are in the main those that they gave us. As age succeeds to age, the past, in its religion, its law, its life, may fossilise, but the petrified matter becomes imperishable.

Chronological tables have been provided to supplement the references of the text. A word of apology for the choice of the date 1250 as dividing two periods may be deemed necessary inasmuch as it may appear to be a date arbitrarily selected for the purpose of obtaining an equal division. It can be defended, I think, upon two grounds. The middle of the century marks a real epoch in the history of thought, inasmuch as it was about that time that Roger Bacon began to lecture and write in Oxford, and, further, it has seemed better to take the era of Simon de Montfort's activity in constitution-making with that of Edward I., who learned so much from his example, than to divide at Henry III.'s death in 1272.

I have drawn up no list of the writers, living or dead, whose works have been guides to me in compiling this book, as in common gratitude I should like to do. That I have drawn freely from many sources, and not least from books that have been published comparatively lately, must be obvious. A long list would be out of place in a book of this size, and a short list would be unsatisfactory. The acknowledgments of those who compile from the original labours of others must generally be silent, and in the present case they would have little worth.

M. B.

CONTENTS

PART I.

NORMAN FEUDALISM, 1066-1154

I.

I *

PART III.

DECADENT FEUDALISM, 1250-1350

XIII.

XIV.

XV.

XVI.

LIST OF ILLUSTRATIONS

xxi

ERRATUM

In the map of London, p. 265, Langbourne should appear as a street, not a stream : see Lethaby, *London before the Conquest.*

COOKING FROM THE BAYEUX TAPESTRY.

MEDIÆVAL ENGLAND

PART I

NORMAN FEUDALISM

(1066–1154)

I

THE KING AND HIS HOUSEHOLD

1. Nature of the Conqueror's feudalism—2. The officers of the royal household and their fees—3. Royal residences and building of the Tower—4. Character of the royal expenses, dress, manners, and education.

1. DURING the reigns of the four Norman kings, England was as it were violently caught up by the irresistible Norman torrent and swept out of its back-water into the main stream of continental civilisation. Saxon England had had a civilisation of its own, and brought a wealth of treasure and of ideas to

its new governors so great as to secure for it the first
place among its lord's possessions. England was no
mere appendage to Normandy, with London suffragan
to Rouen ; from the first it was clear that the kingdom
would precede the duchy. To the newly-conquered
kingdom the conquerors brought all they had to give,
and the chief part of their wealth lay in their continental ideas, which put new life into Church and
State. As he owed much to the papacy, which was
now to enter upon a new era, characterised by novel
and ambitious schemes, it was certain that William I.
would bring the English church into line with his
Norman church : he was prepared to distinguish
things spiritual from things temporal, and let his own
masterful wielding of the temporal sword measure
the strength of the spiritual. In his time there would
be no war on the frontier of the spiritual and temporal
kingdoms. Further he brought with him men of all
ranks of society and from many countries, imbued with
the doctrines of continental feudalism. William and
his ministers found English society already half
feudalised, but without cohesion and almost anarchic,
with tribal elements still only half absorbed, a
society so wanting in symmetry and system as to
have little to commend it to Norman ideas of government. But as in feudalism there was danger of
conflict among the many temporal swords, here, too,
William the Conqueror saw to it that the royal sword,
while he wielded it, should be supreme. The feudalism which he brought with him placed him merely
as " primus inter pares " : that was a position not good
enough for him ; he aimed at and secured a mastery.

The fabric of society as it was woven by him was of course to be woven of tenurial relations, for no western European could conceive of social relations of any other web, but in woof and warp he introduced a strand of governmental power which was not of tenure.   With marvellous vigour king after king carried on his work.   Only the reign of Stephen shows by contrast how great was the accomplishment of his predecessors and successors.   It was then and then only that the spiritual sword and the baronial swords were uppermost.

What manner of men were these great rulers ?   Can they be approached at all in their daily lives and be seen otherwise than as governors?   Little attention, comparatively speaking, has been paid to the social life of the Normans in England, and yet many difficulties in the understanding of larger themes are best removed by understanding the many characteristic phrases or expressions descriptive of daily life which give colour to the chronicles of the past.   The Normans were capable of carrying out schemes of a particular nature, partly by reason of their peculiar domestic civilisation.   The evidence descriptive of the life of the Norman kings in England is not abundant, for their palaces are almost wholly swept away ; almost all the records of their expenses have vanished ; their letters are few in number and formal in character ; ·no chronicle describes their courts in detail.   Furthermore, much of their life was spent across the Channel, and their interests were centred largely in the land they came from, so that some of the evidence we have is relevant rather to the Norman duchy than to the English realm. Nevertheless, the fragments of evidence that remain, the entries in Domesday Book, and the statements made touching Henry I.'s reforms in his court are not inadequate to give a detailed picture.

2. The increase in royal dignity which followed on the Norman Conquest was merely one symptom of the nature of the change that had come over England. The Norman court was better planned than the royal household of Anglo-Saxon times, so far as we know it. Both had grown out of the Germanic idea of the household, with its reeve, dish-thegn, cup-bearer, and staller, but in the Norman ducal household these officers had been reinforced by many others. Household departments were multiplied, and under each head of a department (whose office tended to become hereditary and one of dignity only), there were the numerous servants doing the domestic duties. The Norman "curia" was capable of Protean changes of character, adapting itself according to circumstance as an ambulatory household, a camp, a tribunal, a council of war, an administrative or political assembly. Inasmuch as the king's household was the nursery in which were trained and reared the great officers of State, a peculiar interest attaches to offices that sound humble enough. The king's household, and the separate households of the queen and the royal children have all left their mark on· Domesday Book, for, in return for services past and future, stallers, marshals, chamberlains, cooks, bed-chamber-attendants, stewards, jesters, managers of the king's transport, of his hunting and hawking expedi-

tions, must all be given a landed provision, in the days when the king is rich in land and not in money.

But a precise description of the daily allowances of the palace servants comes from an Exchequer record of a somewhat later date. The record is believed to represent the reformed household of Henry I., and there is evidence that it was written soon after his death in 1135. Henry found it necessary to correct many abuses that had come in under Rufus's management and he ordered that his Chancellor should receive five shillings a day, and bread, wine, and candles in fixed quantity. The stewards had a like "livery" or stipend, and so also the butler, master chamberlain, treasurer, and constables. The solid part of the board, which is not mentioned, was of course provided at the king's table ; these liveries, or "buttery commons" as we should call them, of bread, wine, and candles were for private consumption. All these officers being *en pension* appear as strictly household officers, though they were, from another point of view, officers of state. This same record shows that in the Chancellor's office there was a master of the writing-room with a staff of clerks and scribes ; it is the office of a man who was Secretary of State for all departments And in close association, for the Chancellor is an ecclesiastic,comes the chapel department, with its two sumpter-men employed in the transport of its furniture when the royal household moves. The supply of lights for the chapel was fixed with precision by the thrifty Norman king at two large candles on Wednesdays and Saturdays, with a torch nightly before the relics and thirty bunches of small candles. The chapel had further a provision of a gallon of wine for mass, and a measure on Absolution Day (Thursday before Good Friday) to wash the altar.

The steward or master-dispenser and his servants got a similar "livery" and a salary which varied according as they were living within the house of the king or without. In the steward's department was a naperer to look after the linen, an usher and a bread-counter. The bearer of the alms-dish or "scuttle" fed in the house. In the larder department slaughterers were employed, receiving "customary" food. In the bakery two bakers fed in the house, and two travelling bakers were at wages. The number of loaves they were to make out of a given quantity of flour was fixed by the careful king, no doubt in order to put a stop to abuses. The making of the royal wafers was the duty of a "nebularius."

The king's kitchen and the great or "hall" kitchen were clearly distinguished, each with its separate staff. The cook of the "demesne" or king's own kitchen fed in the house and had $1\frac{1}{2}$d. a day for his man ; ushers and vessel-keeper and sumpter-man or pack-carrier had the same. The "great" kitchen had a larger staff with numbers of spit-men. The kitchen spits played a large part in the mediæval table-service as many contemporary illustrations remind us.

Owing to the disorder which reigned at William Rufus's great feasts at Westminster Hall, even he, who was not a reformer like Henry I., appointed ushers of hall, and kitchen, and doorkeepers, in all three hundred of them, armed with rods to use upon occasion, for the protection of guests and cooks alike from the press of the rabble. Such is the story of Rufus's contemporary Gaimar, who gives an amusing description of the scenes at royal feasts, of the greedy clutching at dishes as they passed from kitchen offices, with many a spill.

Each department had its own carters and sumpter-men, answerable for the transport when the king travelled, and perhaps also for the provision of supplies. The chamberlain's department was answerable for the king's bedroom service, and included the king's bed-bearer and a water-man who travelled with the king and got an extra salary when his master put him to the trouble of preparing a bath, except on the three great Church festivals when the king was bound to bathe, and the water-man must bathe him without extra charge. "Concerning the washer-woman there is uncertainty," says the writer of this curious record ; that is, it is not clear whether she belongs to the household and has court-rations or not. The treasury is spoken of under the " camera," for the idea that in the sleeping quarters treasure is safest is a very old one. It was the bedchamber staff that was to provide most of the officers of the Exchequer.

Coupled with the " camera " comes the Constable's and next the Marshal's department. The first seems to have already lost its association with the stable (*comes stabuli*), while the Marshal (*marescalcus*, horse-servant) retains his link with the stable and farriery department (compare Fr. *maréchal*). It seems probable that horseshoeing first became customary in England after the Norman Conquest.

Both Constable and Marshal were to be prominent
in the Exchequer department, for their chief duty is
the payment of the king's knights and hunting-
servants. By Henry I.'s " constitution " the wages of
the Marshal's servants when the king's household
moved from place to place were precisely determined,
and the perquisites of the watchmen, the fuel-man,
the tent-keeper, the four horn-blowers and twenty
servants, whose duty was probably that of bodyguard.
Then follow the servants who were responsible for
the king's sport, the fewterer or keeper of greyhounds,
keepers of the hawks' mews, the wild-cat hunters, the
" berner " in charge of running hounds, the huntsman
of the hart, the keeper of the " braches," dogs of
keen scent ; these and the wolf-hunters all had their
" liveries " for themselves and their horses and dogs
and hounds. The archers carrying the king's bow
took 5d. a day.

Subsequent records of the organisation of the king's
household, of which there are several of various dates,
show how the above scheme expanded, and go to
prove that the Norman royal housekeeping, though
an advance on the Saxon, was still rude. The list of
liveries, for instance, becomes much longer in later
times.

The household offices were at least nominally
presided over by the highest of the king's men, but
undoubtedly they delegated to others the services
which they did not care to do themselves. We must
not credit the legend of the Colchester monks, that
their earl became " dapifer " because William fitz-
Osbern, the king's trusted minister, served up an

underdone crane before his master. But Gaimar's story of the origin of the Earl of Chester's golden wand may be truer. Four earls, he tells us, were to carry state swords before Rufus to the great feast at Westminster Hall. Earl Hugh, of Chester, was too proud to carry anything, for he said he was not a servant. Thereupon the king offered him a golden wand and made the bearing of it an office for him and his heirs.

It will be seen that this scheme for the royal household took its character largely from the fact that the court was ambulatory, as it remained when far more highly organised. The story of Henry I.'s reorganisation is borne out from several independent sources. Eadmer, as the biographer of Anselm, claims that the change was due to his beloved patron's advice, and he gives a vivid account of the sufferings of the people when called upon to provide for the necessities of the ravaging horde of courtiers under the old system. Till the number of hangers-on was reduced, the villagers fled before the advent of the court, taking refuge in the woods. William of Malmesbury, writing as a contemporary, and Walter Map, writing under Henry II., both speak of Henry I.'s new system as marking progress in discipline and economy. In his time the royal travels were so regular that as the " camp " moved along its needs were supplied "as easily as at a fair." The officials were sure of their wages, and the merchants who sold food to the court were sure of their pay.

This " Constitutio Domus Regis " of Henry I. has seemed worth analysing carefully, because it is the earliest account, and one full of vivid detail, which describes the royal housekeeping. It serves as a picture not only of the royal household, but, as will be shown later, of the household of the king's great men.

3. The three first Norman kings spent the greater part of their time out of England, and when in England their travels were seldom broken by periods of repose. Punitive expeditions summoned the Conqueror over the length and breadth of his realm, and his successors were scarcely less active within a more limited area. These travels were partly a means of supporting the court, partly for judicial purposes, partly to make known the king's power. All the great forest districts were visited in turn for the pleasures of the chase, and in each the king had a fixed habitation. Thus the great Councils, such as those held at Rockingham, Clarendon, Woodstock, take their names from favourite hunting-seats, for all the kings knew how to combine business with pleasure.

William the Conqueror, after his not too peaceful coronation at Westminster, withdrew to the safety of a camp, and before London could be made a safe centre for operations, fortifications, which resulted in the building of the Tower, had to be begun. The first defences seem to have been temporary, but after the advantages of the site had been experienced, the Conqueror decided to build a great keep or tower, such as probably already stood at Rouen. This was the first keep to be built in England, and the architect was Gundulf, bishop of Rochester, 1077–1108, at one time a clerk of Rouen cathedral, and a monk of Bec, when Lanfranc was prior.   Lanfranc brought him to England in 1070.   That he was still presiding over the works of the White Tower when bishop, is known from an agreement made between him and a London burgess in whose house he was lodging, a record which his Rochester monks preserved.

The White Tower as it now stands is Gundulf's work, adapted to the needs of succeeding centuries. The wall of the keep (12 to 15 feet thick) is said to have taken six weeks to pierce with modern appliances.   The walls, diminishing in thickness at each stage upwards, were built of rubble, rudely coursed, with very open joints, while the plinth, quoins, and pilasters, characteristic of the Norman rectangular keep, are believed to be of Kentish rag.   The chief features to notice in the plans, both because they are characteristic and because they show the creator's architectural power, are the intersecting wall, the three well-staircases, the mural staircase to the chapel, the mural gallery on the top-floor (the lord's dwelling), which communicated with the three well-stairs and with the chapel ; the dark cellars used as storehouses of food and arms ; and the loops, wide enough to shoot from, but not wide enough to admit fire-brands thrown from without.   The floors, now brick, were originally doubtless of timber.

The account of Ralph Flambard's escape from the Tower in 1100 goes to prove that the inner arrangements were then in the main much as they have remained.   This splendid building stands alone to mark the highest point attained in castle architecture in the Conqueror's day.   Under Rufus in 1097, a great wall was built encircling the Tower ; and later a palace was included within one of the castle wards, to which Stephen at one time withdrew.

But the Tower was not often the Norman king's dwelling-place.   At the time when Rufus was levying forced labour for his castle-work from the shires round London, according to the old English plan, he took the opportunity to raise for himself a new palace at Westminster, with a hall of proportions magnificent enough to be thought very grand by his contemporaries.   His famous boast that this hall should be completely surpassed by the rooms which he meant to build round it, he never carried out, and later sovereigns even deemed it necessary to rebuild his great hall on a statelier scale.

The Saxon royal house at Winchester was left to the use of the mother of the Confessor and his widow, and a new one was built for William, on ground which encroached upon the New Minster, and from which twelve burgesses had first to be evicted.   The New Minster was strong enough to obtain compensation ; not so perhaps the burgesses.   Besides this palace, to which a great hall, the essential part of a palace, was attached (as we learn from the account of the destruction of this palace in Stephen's reign), a castle was also built where the treasure, together with the regalia, was kept.   When the king wore his crown at the three great Church festivals, it was fetched from Winchester, and when the Empress Matilda entered Winchester in Stephen's reign to seek to reclaim her own, her first business was to go to the castle for the

crown, as her father had done on William Rufus's
death. Other favourite dwellings were Windsor,
improved by Henry I., and styled New Windsor, and
in the Isle of Wight, a favourite starting-point for
Normandy, a hall was early made at Carisbrooke.
Henry I.'s name is also closely associated with
Beaumont Hall, Oxford, now totally destroyed.

4. William the Conqueror, whilst he was in England, was oftener in camp than under a roof. Rufus's
court was less purely military, and if we may trust a
mass of hostile evidence, it was degraded by scenes of
debauchery that created the profoundest impression
upon his time. Henry I. restored decency to the
court, although he could not boast a clean domestic
record like his father. He had, however, the tastes of
a collector, and the arts prospered under his patronage.
That he collected jewels is known from a letter
written by a prior of Worcester to Eadmer, Anselm's
biographer, in which he suggests that for money
Henry might be persuaded to part with some pearls ;
he collected also plate, and had a menagerie of rare
animals at Woodstock, his favourite place for privacy
and retirement ; to Woodstock foreign kings sent
lions, leopards, lynxes, camels, porcupines, and an
ostrich.

A minute account of his expenses, where these were
deducted from the sheriff's accounts, is entered on the
single Exchequer record which comes from his reign
(1130). It states the cost of conveying wine, wheat,
and garments for the king and queen from hunting-
lodge to hunting-lodge, of carrying cuttle-fish, cheeses,
venison, of "transportations" to Normandy, of building

done at the king's expense, whether of castles as at Arundel and Carlisle, or of lodges of timber and daubed lath. The building or repair of London Bridge (Rufus had begun it), of Rochester Bridge, to be ready against the king's coming, is noted here, and in these, our earliest building accounts, the minute particulars into which the sheriff enters are often of great interest for the history of prices as also of architecture.

The liveries or payments in money, food or clothes, which were due from the king, are likewise deducted by the sheriffs on their accounts, and from this source many curious particulars may be collected.

As recipients of livery, the watch and the porter and the servants of St. Briavel's castle in Gloucestershire are spoken of, and in London there were large deductions for the livery of the future King Stephen, of servants keeping the watch, and the porters of the Tower, of the wife of the naperer, of the engineer ; payments to goldsmiths ; and for fuel, herring, onions, oil and nuts to be taken to Woodstock ; for wine, pepper, cummin, ginger, cloth, basins, shirts, bought for the king's use. The sheriffs deduct, further, liveries for the men working in the royal vineyards, which appear always to have been brought more closely under the lord's eye than the less highly cultivated part of his manors. There are also to be deducted the fees of the guardians of the parks, of the feeding of game-birds in the park, and at Windsor, especially, these charges are heavy. The costs of restocking the royal farms are rarely closely specified, though now and again there may be a special entry. The fee for a costly stallion to leap the king's mares serves to show that some attention was paid to breeding from good stock. Upon the Pipe Roll, too, there are entered those charitable donations which the king's "farmers" were authorised to make in his name; for instance, for the "vestiture" or clothing of nuns at Berkeley, for "corrodies" or grants of food and clothing, as well as less regularly paid alms to the poor and needy.

All these curious side-lights come from an isolated Exchequer roll of a single year, and may serve as specimens of the wealth of illustration which is offered by these records when under Henry II. the stream of them becomes almost continuous. For the Norman period alone do we have to be content with mere scraps, but they are scraps which show the nature of the Norman civilisation in quaint detail.

Although little can be known of the daily life of the Norman palace, the chroniclers have not failed to bring the personalities of kings, queens, and princes vividly before us. Nor is evidence on dress deficient. The seals of the Conqueror and his successors show the king in his military and in his civil dress. On the one side the king is seen mounted and clad in a shirt or hauberk of mail, with long breeches of mail, a helmet, a lance with three streamers, and a kite-shaped shield. Stephen wears the hauberk with continuous coif. On the reverse, in robes of state, he is seated on a throne. The nature of the robes is described by Ordericus Vitalis; for the king sent his robes to Roger de Breteuil, and they consisted of a surcoat or chlamys, a silk tunic, and a mantle of ermine. Henry I. received from the bishop of Lincoln

a cloak lined with sable worth £100 of Norman
money, according to Gerald of Wales, but the sum
is perhaps fabulous. The use of fur-lined clothes was
necessitated by the mediæval custom of living
exposed to the weather, and the sorts which are

SEAL OF WILLIAM, DUKE OF NORMANDY.
From Hewitt, Ancient Armour.

spoken of continually throughout mediæval literature
are spoken of also in Norman times; for instance, in
Gaimar's description of the clothes worn by noblemen
at Rufus's feast, and in the English Chronicle's account
of the furs which Margaret of Scotland gave to the
Norman king.

The seal of Matilda, Henry I.'s daughter, shows a royal lady's dress of the same period ; or we may turn to the statue, believed to represent her mother, which flanks the great gate of Rochester cathedral. A similar figure, possibly by the same hand, is in the wall of the old Moot Hall, Colchester. This hall is said to be the work of Eudo Dapifer, a friend and ally of Gundulf at Rochester.

The tendency to effeminacy in men's dress, which consorts so curiously ill with all we know of Norman energy, an energy which no debauches could quench, was frequently referred to by contemporaries, and in terms which seem to show that the complaint was one better founded and more generally felt to be true than is always the case when contemporaries decry the new fashions. The outward changes were held to be indicative of those far deeper-rooted evils which Rufus's licentiousness (so men said) had made common in England. As a matter of fact, the new fashions had spread all over Western Europe, so at least says Ordericus Vitalis. He speaks of long curled and plaited

STATUE OF
QUEEN MATILDA AT
ROCHESTER.
*From Hollis, Monu-
mental Effigies.*

3

locks, parted down the middle of the head, of trailing
skirts which made all active exercise impossible, of
shoes with pointed toes as long as the tails of
scorpions, filled with tow, of large wide sleeves which
made the hands useless, of fillets in the hair that
curling tongs had crimped ; and equally hateful in
the eyes of many were the long beards which contrasted with the close-shaven faces of the Conqueror's
day—beards that were allowed to grow, a bishop
said, in order that the stubbly chin might not prick
the mouths of ladies in kissing.

Rufus was extravagant in dress, and William of
Malmesbury has a story of his refusing a pair of hose
at three shillings because they were not dear enough.
Some confused reminiscence of this seems to lurk
in Iago's ballad :—

> " King Stephen was a worthy peer,
> His breeches cost him but a crown."

The fashionable robes were worn loose and open,
and the effeminates walked with mincing gait, encumbered by their flowing skirts.   Many bishops are
reported to have preached upon these topics, and
Anselm, archbishop of Canterbury, among others ;
but the most famous incident was the scene after a
sermon preached before Henry I., when he and all
his courtiers submitted their heads to a bishop's
shears.   Of Wulfstan, the saintly bishop of Worcester,
it is recorded that he often used a knife, which he
carried to clean his nails or to remove dirty spots
from books, to crop those whom he could bring to

submission.   Even Rufus amused himself by setting
a passing fashion of lock-clipping at court.   When
in Henry I.'s time long hair was again in vogue the
cropping of Robert, count of Meulan and lord of
Leicester, Henry I.'s principal confidant, was thought
to augur well, for he was in the pink of fashion.
Indeed, such was his power to sway fashionable
circles that he succeeded in reducing the meals of
the nobility to a single long repast, in imitation of
the example of Alexander Comnenius.   This was
wholly contrary to English notions, which encouraged
frequent heavy feeding and drinking.   It is said that
in Hardicnut's time the meals were four a day, and
some of the Norman settlers, whose digestions were
differently planned from that of Robert of Leicester,
elected to follow the English system.   Their leader
was Osbern, bishop of Exeter, brother of William
fitzOsbern, William I.'s right-hand man.   Some
people were bold to say that the new Leicester
fashion was due to stinginess, and William of
Malmesbury was at pains to show that this accusation
was unjustifiable.   But if sparing in food, the Norman
courtiers did not spare their potations, and Robert of
Normandy is said to have been tricked of his duchy
while drunk.

Although the treasures in plate accumulated by
the Norman court as booty after the Conquest give
an idea of luxurious furnishing, further indications are
few and far between.   The French charters mention
the Conqueror's " tapet " and Henry I.'s down quilt,
but likewise the straw for the royal "thalamus."   Of
the tapestry that adorned the room of William I.'s

daughter, embroidered in gold, silver, and silk thread, a life-like account is preserved in a poem by a contemporary. The scenes represented her father's conquests, and some of them must have been almost identical with those of the Bayeux tapestry. But there is sufficient evidence to show that this set of tapestry is not that described in the poem.

Of the amusements of the Norman royal household little trace has been handed down. The dicing and backgammon of Rufus's court was considered one of the many manifestations of his inferiority. In his father's busy reign there had been no room for amusement. In place of these "idle sports" Henry I. is said to have restored active exercises, and the leisure of the court was spent in hunting and practice for the arduous hand-to-hand encounters of serious warfare.

The queens of the Norman period were women of character, and the chroniclers have thought their works and ways worthy of some note. Of the merits of William I.'s queen the best evidence is her husband's confidence and devotion. Vicegerent for him in Normandy, holder of his pleas in England, she was clearly a woman of good sense, tact, and experience. It was the learned Henry I. whose wives achieved some position as patrons of literature. His first wife, Matilda, English born, took great delight in minstrelsy, and encouraged the members of a fraternity which was regarded by the superior persons of that age as of worse than doubtful repute. " Happy he who could soothe the ears of the queen by some new song." It was complained of her that her patronage was extended chiefly to foreigners (the poet Guy of Amiens was her almoner), but as it was the clerks of melodious voice, the scholars famed for verse and for singing, who, according to William of Malmesbury, were the recipients of her charity, we may believe rather that her discrimination in patronage was justified. The low character of the fraternity of minstrels was a familiar theme, and the good religious queen preferred perhaps the better educated of the singers of romantic lays. The queen's letters, whether from her own pen or not, give a favourable idea of her intellect. Six are to Anselm, to whom she never failed to show every mark of friendship. Neither worldly business nor pleasure, it is recorded, could keep her from hurrying to meet him wherever he passed, that she might prepare convenient lodgings for him. Hildebert, bishop of Le Mans, was also one of her correspondents. Her charities, her hospitals, and maintenance of bridges have secured to her always a favourable memory.

Not only Matilda, but her Flemish-born successor, Adeliza, cultivated the romanticists. It was the poet Gaimar's boast that he knew tales which Adeliza's troubadour David did not know, "nor had he them in writing." The "bestiary" of Philip de Thuan, perhaps one of her countrymen, is dedicated to her.

The indifference of William I. to the poets is recorded by one who wrote under the patronage of his daughter Adela. William was concerned rather to choose active men of affairs for the public offices of his new kingdom than to extend his patronage to learning. Neither his name, nor that of Rufus, is associated with any literary enterprise. But the men of affairs attached to the Norman churches, who came over to fill bishoprics and abbeys, were almost without exception men of learning and all were of his choosing. The school of historians that wrote of the Conqueror's reign alone would testify to the fact that his circle was intellectual. Rufus's education was purely military ; but all the chroniclers agree in describing Henry as well educated, though the name Beauclerk was a late addition. What exactly this literary education amounted to is another question. Ordericus Vitalis styles him " litteratus rex " because he could read a letter in Latin. William of Malmesbury says he was not a good reader aloud, and his Latin was not of the best. A curious story has been adduced in proof that he understood English, but it will not bear that interpretation. A clerk reading out of a charter came to a list of customs in English, granting " sac and soc," " toll and team," " mundbryce," and the like. He came to a standstill, but the king, who was well-learned, was able to explain it all. The story testifies rather to his legal than to his linguistic attainments. Of the Conqueror it is recorded that he tried to learn the English language, but found that he was too advanced in life to make much progress.

Henry I.'s education was in all likelihood that of a business man and a lawyer, and his age was a great one in administrative reform. Through his skill in selecting organisers who rose through his chancery, and came under his eye in his chapel, it is to his reign that are traced the development of the Exchequer,

of the national councils and courts, and the beginning of judicial circuits. He attended to despatches
even during mass, and it was to speed in getting
through the service that his greatest servant, Roger,
bishop of Salisbury, owed his early promotion. In
Henry I.'s time illiteracy was considered by some a
positive aid to ecclesiastical promotion by the king
(who wanted no second Anselm), if we may trust the
story of a king's chaplain who deliberately misread
the service in order to gain advancement. He read
so grotesquely that Henry asked the reason. On
hearing the truth, the chaplain received at once the
reward of his humour and penetration, the priory
of St. Frideswide's, Oxford.

DINNER FROM THE BAYEUX TAPESTRY,

SEAT FROM THE BAYEUX TAPESTRY

II

THE NOBILITY

1. The supplanting of the English nobility—2. Baronial households—
3. Evidences of literary taste among the barons—4. Nature of
their castle-building: armour—5. Private war: ideas of honour—
6. The military orders—7. Ladies.

1. IT was part of the Conqueror's scheme that as far
as possible the whole frame-work of English government and English society should be maintained and
made the basis on which the strengthening and
systematising Norman genius for government should
be set to work. The principle of retention was
carried so far that in the distribution of lands to his
followers William did not map out the country into
compact military districts, suitable for military occupation, but gave as a rule to each Norman the
holding of an English predecessor, a holding that

had been casually and unsystematically pieced
together, whose portions lay scattered far and wide
and were held on many various conditions. Surrounded by his own relatives and by adventurers
from all parts of Gaul, William was obliged to give
to the greedy, but he gave in such a way as not to
weaken himself.

The process of supplanting the English nobility
and the English official class was carried out with
great completeness, though the method of the change
varied in different parts of the country.   In Kent,
the most civilised part, many non-feudal characteristics were allowed to stand, to trouble lawyers in
aftertimes : on the marches of Wales and in the
least civilised parts of the country the king accepted
an unmitigated feudalism, with all its dangers, as the
best guarantee, at the moment, of his own peace.
He delegated to the lords of lands the sovereign
powers he could not exercise himself.   The great
feudalists, whom William endowed, shared with him
the racial genius for government, which showed itself
not in England only but likewise in Sicily, where
at this very time " the best organised and most
united " state in Europe was being built up by
them.   Their law and their architecture are the
most eloquent witnesses to their character.   Bold
and stern, ruggedly simple, what they built was
destined to endure.

2. Of their domesticity we can know less even
than of the king's.   Not a single account of baronial
expenses comes from this period or from the next.
But the Normans did not create many different

types of domestic life. The scheme of the king's household was that of every baron. The "Laws of Edward the Confessor," not always trustworthy, speak truth when they tell us that archbishops, bishops, earls, barons had in their households their knights and servants, namely dapifers, butlers, chamberlains, cooks, bakers. So great an earl as he of Chester is said by Henry of Huntingdon to have owned a third of the kingdom. Whether this be true or not, Ordericus Vitalis has a good deal to say of his style of living. Hugh of Avranches, earl of Chester, "the Wolf," "the Fat," gathered about him a vast household of clerks, knights, and young men : his court was a school of manners of a boisterous kind. A lover of riotous sport, he was before all a lover of minstrelsy, romance, and jest. He engaged the best narrators of historic feats, to spur on the young to rivalry. Gaimar bears out part of this story, and describes his house as open to all, a place where wine flowed like water. The earl's friendship for Anselm proves that his character was many-sided. A careful collection of rather scrappy evidence might show that some of the Norman barons had their peaceful interests which give relief to that picture of their turbulence, violence, and cruelty which doubtless cannot be painted in colours too dark. Even Robert of Bellême, one of the worst specimens, made it his interest to improve the English breed of horses by introducing Spanish stallions, and Gerald of Wales a century later praises the result of his work.

3. Although there were but few, comparatively

speaking, among the Norman laymen, who cared
aught for cultivation of mind, the names of those
who are associated with literature deserve the more
to be remembered.   Henry I.'s illegitimate son,
Robert, Earl of Gloucester, has earned for himself,
through William of Malmesbury's dedications, a
lasting fame.   William tells in terms of unbounded
praise of Robert's devotion to literature, of his copious
draughts from the fount of science.   And his story is
borne out by Geoffrey of Monmouth's dedication of
his History of the Kings of Britain, addressed likewise
to Robert.   Geoffrey's history, according to his own
account, was based on oral traditions, recited by heart
"as though they were written," and on a Latin
rendering made by Walter, archdeacon of Oxford,
from a Breton or Welsh chronicle.   Gaimar, who
used Geoffrey of Monmouth, says likewise that he
used Walter's work, and that it was rendered from
the Welsh at Robert of Gloucester's request.   Neither
Welsh nor Breton original, nor Walter of Oxford's
Latin, is extant, nor indeed seems to have been
known to any of Geoffrey's successors, so that doubt
has been thrown on the whole story.   But whether
Geoffrey is to be credited with more or less imaginative power, or more or less respect for historic truth,
we may believe that in Gloucester he found a patron ;
and from Gaimar's account it is clear that in Lincolnshire also there was a group of nobles and ladies
interested in romantic literature.   Gaimar records his
indebtedness to the patronage of Dame Custance
wife of Ralph fitzGilbert, the founder of a Cistercian
abbey, Kirkstead, in Lincolnshire.   He used many

books before he finished ; indeed he never could have
finished, he says, had it not been for her aid.   For
his use she sent to Helmsley for a book belonging
to one Walter Espec (the Woodpecker).   This work
was the translation made from the Welsh at Robert
of Gloucester's request.   Custance prized the volume
so much that she paid a mark of silver, burnt and
weighed, for a copy, and kept it always in her
chamber.   The book-lender Walter Espec is introduced to us in another capacity by the historian of
the Battle of the Standard, who describes him as a
man of gigantic stature, with raven-black hair and
a voice like a trumpet.   The fine speech which
Ailred puts in his mouth may well be his, at least
based on his own words ; he bids the Normans
remember that they have seen the King of France
turn tail, that it is they who have subdued distant
Apulia, Calabria, Sicily, and will their mailed
knights be beaten by the bare-legged barbarous
Scotch ?

Another Lincolnshire patroness of literature was
Adelaide de Condé of Horncastle, who employed in
her household the trouvère Samson of Nanteuil.

A baron who was himself a writer was the clever
Breton, Earl Brian fitzCount, reared and knighted
by Henry I., an Exchequer auditor and a supporter
of the Empress Matilda against Stephen.   He composed a treatise (now lost) in defence of her rights,
so eloquent that a very learned man, Foliot, bishop
of Hereford, writes that it kept him engrossed to the
neglect of his duties.

But the best evidence that lay education was not

wholly neglected is the number of barons who were famous lawyers, like Alberic de Ver, "causidicus," chief justiciar and chamberlain to Stephen, one of whose judicial speeches remains on record. Such another, Henry I.'s councillor and judge, the earl of Leicester, though no great Latinist, could see through many a legal subtlety in lay and ecclesiastical controversy. For this man's sons Henry I. provided an education, bringing them up " like his own children " ; and when these youths were sent to dispute with the cardinals in logic, they beat them " in sophisms and lively argument," so says William of Malmesbury.

Another of Henry I.'s bastard sons, Richard, was educated by Bloet, bishop of Lincoln, together with the historian Henry of Huntingdon. The Empress Matilda's son, the future Henry II., was given the greatest continental teachers in the Latin classics, natural philosophy and versification, and while under his uncle, Robert of Gloucester, likewise, he had in England excellent teaching, together with that earl's sons. One of these sons, Roger, became bishop of Worcester ; another, William, had for his chaplain that same Geoffrey of Monmouth who was to be chief of a school of quasi-historical romance.

But there were few learned knights, such as the friend of Paul, abbot of St. Alban's, who delighted to buy books for the church, few ladies like the Countess Goda, wife of Eustace of Boulogne and sister to the Confessor, who possessed a choice copy of the Gospels, worthy to be presented to such a library as that of Rochester cathedral.

4. What is more characteristic of the baronial spirit of the Norman era is their building of castles, whose ruins remain to show the dominance of force in everyday Norman life.

Modern scientific inquiry inclines to ascribe more and more of the earth-works, *motae*, to the Norman rather than to the Anglo-Saxon time. The castle

HEDINGHAM CASTLE.

towers, none of which were pre-Norman, fall into two well-defined groups, one solid and rectangular, floored and intended for habitation, the other hollow and generally round, a shell-keep, built as a defence added to an artificial mound. The rectangular keep, requiring solid foundations, is not found in conjunction with the artificial *mota*. The majority of the

barons seem to have been content at first with an
enclosed camp, planted in a defensible position, and
protected only by an earthwork or palisade.   Within,
wooden cabins furnished shelter from the elements.

William I. had employed Gundulf to build him the
Tower of London, and Gundulf, imitating his own
tower built himself the square keep of West Malling,
where he lived as bishop of Rochester.   To his
influence the keep of Colchester, known to have
been in existence in 1101, may very possibly be due.
The De Veres followed suit with the square keep
of Hedingham in Essex ; at Norwich the keep
was added to the castle 1120–1140.   At Rochester,
where Gundulf had built a wall in part-payment of
a fine of £100 to Rufus, William de Corbeuil, archbishop of Canterbury, added a keep 1126–1139.
Ordericus has described the horrors of a siege at
Rochester before the keep was built ; the accumula-
tion of filth from men and horses ; the heat ; the flies,
so numerous that men could not eat by day or night
unless flappers were used.   Such troubles were
avoided by those who could shelter themselves in a
floored keep, with fire-places and bed-chambers in the
thickness of the walls, with privies likewise, arranged
with shoots to keep the filth from the wall.   By the
end of the period there were such keeps in the west,
Bristol and Gloucester (both destroyed), Bridgenorth,
Ludlow, Chepstow ; at Sherborne, Devizes, and Old
Sarum, Roger of Salisbury's castles were considered
miracles of masonry ; his Devizes was called "the
glory of Western Europe."   At Sherborne his keep
was octagonal.   Of the castles of his nephew

Alexander, bishop of Lincoln, Sleaford, Banbury, Newark, praised in similar terms, only a part of Newark remains. At Porchester the fine keep stands ; near Winchester, Henry the bishop built Wolvesey, from the stones of the destroyed king's

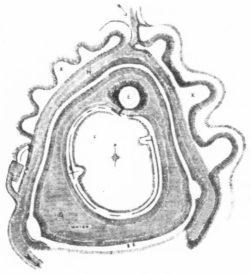

PLAN OF BERKHAMPSTEAD.
From Sir J. D. Mackenzie's " Castles of England."
(Reproduced by kind permission of Mr. Heinemann.)

palace. The keeps of Bamborough and Newcastle belong to the next period, but in the north, Norham received its solid keep from Ralph Flambard.

Where a shell-keep suited best the nature of the ground, the occupants need have recourse to its protection only during siege ; in times of peace the garrison was housed in timber buildings in the several wards or separate enclosures which surrounded it. At Cardiff the shell-keep was further defended by a great enclosing wall, 40 feet high and 10 feet thick.

In the lower scale of castle-building came small "peles" for a captain and slender garrison, or a "baile," such as that of York, which was built in eight days in William I's. time. Lower still came the "domus defensabilis," which was generally not strong enough to stand a serious siege. In Stephen's time a lord, whose house was too weak to protect his people, moved with all his following into Exeter. The county-town in troubled districts, now and for a long time after, was a place of shelter for the people of the county. There is reason to think that the county-towns were carefully schemed by the Saxon kings to fulfil this object. At Shrewsbury a payment towards the repair of the borough walls was long levied on the county, and in the fifteenth century Hereford still acknowledged its responsibility for the protection of the county residents above the rank of cottier.

Numbers of castles which in the early Norman period were seignorial, were destined to become royal by the process of confiscation. That the policy of bridling the people by strongholds was one likely to turn to the weakening of the royal power was quickly perceived, as rebellion followed on rebellion, each with a castle as its centre. At Bridgenorth, for instance, Robert of Bellême had strongly protected a vast space capable of holding thousands of men. When in Stephen's time the multitude of castles became a danger, threatening all alike, the necessity for control was realised, and the work of destroying those that were unlicensed by royal authority had to be taken in hand as the first duty of his successor. The possession of a castle, even though a castle in little more than name, implied feudal rights of a high kind ; and Henry II., in determining what castles were "adulterine," took in hand a "quo warranto" enquiry of a searching kind. Unlike Edward I. he collected no great volume of evidence as to the warrants for castellar rights, but, backed by a national feeling that had been disciplined by civil war, Henry accomplished where Edward merely recorded.

Three principal dangers had to be encountered when the fortifications were put to the test of a siege. First there was the danger lest the water supply should give out. This happened at Exeter, and a terrible description of the horrors men endured remains to us. Wine had to be used to make bread, and to put out fire-brands. This last, the danger from fire, was a principal cause for the erection of stone buildings. Thirdly, for use against stone buildings, the Normans fully developed, at an early date, the possibilities of mining, and with the exercise of much engineering skill arranged cover for the miners. In victualling castles for prolonged sieges no great difficulty seems to have been encountered. Provisions were levied by compulsory sale, from the surrounding country, as part of the castellan's right, and bread and salt flesh, wine, beer, and flour

HEDINGHAM CASTLE.   FIREPLACE.

were deposited each in its proper place, as Laurence of Durham describes in his versified account of a castle's organisation. Hall, kitchen, stables, barracks, and lodgings for soldiers, were arranged in orderly fashion, and every need was supplied by a levy of feudal service. It was due to these services that the word "castellum" carried to English ears a dread significance.

The military dress of the "loricati" who garrisoned these castles consisted of a conical helm with a nose-piece, a mail-shirt (lorica) or coat with short mail sleeves, and mail breeches, the mail consisting of lozenges of steel, perforated, and sewn on to a leathern vesture. The armour was practical and did not call for training in military exercises like the suits that developed later. But military exercises of an artificial and half sportive kind, were already used in the Norman period. According to William of Newburgh they were introduced under Stephen, and discouraged by Henry II., but the so-called laws of Henry I. describe exercises with the dart that might lead to an accidental death. The continual opportunities for private war were adequate enough in Norman times to offer abundant practical training. Fealty to the liege lord is a doctrine more readily instilled than fealty to a distant king, which may or may not have been directly sworn. It was urged on behalf of the Exeter rebels that they never had sworn fealty to the king, but took up arms in obedience to the orders of their liege (or immediate) lord. This was the doctrine of a feudalism which the kings, supported by the lawyers, set themselves to break.

5. In a feudalism that still regarded private war as legally justifiable, there was no place for the half fanciful and romantic ideas indulged in at a later time. We meet already in the Norman age the sworn brotherhoods and comradeships which savour of " chivalry," but the brotherhood of a Baldwin de Réviers and a Joel of Totnes was a political reality. Between rival lords it may need a bishop to arbitrate in order to secure a compromise as elaborate as a treaty between kings. Such diplomatic records attest, as nothing else can do, the power of the parties. The long strife between the Earl of Chester and the Earl of Leicester was settled in 1151 by a covenant of " final peace and concord," sworn to by an " affidavit," an oath on their Christian faith, made before the bishop of Lincoln. The two agreed to allow either to enter the mound and wards (the burh and bailes) of the Castle of Mountsorrel, with a full household, and for the purpose of warfare. But neither might make war on the other with more than twenty knights, and neither might take any goods of the other. Each was to give the other a fortnight's notice of attack, and the aid that each might give to other lords was limited. Thus by agreement their private war was reduced to comparatively meagre proportions. To take another case, both offensive and defensive was the " confederation of love " made between William Earl of Gloucester and Miles Earl of Hereford and between their sons ; here for the securing of the conditions there was a solemn interchange of hostages.

In the Norman period already there are not want-

ing signs of the development of a spirit of chivalry.
Civilisation, among kings and nobles at least, had
advanced far enough to invent a code of honour of
a rather arbitrary kind.   There is knightly courtesy
inter pares; there is a scrupulousness about slaying
brother-knights.   Rufus will not break certain kinds
of promises; Robert of Normandy will not besiege
a castle when the besieged are waterless; he will not
besiege a castle when Henry I's. queen is in child-
bed, and thinks that he would be a *villain* so to do.
Matilda the Empress is accorded safe conduct, which
no honourable knight can refuse an enemy.   Personal
bravery, and the moral bravery shown by readiness
in retort, are the great Norman tests of merit.   With
all this there goes a large measure of barbarous
cruelty.   In Stephen's reign the castellans invented
horrible tortures; to gouge out a child's eyes with
the fingers, or to bridge a moat with live horses and,
when their bodies proved insufficient then to order
villains likewise to be thrown in, such was the handiwork, such was the command of a Bellême, a person
of exceptional cruelty; but to order blinding, castra-
tion, the cutting off of noses and limbs, such was the
ordinary work of the law.

6. Amid this fierce and restless society the crusading
fever spread wildly, and by many of the better spirits
it was welcomed in sternest discipline of mind and
body, as a means to reconcile the world and religion;
for the religious object of the new warfare kindled a
fire of spiritual enthusiasm among all classes of the
laity of Europe, such as has never been kindled before
or since.   "The Welshman left his hunting, the Scot

his fellowship with lice, the Dane his drinking party, the Norwegian his raw fish ; " rich and poor, men and women and children of all races, went flocking eastward. The hunger and thirst after Jerusalem that swept away humbler desires, made many of the nobles seek to change their lives in entirety. Among the knights in this "army of Christ" were many who could not willingly (now that their eyes were opened) pass over laxity and worldliness, the passion for dress and gorgeous display, for all the paraphernalia of feudal rank which was seen to be undermining their virility. Vaingloriousness would not consort with their new duties. They sought to humble themselves before all men and become the *serfs*, not indeed of a temporal lord, but of the invisible lord Christ. Monks and regular canons had already shown the way in submission to a discipline under vows of implicit obedience, of chastity, and humility, and it was a monastic rule adapted to military exigencies that now provided what was wanted. Two "military orders," that of the Knights of St. John of Jerusalem and that of the Knights of the Temple (the first taking precedence in point of time) had become widely fashionable in England by Stephen's reign. Those who did not care to take the vows of either order might acquire merit by giving a benefaction.

The common funds of the order of St. John were devoted at first to the support of sick Christians in Jerusalem, those of the Temple to providing armed protection for pilgrims. Both these purposes appealed strongly to a laity who might at any time be in the enjoyment of these benefits. The rule of the Temp-

lars, revised more or less under the influence of St.
Bernard (not by his hand as was once supposed),
warns the knights against using gold and silver on
their bridles and mailcoats and spurs, and paint, silk,
and gold in their horse trappings. If rich armour
be given to the order, its glories must be deliberately
dimmed. Hawking and hunting are forbidden, and
all stories of past feats and gossip and tale-bearing
concerning each other's vices ; for in a society of
knightly adventurers there was all too much to relate.
In warfare the action of the Templar knights is to
be united : no brother may prick forward to the fight
without leave, and if any harm should come of his
impetuousness he may lose his habit. Only if he
sees a Christian in peril of death and his conscience
moves him to go to the rescue, he may do so. The
rule enforced no general silence except at table, but
noisy talking, gambling, jesting, and soothsaying,
scurrilous songs, shows and games were forbidden.
There was to be a common refectory and property
was held in common, but close confinement to the
walls of the house was of course not part of the rule.
The master of each house had absolute power to
direct the incoming and outgoing of the brethren, as
in a monastery. The difficulty of requiring celibacy
was obvious : on the other hand, there was the difficulty of securing the property of married knights for
the order. Arrangements were made accordingly :
the married were admitted but not to the right to
wear the white cloak and the full honour of the order.

The " nourished " hair and carefully dressed curls
of the secular knights were derided by these "regulars,"

who gloried in their rough beards, their short hair,
uncombed and unwashed. Their churches were to
be decorated by none but military ornaments, shields
and weapons, in the place of glories of marble, wood-
work, painting and gold. The English preceptories
and commanderies were centres for the management
of estates and for the collection of funds; here the
knights who were not engaged on active service found
shelter under the rule of the preceptor or commander,
and spent their time in mending their armour and in
field labour.

The order of St. John, as a hospital order, admitted
women to affiliation, and in the first instance they
were attached to the men's preceptories; later on the
English members were located at Minchin Buckland,
Somerset.

7. Concerning the aristocratic ladies of the Norman
period, who were not subject to monastic rule, nor
attendant upon the court, we know next to nothing:
but here and there we get the name of a heroic wife
capable of taking the lead when her husband's castle
was besieged, an Emma of Breteuil, a Matilda de
l'Aigle, the defenders of Norwich, of Bamborough.
It is a mere accident if the name of a famous em-
broiderer has survived to add reality to the well
known fact that English women had earned a continental fame for their taste and skill. Queen Matilda
gave to Caen the vestments made in England at Winchester by the wife of Alderet. Heldisenda, "the best
orfrey worker" in England, was carried to Scotland
as "cameraria" to King David's queen. Just be-

cause a miracle happened to her at St. Cuthbert's
tomb, her name has survived.

John of Salisbury observed that women excelled
men in the art of falconry, a fact which he adduced
to prove that it was an effeminate sport, not worth the
pains spent upon it.   His remarks passed unheeded ;
but a good lady found a more practical way to stop
her husband from preserving his venison and taking
too much pleasure in the chase.   She pretended that
stags destroyed her lord's sheep, and to prove her point
put wool in a stag's stomach.   Thereupon the deer
were sacrificed in the cause of economy.

THE DEVIL DRESSED AS A LADY OF FASHION.

WILLIAM OF MALMESBURY'S WRITING.

III

SECULAR AND REGULAR CLERGY

1. Relations of Church and State—2. The new monasticism and the hostility of seculars and regulars—3. Rise of orders of canons—4. Cathedral chapters and collegiate churches—5. Episcopal households—6. The monastic orders—7. Hermits.

1. THE influx of foreign clergy and monks, coming at a time when strong ecclesiastical movements were stirring on the Continent, brought to the church of the conquered country the breath of a new existence. The world of learning, with very few exceptions, was a world of ecclesiastics, and hence it is the life of the church that is known to us in fullest detail. Many hands were at work penning biographies of bishops, annals of religious houses, rules for the guidance of monastic daily life, and the records of the learned church have endured where the records of the unlearned laity have perished. We would gladly forfeit some contemporary lives of ecclesiastics for a single biography of a lay Norman baron, for what is lost is more desired than what is kept. But for good or ill, clerical and lay persons, whatever be the differences in their view of life, have always much humanity in

43

common, and after all the Norman king's bishops were likewise his barons. Not the most bitter opponent of lay "investiture" forewent the "barony" attaching to his see : that would have been negligent stewardship of the church's property. The mediæval church was not prepared to measure its power in spiritual terms, but sought to increase its influence upon the state by secular means. Men saw the readiest means of access to spiritual power through temporal power, and failed to perceive that in this source of strength lay also a source of weakness. All the bishops and many of the abbots were the king's tenants-in-chief, holding their lands of him, answerable to him for the services due from those lands : upon these lands the whole of the tenant-in-chief's income depended. The greatest ecclesiastic had it constantly brought home to him that he was, if a bishop, likewise a subject, and the servant of two masters, pope and king. The attempt to harmonise these incompatibles absorbed a large part of the abundant energies of mediæval bishops, and much legal, metaphysical, and theological subtlety went to the solution of the problem.

2. The new life infused into English monasticism a century before the Conquest had ebbed when the Normans came over. They found Benedictine monks in possession of the larger number of the English cathedrals ; a few in the hands of the clerks who were not subject to monastic rule ; a few divided, with clerks in the bishop's household, and monks in the cathedral cloister. In Normandy it was the "secular" clerks, not the "regular" monks, who were the members

of cathedral chapters, and the long-standing feud between the two sets of churchmen became accordingly
more than ordinarily acute in England.   At the back
of their differences lay a deep-seated rivalry between
lovers of the active and the contemplative life, a rivalry
which divides many even nowadays.   Then the strife
was sharpened, into a bitter struggle for place and
power, which gives colour to all the writings of the
time and largely vitiates their reliability when the
party question is prominent.   The monks, being the
more learned party, have left their views on record in
abundant detail, but though the seculars, as men of
affairs, wrote less, their side has not gone unrepre-
sented.   Theobald of Étampes attacked monastic
appropriations, the   policy   of   exploiting   parish
churches to enrich the monks.   He uses unsparing
language of the convents, " prisons of the damned,"
who have condemned themselves to prison in hope
of escaping eternal damnation.   With other clerks he
sought to show that monks had no right to fulfil
sacerdotal functions.   The monastic reply to this
" tantillus clericus " was to call him a wandering
chaplain with a pointed beard, curled hair, and
effeminate dress, ashamed of the proper ecclesiastical
habit and tonsure ; for the clerks were less uniform
in the matter of dress than the regulars.   More to
the purpose was the forging of canons to prove that
the monks are the best priests because their lives are
nearest to the divine.   Dr. Böhmer has lately shown
how much reason there is to trace these and other
forgeries to Lanfranc's necessities.

The strength of the monks lay in their union, for

there were as yet no mutually hostile orders priding themselves upon special features which distinguished them from unreformed Benedictines. The existence of a " Cluniac congregation " showed that something of the sort was coming, but they as yet had no reason to be exclusive. Wishing to spread their reform everywhere, they admitted to a loose association with their house many monasteries that were not destined to become affiliated when a choice of " orders " offered. The seculars, on the other hand, though a more numerous body, including all the parish clergy, were forced into a merely artificial union, the result of the hostility of the regulars; and this union rather injured the cause of the best of the party, for it exposed them to all the contempt which the inferior members deserved. It is difficult to conceive the true position of the secular priest at a time when churches take a Christian name from a patron saint and a surname from the name of the founder and builder,[1] whose rights in the church seem altogether to swamp those of the officiating priest. Multitudes of priests whom we should call parish priests must have been more like chaplains attached to private families than like the parochial clergy of a later time, who knew of no such feudal relation. In a class of persons so dependent and so ill-provided (for on the tithes the church had not yet laid firm hands), it is not surprising if the standard of morals was low. Church councils were unwearied in

[1] Compare in London St. Benet Fink, St. Margaret Moses, St. Mary Woolnoth ; All Hallows Staining, All Hallows Barking, belong to another proprietary group.

planning means to amend the vices of the secular clergy, and the list of these vices is a list that could only be drawn up in an age of ungoverned lusts.   For the evils which were notorious the councils sought a remedy in the same cast-iron system to which many who joined the regulars voluntarily submitted themselves.   The regulars had found the severities of their rule an armour against worldly temptations. Total abstinence from sexual intercourse was for them a panacea, and in their eyes there was no choice between a celibate clergy, bound by rule, watched by a crowd of fellow-clergy at every moment of the day and night, kept under lock and key, denied the enjoyment of private property, and a clergy drunken, debauched, and dissolute, the clergy of the penitential literature.

3. The best measure of the truth of the regular monk's criticisms is the evidence which shows that the better sort of secular clergy were seeking the identical way to which the regulars pointed.   From the eighth century onwards attempts were continually being made to bring the secular clerks into groups under a closer system of discipline, and especially to do this for the canons of cathedral churches, where common service and a common source of income seemed to overcome the practical difficulties which stood in the way of regulating the poor and scattered country priests. In the Norman churches the secular canons had been brought under regulations varying in severity from see to see ; and when vows were taken which deprived the canon of the separate enjoyment of property, and brought him under rules that were quasi-monastic,

the term " regular canon " began to be used, for want of a better phrase. The movement had already made progress in England before the Norman Conquest.

The hostility of the Benedictines was nevertheless unremitting, especially in England, for they dreaded lest the regular canons should be placed over them as bishops, a position for which their disciplined training, both active and contemplative, seemed likely to mark them out. It was feared that the English practice of choosing monks as bishops would be set aside as incompatible with monastic strictness of life. If that happened, the Benedictines saw that they would be removed from some of their wealthiest monasteries, from those in particular where in past times they had themselves with difficulty ousted the despised and disgraced seculars. William I., however, had chosen for his archbishop of Canterbury Lanfranc, a monk of Bec, and although he himself introduced regular canons where he deemed them useful—for instance, to serve the spiritual needs of a hospital of men and women—he used his influence with William to maintain the existing state of affairs. Here and there a chapter of seculars was ousted in favour of Benedictines, for instance at Durham, Norwich, and Rochester ; but here and there a Norman secular was made bishop over a cathedral convent, for instance Walkelin at Winchester—a man much feared as a possible opponent of regulars ; here and there, too, regular canons were later on allowed their chance. Henry I. placed them in his new see of Carlisle, and in many places this " via media " was favoured by founders in the twelfth century.

When some brethren from St. Botulf's, Colchester, were sent to learn more of new rules for regular canons from the Arrouasians at Mont St. Eloi and at St. Quentin de Beauvais, and returned with a written rule believed to be that of St. Augustine, a new impulse was given, and teachers of the rule of the " Austin canons " were provided for Queen Matilda's foundation of Holy Trinity, Aldgate, for Dunstable, Launceston, St. Frideswide's, Oxford, St. Osith's, Essex, and Merton, Surrey ; Barnwell, Cambridge, and Nostell, Yorkshire, were probably similarly provided, and many of these sent out teachers to other places. The hospitals, of which several were founded soon after the Conquest, all came under this looser rule, which lent itself to many forms of adaptation. It was a great triumph for these Augustinians when they produced a bishop of London and an archbishop of Canterbury, successor to Anselm. From that time the cathedral monks at Canterbury were less eager sharply to differentiate the regular canon from the monk.

How far the regular clerk could combine active parochial functions with a contemplative life, closely restricted by rule, was early seen to be a difficult question. In the view of those who, like Ivo of Chartres, were chiefly instrumental in introducing " regularity " among secular clerks, it was intended that after they had been first thoroughly disciplined and tried, those that were found to be hardened and fit should be given parochial work. As the number of regular canons swelled, and greater strictness of rule developed, two classes of houses appear, the

5

large and wealthy houses which were in every sense strictly monastic, and the smaller groups, attendant on hospitals, or nunneries, of the Augustinian order, or gathered in remote villages in scanty numbers. These smaller groups took over duties that were scarcely to be distinguished from parochial duty.

St. Norbert, in the first quarter of the twelfth century, created a new order of canons, who were directed to make pastoral duties in the cure of souls their ultimate object ; their suitability was to be tested by a period of severe discipline under rule in a retired place. His rule was more severe than that to which any other canons of his day submitted ; he ordered a total abstinence from meat, additional severe fasting in Lent, and a dress of sheepskins, to be worn without any linen shirt underneath. The wearing of linen had hitherto been characteristic of canons as contrasted with monks. Over their sheepskins the " White Canons " of St. Norbert wore a white wool tunic. Thus the Premonstratensian or White Canons were contrasted with the Black Canons of St. Austin, who followed a milder rule. The new order found many supporters in England and still more in Scotland.

4. The Conquest had enduring effects in the changes introduced by the clergy from Rouen and Bayeux into the constitutions and ecclesiastical rites of those cathedral churches where secular canons held their ground. At York, Lincoln, and Salisbury, three churches which served as types for many others, the erection of cathedral establishments on the Norman pattern took place almost simultaneously.

The prevailing tendency which showed itself even
in the monasteries, to divide the funds into separate
" prebends " or provisions, attached in the monasteries
to certain offices, in the cathedral chapters to each
canonry, was accepted in most cases.   Where a single
manor was so rich as to provide many prebends, then
it was apt to remain as a single *corpus* managed by a
provost in the interest of a group of canons.

The powers which bishops, occupied with public
affairs, and absent for long seasons, could not be
expected to exercise regularly, were given to the
group of clergy who had formed his council.   Under
the Dean was a "cantor" responsible for the elaborate
services which required one well-versed in a highly
complicated ritual.   There was also a chancellor or
secretary (who sometimes acted as a schoolmaster to
teach young clerks in the cathedral school), a treasurer, and canons, resident or otherwise.   In some
cases greater stress was laid on community of life,
on the common refectory, on common sharing of
the cathedral property, in others less.   But common
living soon proved impossible without celibacy.

The other English chapters of the secular group
were St. Paul's, Hereford, Lichfield, Chichester, Wells,
Exeter.   Three great collegiate churches, governed
on a similar plan but without bishops, were subject to
York, at Beverley, Southwell, and Ripon.   Waltham
and Christchurch, Hants, are other famous examples,
both becoming Augustinian at a later date.   In the
castles of the king and of many great earls the
collegiate groups of secular clerks or canons were in
high favour, and to the needs of the castle chapel

we owe Windsor, St. Mary's Warwick, St. Mary's de Castro at Leicester, and others. In London, St. Martin's the Grand was early famous for its school. The collegiate church of secular clerks was chiefly popular in towns, where the demands of

DRESS OF ECCLESIASTICS c. 1150.

parochial work were large, where the economy of common living was obvious, and where a large endowment made it possible to build a large church, which required a number of clergy to serve its altars.

The secular clergy were bound to celibacy by repeated canons of the church, passed both in national and in Roman synods. No priest who disregarded the canons might celebrate mass, and, if he celebrated, he might not be heard. Periodically reissued in slightly varying forms, they were continually set at nought, more especially by the isolated village clergy whose proceedings could not be constantly watched. The illicit unions of the priests were more or less tacitly condoned. Henry I., according to Eadmer and the English Chronicle, used his power on behalf of the canon law and took such heavy fines from married priests that two hundred of them in albs and stoles went barefoot to his palace to plead for mercy.

5. Whether attached to a conventual or a secular cathedral, the household of the bishop was arranged on the same plan as that of the king or great noble. He had his cook, butler, chamberlain, chancellor, and receiver, accounting to his Exchequer, and likewise his own dancers and minstrels. When Gilbert of Sempringham (the future founder of a monastic order), as a clerk in the Bishop of Lincoln's household, rose in the night watches to wrestle with his soul in prayer, his strange gesticulations cast shadows on the wall which a watcher took to be those of one of the bishop's "saltatores." Further, the episcopal household contained a full suite of knights, whose services would be called for when the bishop sent his quota to the host. When travelling, a bishop took with him gold and silver, costly plate, and horses, arms, clothes, dogs, and hawks ; these items were all named in the catalogue of necessaries required to be covered

by the royal safe-conduct in the case of an exiled bishop.

From Lanfranc's days come reports of the oppressions and greed of episcopal officials. But likewise there come reports of the efforts made by a Gundulf or an Anselm to improve the state of their dioceses by building stone and wooden houses, by constant travel and visitation. Distant manors were exchanged to make the payment of food rents less difficult : the coming of the bishop was a time when oppressive bailiffs were brought to account.

6. The unity of the monastic interest was destined to be but short-lived. Already, by the second half of the eleventh century, the practice of affiliating new monasteries to the famous house of Cluny, the centre of a reform movement in Benedictine discipline, was widespread, and it was to Cluny that William I. sent for monks, saying that he would pay their weight in gold for them. The abbot replied that rather than sell any he would pay to get more, so much were they in demand. Instead, English monks were sent abroad to learn the stricter Cluniac rule of silence, the minutely ordered clothing, the ritual observances, the system of a chapter - general at Cluny, where visitors were appointed to the several provinces, and the accounts of each dependent house were heard.

The great Norman lords in the first period of settlement showed much favour to the reformed order, and in Devonshire Joel of Totnes, in Surrey and Norfolk William of Warrenne (who had seen and admired Cluny), Peverel at Lenton, Lacy at Pontefract, Bigod at Thetford, Roger of Montgomery at Wenlock, the Count of Mortain at Montacute, and Simon of Senlis in several Northamptonshire houses. were founders within the first three Norman reigns. From Lewes, Castleacre, Wenlock, Thetford, branch houses again went out. In London before the end of the eleventh century Aylwin Child, supported by a number of English citizens, richly endowed Bermondsey. But the English houses of the Cluniac order were not destined ever to number more than thirty-five ; for a reaction came, as the result of their excessive wealth which led to splendid display and consequent loss of popularity. A new party of ascetics was again organised, anxious to reform once more the Benedictine original ; from this, the Cistercian order, came a multitude of English settlements.

The original founder of the order was an English-man, Harding, who was at first a monk at Sherborne, and left the monastic life to travel. After journeying in Scotland, he passed through France to Rome. He returned to the monastic life at Molêmes in Burgundy, where he and others discussed in chapter how to discover and adhere to the essential features of St. Benedict's rule. Those of the community who were bent on a severe asceticism formed a separate establishment which seemed likely to have no offshoots, until it came under the inspiration of St. Bernard. Soon after his foundation of Clairvaux, in 1115, colonies were multiplied, and in 1119 a written collection of customs was promulgated. The dress consisted of two tunics only, of undyed wool,

whence the name White Monks.   They rejected any
additional coat for winter, the use of linen and fur.
The refusal to wear breeches except on journeys was,
like the Cluniac's extra coat, a constant subject of
ridicule at a later time when the order had become
large, wealthy, and luxurious.   By rule they slept
clad and girded, to save bed-clothing and to be ready
instantly for mass somewhat before dawn.   No
mid-day sleep was allowed, contrary to nearly all
rules that took their origin on the Continent.
Another early feature was the rejection of artificial
light.   The order of services was of course minutely
regulated, and no excuse for absence was admitted
except on the ground of illness.   The silence was
stricter than that of the Cluniacs ; the monks were
ordered never to speak in cloister or elsewhere except
to the abbot or prior.   The abbot subjected himself
in all things to the same rule, save that he took his
meals with the strangers and the poor.   His party
was waited on in silence, and his conversation with
the guests was to be sparing.   Two kinds of food
were served at the most to the abbot and guests,
meat and lard never, except to the sick.   Throughout
autumn and winter, till Easter, one meal a day only
was allowed, except on Sundays.   The services were
recited to the Ambrosian chant as used at Milan.
Other monastics had been using the new system of
Fécamp, the introduction of which, by a Norman
abbot at Glastonbury, led to a great disturbance
among English monks accustomed to the Gregorian
chant.   The Cistercian churches were to be of the
plainest, to contain no lights save one on an iron

CISTERCIAN MONK.

From Dugdale's "Monasticon."

stand, no jewels, gold, silver, or crucifixes, only painted wood and brass or iron censers, and a chalice of silver gilt: the vestments were to be plain and unembroidered. The bareness of a dissenting chapel would have consorted with the Cistercian fancy.

As soon as the Cistercians grew prosperous, the rivalry between them and the Cluniacs, who had hitherto held the highest place, became embittered, inasmuch as there was competition for benefactors. These last showed as a rule catholic taste, founding here a Cluniac, there a Cistercian or an Augustinian house. The Cluniacs were further made to feel that there was a rival in the field, by the papal exemptions which released Cistercians from tithe, and which gave them a right to celebrate mass with closed doors in time of interdict. The exemption from tithe was due to the original Cistercian intention to reject support from lay tithes and oblations that should support the parish clergy—a self-denying ordinance which was not kept.

Each order hoped by fresh reforms to keep its hold on the popular taste, but among the Cluniacs there was a conservative party who refused to go further on the path of asceticism, and scoffed at the Cistercians' "novelties" and their desire to make themselves conspicuous. If some of the Cluniacs strove to match the Cistercian severity, the Cistercians learned too from the Cluniacs, taking from them their idea of an annual general chapter, perhaps, too, the association of a large body of "conversi," or unlettered brethren, who could not take part in the religious services. But unlike the

Cluniac system, each Cistercian abbey was self-governing and the bond of union was merely federal.

In England the first Cistercian house was founded in 1128 by Giffard, a secular Bishop of Winchester, at his episcopal manor, Waverley, in Surrey. An abbot and twelve monks came from " le petit Cisteaux " to introduce the rule at his request. From this house sprang some offshoots, but the greater number came from the northern foundations, of which Rivaulx was the first. It was planned in 1132 by an Englishman who had come from Clairvaux, and the land was given by that Walter Espec who has been named above as a reader of romantic history. It was in accordance with the spirit of the Cistercian rule that the Yorkshire foundations were all placed far from the haunts of men.

Many Norman monasteries, without affiliating to Cluny, had come more or less directly under its reforming influence before the Conquest took place. Bec, Fécamp, Jumièges, which sent some of their best men to England, were of a reformed model, which, no doubt, had written customs drafted to deal more explicitly with some of the open questions of the Benedictine rule. Lanfranc, when he came to Christchurch, Canterbury, found the English monks accustomed to a very easy life and a liberal diet, to outdoor sports in summer, to gambling in winter. With his usual worldly wisdom he introduced changes gradually, and, after practical experience, he drafted (c. 1082) a detailed custumal, which became a model for a number of the great monas-

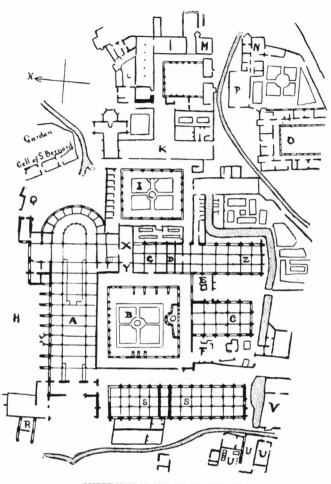

CISTERCIAN PLANS OF CLAIRVAUX.

By permission of MM. Quantin, Motterot, Morel and Matinet.

A. Church. B. Great Cloister with covered Lavatory. C. Chapter-house with garden in rear. D. Parlour. E. Calefactory. F. Kitchen and Court, Washhouse and Larder. G. Refectory. H. Cemetery. I. Little Cloister of 8 cells for copyists. K. Infirmary. L. Noviciate. M. Old lodging for strangers. N. Old Abbot's lodging. O. Cloister of old and infirm. P. Abbot's hall. Q. St. Bernard's Cell and Oratory. R. Stables. S. Granges and Cellars. U. Oil Mill and Sawmill. V. Currier's Shop. X. Sacristy. Y. Library. Z. Dormitory over dayroom.

NOTE.—The shaded channels are watercourses.

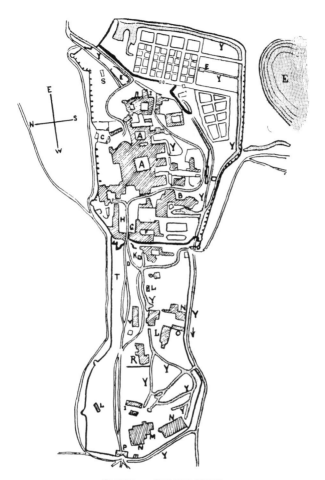

SECTION 1.—FOR THE MONKS.

A. Church Cloisters. B. Oil and Flour Mills, Ovens. C. St. Bernard's Cell, Oratory and Garden. D. Chief Entrance. E. Fishpond. F. Guests. G. Abbot's house. H. Stables. I. Storehouse.

SECTION 2.—SEPARATED BY A WALL FOR CONVERSI AND SERVANTS.

K. Parlour. L. Lodgings and Workmen's Rooms. M. Shambles. N. Granges and Stables. O. Clothes Store. P. Chief Gate. R. Remains of old monastery. T. A garden. V. Tileworks. X. Oven. Y. Watercourses.

teries, which rejected the idea of affiliation to Cluny, but accepted a severe system of rule.   Lanfranc raised the number of monks at the cathedral to 150, and in many of the more flourishing abbeys there were from fifty to a hundred monks, a number which did not include the novices, schoolboys, choristers, and semi-attached servants and unlettered brethren. Such communities, it must never be forgotten, were larger than most English villages of that time.   The organisation of the commissariat alone, for the monks and their many dependents, required elaborate systematising ; in those days the possession of money wherewith to buy food was by no means a secure means to the purchase of food.   The danger of starvation was a real one not only to the poor but to the rich.

Their size alone makes it difficult to exaggerate the influence which mediæval monasticism had in the development of national civilisation.   The influence of these groups of men, who in theory had withdrawn from the world and were dead to it, yet from the shelter of their cloister shaped the course of society, was more varied and wide-ranging, and more powerful, in the Norman period at all events, than that of any of the other groups of living persons.

The most detailed account we have of the life as ordered in an English Benedictine house is the custumal from Lanfranc's pen.   In his preface he urges in fine language " that the letter killeth but the spirit giveth life," and he specially desires that what he writes shall not be viewed as binding or final. Nevertheless a large part of his treatise is devoted to liturgical regulations, to careful rules on the times and places for speech, the intervals for meals, the diet, the frequent, probably monthly, bleedings, the relaxations for the bled. We may notice incidentally that periodic "minutions" were not ordered solely for the reduction of the monastic flesh. The Norman kings retired periodically for the same purpose.

Lanfranc's cathedral monastery is pre-eminently a school in which numbers of boys were being educated, no doubt with a view to entering monastic or holy orders should they prove suitable. They are grouped under masters, one for every two (at least of the younger children) if possible, and the rules for their washing and combing, teaching and continual supervision are minute. The boys may not make signs, and must sit far enough from each other to be prevented from nudging ; a master must walk between every two ; only the abbot, prior, or precentor may smile at them. Their beds were at the foot of the masters' beds ; they might never talk to each other except when a master listened. There were boys " offered " by their parents with religious ceremony, who wore the shaven crown ; and likewise there were youths who were, presumably, free to rejoin the world. The children held their own separate chapter-meeting daily, when the rule or " chapter " was read, and, like the monks of the elder convent chapter, they told tales of each other there and took their whippings.

The occupations of the monks are not precisely described, but handiwork and reading and writing are clearly contemplated. The arrangements for the library are careful ; books were given out to be read in Lent, and a catalogue of these loans was kept. In order to keep strictly to the minute time-table of the day and night, the convent had a variety of bells, small and large, each for an appointed purpose. The arrangements for cleanliness were precise, and as the standard of monastic life was probably that of the social life of the day, these rules throw a favourable light on Norman manners. The washings of face and hands were frequent, and the arrangements for bathing before great festivals were regulated with scrupulous decency. At festivals the seats of the refectory, chapter-house, and cloister were draped, and fresh rushes were strewn ; the tablecloths were changed on the day when heads were shampooed in the cloister. The cloister was the great centre of the strictly monastic life ; in this large and airy sitting-room all the work was done for which no other place was appointed.

At Christchurch, Canterbury, the regulations for almsgiving and hospitality were on a most liberal scale. The poor were freely invited into the cloister for the ceremonial feet-washing of weekly occurrence, and at this time an alms of 2d. each might be given if thought desirable by the cellarer or chamberlain. After the Maundy, the "cup of charity" was handed.

The almoner was responsible for visiting the sick poor of the neighbourhood in person (accompanied by two servants) or by deputy. Women had to leave the sick-room before the monk might enter and inquire what was needed for the sick man's comfort.

Sick women might be visited by one of the monastic servants, and what they asked for was to be sent if the almoner approved.

Lanfranc expected his monks to travel on business, and arranged a special dress for the purpose, which included leggings and gloves. In his scheme there was a " hostrey," who looked after the guests housed in the monastery, and provided their beds, seats, tables, clothes, towels, dishes, "scuttles " (for bread and meat), spoons, and basins. He introduced strange monks into the cloister, and secular men, about to enter the society of the brethren, into the chapter-house.

The sick, of whom large numbers were expected to continually occupy the infirmary of the monastery, were under a monk, who superintended the infirmary-cook and kitchen. He helped the sick to their food, sprinkled them daily with holy water, saw that none malingered, and brought all complaints before the chapter of brethren.

The chamberlain was answerable for finding all the monks' clothes, shoes, beds, bedclothes, razors, and dormitory vessels ; he had to repair the dormitory windows (of glass) and to find horseshoes for the abbot, prior, and guests' horses, and travelling clothes for the brethren. Once a year he had to provide new hay for all the beds. The cellarer was answerable for the monks' food and drink and kitchen vessels. The precentor was to warn him when specially good provision was to be made in the refectory in order to celebrate a feast. Under the abbot and prior and sub-prior the chief officer was the precentor (cantor), answerable for the services of the church and for the secretarial work of the house. The books were under a special custodian, and a sacristan was responsible for the ornaments of the church, to keep them clean, to provide specially pure bread for the sacrament (after the fashion of Cluny), to ring the bells, light the candles, and in general to serve the church. Hence in most monasteries he became the officer responsible for the maintenance of the monastic fabric.

One indication of the unity of the monastic houses was the elaborate system of confraternity kept up between remote houses. Besides the living monks who asked to share the benefits of societies other than their own, there were also the houses attached in a systematic prayer-union for the dead. Further the laity, alive and dead, were admitted to share like privileges, after a formal ceremony of enrolment accompanied by a gift. The seculars who applied in the chapter-house in person were received with kisses, and women were admitted to the confraternity, but, according to Lanfranc's rule, did not receive the kiss.

Lanfranc's example in drafting rules was imitated by his kinsman Paul at St. Alban's, by Gundulf at Rochester, and very skilfully by the prior Simeon (bishop Walkelin's brother, from St. Ouen, Rouen) at Winchester. Simeon cancelled the use of meat at his cathedral church, but introduced such dainty (French) cooking of fish that the English monks were mollified. At Worcester the change came probably through the prior Nicholas, whom the English bishop Wulfstan sent to Lanfranc to receive instruction.

Other reformed monasteries, besides Christchurch, set almsgiving before them as a primary duty. At Evesham, according to rule, the abbey was charged with the support of thirteen poor people, fed from the leavings of the abbot's table, besides the twelve "maundy" poor who had to be clothed and fed, and fifty sick persons who were supported at the convent's expense.

A pleasing aspect of monachism is seen in such a story as that of the missionary colonising of Northern England by a prior of Winchcomb and two Evesham monks. But many dangers of monastic abuses were already preceived. Men were still at liberty to allocate their tithes at pleasure, and handed them over to the monastery from which they could hope for the largest measure of spiritual *quid pro quo*. A place was secured to the monastic benefactor in a splendid " Liber Vitæ," and systematic and punctual prayers were guaranteed to the donor. Questions affecting the repair of the parish-church fabric, the stipends of parish priests, seemed of more remote and slender interest to the lords of lands. The laity were short-sighted and the monasteries greedy.

Within, the convent was troubled with a complaint known as " accidia," which may be translated by the English word boredom. A special stone was provided in the infirmary on which sufferers from this disease were required to sit in order to effect a cure. Then there was the risk that some monks might seek a way to avoid an attack of this disease by improper means, for instance by taking paid work in the shape of copying. Herbert Losinga's letters are full of these secrets of the prison-house. A young monk enjoys himself too much composing the private correspondence of his fellows : he should stick to Augustine and learn grammar. Henry I. in his charter to Reading says that, instead of spending money on his relations, the abbot should see that it goes to the poor, to pilgrims and guests. Further, he warns the abbot to beware of putting children " in sacra veste Christi."

The bitter hostilities between monasteries, for instance between Christchurch and St. Augustine's (the Canterbury neighbours), the passion for litigation, the quarrels for precedence, the competition for the benefactions of rich and poor, the simony which should have been impossible where there was community of goods, were all sources of obvious weakness. But these weaknesses were not confined to the monastic side of the church. The archbishop of Canterbury and the bishop of London had to be sent away from the king's dinner-table to dine alone because their rival claim to say grace threatened to disturb the peace. The buckle that fastened on the king's crown was broken in an unseemly scuffle between church dignitaries anxious to crown him. The terrible anathemas uttered by bishops in defence of their private interests, as for instance by Herbert of Norwich against poachers in his park, are choice examples of man's zeal in the use of religion as a means to serve personal ends.

7. For most of those in whom the religious sense was highly developed, the disciplined life of religious communities had unrivalled charm, but a consider-

able group of the more extreme ascetics desired
solitude rather than the cloister. The literature of
the English Middle Ages, early and late, is full of
references to hermits, recluses, and anchorites, dwelling
either in desert-places or immolating themselves in
chambers attached to churches or monasteries. Those
who could not go on crusade or pilgrimage would
disturb the hermit's solitude by crowding to the neighbourhood of his cell, and as soon as the temporary
dwellings of such visitors became thickly clustered,
monastic discipline was generally introduced and the
original character of the settlement changed. The
foundation of Selby is an example of this.

WEST DOOR OF IFFLEY CHURCH (OXON.)

DETAIL FROM THE CAPITAL OF A PILLAR
IN SHOBDON CHURCH.

IV

LEARNING, ART, AND EDUCATION

1. The foreign ecclesiastics and the schools whence they came—
2. Range of learned interest — 3. Norman architecture and
church ornaments—4. Bookbindings—5. Work of the nunneries—
6. Schools—7. Oxford studies.

1. WILLIAM THE CONQUEROR allowed many of
the English abbots to keep their places ; of 21
abbots signing the London synod of 1075, 13
were natives. But by Rufus's reign the number of
natives was greatly reduced. Foreigners, chiefly from
Normandy, were everywhere, and the first group of
bishops and abbots that came over contained many
of the most remarkable men Normandy had to send.
Their activity was boundless and much of their

learning was wholly new to the English, who, while
retaining a naïve freshness of thought, were no match
for the continentals in scholastic learning. With
scholasticism, the foreigners brought an architectural
knowledge which was a further revelation to the
English.

The schools of Caen and Bec sent not only the
Lombard Lanfranc, learned in the law, a contro-
versialist and pre-eminently a statesman, and, later,
Anselm, a spiritual theologian of the most refined
and cultivated type, but many lesser lights came
crowding in Lanfranc's train. For instance, there
was Gundulf, the architect, and the Italian Paul of
St. Alban's, Lanfranc's kinsman, and Walter, Lanfranc's chaplain, abbot of Evesham, where he proved
himself a capable organiser and builder. There was
Gilbert Crispin, Lanfranc's clerk, a man of noble
family, connected with other famous Crispins, a man
learned in secular knowledge · as abbot of Westminster he entered into public discussion with a
learned Jew, and Crispin himself set the formal
points in dispute on record. There was also Ernulf,
prior of Christchurch, Canterbury, then abbot of
Peterborough, and there a great builder and hospital
founder, finally bishop of Rochester, and there the
compiler of the famous *Textus Roffensis ;* his early
training had been at Bec and Beauvais. Thurstan
of Glastonbury, a lover of music and song, with
many writers of verse and others too numerous to
specify, came in this swarm of ecclesiastics who
traced their education to Bec or Caen. In the next
century Theobald, archbishop of Canterbury, like

Lanfranc a lawyer, continued the connection with Bec.

From the regular and secular schools of Rouen came a crowd of king's chaplains ; among the most notable figures were Walkelin, bishop of Winchester, and his brother Simeon, famous at Ely ; Giffard, Walkelin's successor ; and Walkelin's nephew, the great secular archbishop of York, Gerard, an opponent of Anselm on the vexed question of investitures. Gerard was the head of a strong royalist and anti-papal school, from which came some important law-books and controversial writings. Too independent a thinker for his contemporaries, his opponents held up their hands in horror that an astrological work by Julius Firmicus Maternus should be found under his pillow when he died.

Mont St. Michel sent Remigius, the founder of Lincoln cathedral, a monk who was won over to support the scheme of secular chapters, and from the same place came others who carried the new monastic discipline east and west through England.

From Fécamp, another reformed house, and a great school where many poor students were supported free of charge, came the Lotharingian Herbert " Losinga," whose reputation is half brilliant, half shady. He found it hard to reconcile the spiritual and the secular view of affairs and used his money freely in buying ecclesiastical preferment for himself and his father. The sums he thought it worth while to expend—£900, £1,000—were large ones in those days, and they give a measure by which to judge what abbacies and bishoprics were then worth. As abbot of Ramsey, as a "sewer" attendant on the king's table, as bishop of Norwich, he served and enjoyed the world. He founded Norwich cathedral and put in monks there, keeping before him Fécamp as a model ; and not only in large but also in small matters ; for he sent one of his serving-men to the Fécamp abbey kitchen to learn cooking. Conscious himself that the world was too much with him, to his danger, he placed his episcopal palace far from the cloister, that the monks might not be disturbed by the worldly bustle inseparable from a great bishop's household. His correspondence attests his zeal as a book-collector and reader. He had to send abroad for a Suetonius ; a Josephus (in Latin form, no doubt) he asked on loan of an abbot, but was refused on the ground that the binding was loose.

In the next century Cluny had the credit of educating the great Foliot, abbot of Gloucester, bishop of Hereford and then of London ; but more characteristically Cluniac in spirit was another who was trained there, Henry of Blois, bishop of Winchester, the brother of king Stephen. Not only was he a first-rate politician who used the disturbances of Stephen's reign to exalt the church in such a way as to necessitate the conflict between Becket and Henry II., but he was also a famous builder, the founder of the hospital of St. Cross, an art-collector, and a patron of letters. He brought Italian statuary from abroad, kept a collection of beasts and birds, built aqueducts, and furnished gorgeous palaces and castles. The Winchester font, believed to be his, represents scenes in the life of St. Nicholas of

Myra, and there can be little doubt that it came from Italy. Some of the fine manuscripts that belonged to the Shaftesbury nuns were probably originally written for Henry of Blois, and some drawings in them in the Italian style are thought to be traceable to his influence.

Bayeux, where William I.'s half-brother Odo was

WINCHESTER FONT.

bishop, sent many of the great seculars; for instance, Thomas, archbishop of York, who had seen the working of all the great European schools, and was himself a teacher, a musician, a philosopher, came from Bayeux with two of his relations. His brother

Samson was bishop of Worcester, and Samson's son kept the archbishopric of York in the family. The monastic annalists viewed the Bayeux contingent critically. Gluttony is more than once laid to their charge, tempered, it may be, by a reference to the too greedy bishop's indulgence for others. Samson of Worcester sat down once to a dish of eighty chickens, but as he could not eat them all the poor fared the better. To William of Malmesbury, who tells this story, abstemiousness and indifference to dress were saving graces in his contemporaries ; and his severity on those who had not these virtues may perhaps hint that excess was then a fashionable vice among the many foreign members who filled the new secular chapters.

The half-secular, yet would-be ecclesiastical extremist, William of St. Calais, bishop of Durham, was originally a canon of Bayeux, but afterwards chose the monastic life and became abbot of St. Calais, in Maine. Apart from his magnificent building at Durham, which Ralph Flambard carried forward towards completion, his name is memorable for the part he played in a great law-suit against Rufus, in which he used the advantage of the new hierarchical arguments to place his fellow-bishops in a difficult position. But Lanfranc had a policy of his own, which recognised some of the merits of the secular point of view ; backed by the king, he was a match for the troublesome bishop, though Rufus's constant interruption of the trial by remarks of an injudicious and highly unjudicial kind made Lanfranc's position more distinctly that of the secular against the spiritual than can have been pleasant for his relations with the sacerdotalists.

The schools of Tours and Laon are no less closely associated with the church. William of Corbeuil, archbishop of Canterbury, who taught the canons of St. Osyth's, Chich, was taught in Laon, and there in all likelihood he was tutor to the sons of Ralph Flambard. Laon too had educated two famous nephews of the statesman-bishop Roger of Salisbury, Alexander the future bishop of Lincoln, and Nigel the future bishop of Ely. And to complete the list, the names of the great men sent by Lorraine and by Liège might be added.

2. Further the Normans brought with them a know-ledge of medicine in advance of that of the English. John of Tours, bishop of Wells (1088–1123), was famed for his medical skill ; the Italian Grimbald, or Grimaldi, was in constant attendance as leech to the court, and he with the Italian abbot of Abingdon, Faricius, attended Henry I.'s Queen Matilda, in child-bed. When Faricius was near being made arch-bishop, it was urged against him that he attended women in sickness.

Faricius had been cellarer at Malmesbury and seems to have started a medical school there, for thither came the famous knight Ernulph of Hesding to consult a monk, Gregory of Malmesbury, how to treat a disease of the hands. Gregory's most successful medicine was some balsam taken from St. Aldhelm's tomb, at the abbot's suggestion. Baldwin, abbot of Bury, a monk of St. Denis and prior of Deerhurst, doctored Lanfranc by King

William's orders, and Lanfranc in his turn doctored Gundulf.

Historical studies had the greatest charm for learned monks, canons, and bishops, as, for example, Robert of Lorraine, bishop of Hereford, an architect and a mathematician, who introduced the chronology of Marianus Scotus. William of Malmesbury, Simeon of Durham, Florence of Worcester are at the head of the list, but several of the larger abbeys had historical schools of their own. Durham produced not only Simeon, but Reginald, Laurence, Turgot, and Ailred of Rivaulx. Of the secular historians, the archdeacon Henry of Huntingdon was one of the best ; but seculars, being more dependent on the laity for appreciation, were inclined to join the school of semi-fabulous history, which had all too large a following.

Many French bishops preached to the people, and must have learned English to do this. The monks who went about the country collecting funds for their churches, secured the gifts of the humble class of the faithful, no doubt by use of the native tongue. Wulfstan the English bishop of Worcester was a famous preacher, and lived down successfully the charge of illiteracy which the Normans had brought against him.

Of the letter-writers whose utterances have remained to this day, Herbert of Norwich, Lanfranc, Anselm, and Osbert of Clare are the most informing, but those who collected volumes of manuscript letters unfortunately collected them rather as specimens of style than for the sake of what was actually said.   Yet there is enough to show that many of the great French bishops were in correspondence with their learned friends who had migrated to England.   Now as later, close intercourse was kept up between many learned people who lived far apart.

William of Malmesbury stands at the head of his generation for the immense range and lasting value of his studies : the library which as a boy he helped to arrange at Malmesbury must have been a very rich one, matched perhaps by that of Gloucester, which the monk Osbern had at hand, at a somewhat later date, to consult for his remarkable dictionary.

William's works show that he had travelled over England, had visited the court, and had been the recipient of information from countless sources.   He aspired to be the Bede of his time and not without success.   Like Bede, he was not merely a historian ; it is by his other volumes, now less directly valuable, that it is possible to measure the extent of the learning of his day.   His collections range over law, philosophy, and theology, and much work upon them still remains to be done before the library which he had at his disposal can be in any way reconstructed; His histories show that the monasteries were in many cases centres of civilisation in every sense : meeting-places of the learned and the lay, the great and the humble.   A glimpse of the character of some of the monkish inhabitants of his cloister is given in his account of the merchant Saewulf, who, late in life, after much travel, entered the Malmesbury convent. There is no doubt that this is the traveller Saewulf whose account of Palestine was written at this time.

From such a man, one who knew much of Europe, William had an opportunity to learn a great deal of current continental politics, and he has made it abundantly clear that he neglected no opportunity to extend his knowledge and his interests.

3. The age that produced Domesday Book produced the first great architectural triumphs : it is in these that men will ever see the grandest expression of what was fine in Norman thought and Norman action. It is difficult to realise that most of the churches which the Normans built before 1154 are destroyed : enough remains to give some measure of the beauty and extent of what is gone. The greatest works date from the close of the eleventh century : by that time England had already shaped the Norman architecture to a new character, in which size, such as Normandy had not known, should be made a first object of ambition : withal a certain primitive severity remained from the English style of an earlier period to lend a peculiar character.

A brief consideration of the greatest churches, of what once was and is no more, or exists in another form, will serve to show how much was done. The great Norman church of Westminster, begun under the Confessor, and deemed of surpassing grandeur, is gone : it was held to be a model for other churches while it stood. The crypt alone, serving as the treasury of the royal wardrobe in Edward I.'s time, still remains, and an inscribed Norman pillar gives a precise date, rare and valuable in the history of architecture.

Of Thomas of Bayeux's church, begun at York in

1070, scarcely anything remains but a portion of the crypt. The cathedral of Canterbury was begun by Lanfranc in 1072, exactly on the plan of St. Stephen's, Caen : Eadmer was astonished that it should have been finished in seven years. Under Anselm, the prior Ernulf—future bishop of Rochester—and prior Conrad, finishing in 1130, extended Lanfranc's short choir, after the manner of that of Cluny. Of this work some columns alone remain. Osmund of Salisbury had built a cathedral church, 1075–1092 ; now all is gone. Remigius built at Lincoln, 1075–1081, but his building fell and the lower part of the west front alone remains to give an idea of the nature of his work. Rochester, 1077–1137, was the joint work of Lanfranc, Gundulf, and Ernulf : it stands, and the great west door shows what wealth of idea the sculptors of that time could lavish. Similar in all likelihood was Evesham : here the work was begun in 1077, but not finished till 1160, though the money-chests had been well filled by the receipts of a grand tour of the Saxon Egwin's bones through England. Such, too, were the buildings at Bury St. Edmund's, where the choir built by Baldwin was 150 feet long, and where the greater Anselm's nephew Anselm built a nave over 300 feet long, eclipsing in length our largest cathedral. At St. Alban's, the Italian Paul rebuilt the church and all the adjacent buildings of the monastery, except the bakehouse and millhouse ; he used up the Roman tile and what materials were at hand, as any one who looks may see, and as the St. Alban's Chronicle bears record. Lanfranc contributed 1,000 marks to the cost. Paul's building (1077–1093) is the eastern end of the church, and the tower ; the western end was completed by 1115, when the king and queen came to the dedication. Robert the mason, on whom the monastery conferred a manor, was perhaps principally responsible for the works of abbot Paul.

At Glastonbury, Thurstan of Caen built a church, probably finished in 1083, when he and his monks quarrelled over the new psalmody. His successor, thinking the building unworthy of the abbey's vast revenues, built another in 1102–1120 at a cost of £480.

Then comes Walkelin's Winchester 1079–1093, with a nave 250 feet long : to build it the bishop's estates were annually oppressed : for its timbering a king's wood was cut to the ground. But most of this nave is hidden now in a later casing. At Ely, Walkelin's brother Simeon built 1081–1103 as much of the church as was necessary for the monks' immediate occupation, the eastern limb, whose broad transepts and great central tower should set the measure for any future additions. His transepts remain, rivalling the finest parts of Durham in dignity. His choir, a short one, is gone. The monks, here as in other Norman monastic churches, were grouped in stalls under the central tower. The choir was occupied by the priests. For the nave the house could afford to wait. Simeon's work, incomplete as it was, seems to have heavily burdened the monastery, which was at a low ebb in his successor's day.

Hereford cathedral, as built by Robert of Lorraine, was planned on the model of his native Aix-la-chapelle, but little of the Hereford he built and none

7

of the Aix he imitated now remains.   At Worcester
we have one perfect specimen of the character of
Wulfstan's building, finished in 1089, and that is his
crypt.

The Norman St. Paul's, begun in 1086 by bishop
Maurice, the Conqueror's chaplain (whose loose living
William of Malmesbury held to be atoned by his
activity as a builder and organiser), was continued by
another great secular bishop, Richard of Belmes,
who had earned a great secular reputation for himself
as governor of the Welsh marches.   His ideas of
building were so grandiose that the St. Paul's of his
day (of which no stone remains), was deemed to take
the first rank among English cathedrals.

At Gloucester the eastern half of Serlo's church
(1080–1100) is hidden in a later casing, while of the
Chichester that was built 1091–1114, a part only
remains.

But now we come to Durham, the unsurpassed :
in three years, so Simeon of Durham plainly says,
William of St. Calais built the choir—as it now stands,
save that its eastern end is changed.   The western
sides of each transept, greatly inferior to his work,
were the contributions by agreement of the monastic
house, whose funds were distinct from those of the
bishop and more sparingly expended.   There is
reason to think that William and the monks had
before them a complete plan, and this vast work
Ralph Flambard finished between 1104–1128.   It was
he, William Rufus's minister of evil fame, who completed the nave, all save the vaulting, and he too
built the exquisite castle chapel.   Before 1133 the

vaulting had been added, for the example of Alexander the Magnificent, bishop of Lincoln, had in 1123 shown that the vaulting of wide spaces was possible. Between 1133 and 1140 there was built at Durham a chapter-house that must have been one of the finest in England. It was demolished in 1796 because it was not comfortable enough.

GROINED ROOF AT PETERBOROUGH.

Soon after Durham, Herbert, of Fécamp origin, planned Norwich, 1096–1101, and much of his work is still visible. In 1100-1117 Faricius was building the church of Abingdon which has vanished. In 1107 Tewkesbury was finished, in 1107 Warelwast's hoary towers of Exeter were reared. The choir of Peterborough is somewhat later. Of the builders of

Romsey, of Malmesbury, we know nothing, but their work remains. Nor was the passion of this period expended on great cathedrals and abbeys only; the parish churches found great builders too. Though later taste may have removed the church, the Norman doorway on which was lavished all the beauty of sculpture which the brain of man could suggest, has generally been thought worthy of preservation by all the generations of artistic and inartistic successors.

Much has been said above of great losses. The wooden roof, with its leaden casing, was often the cause of this mischief. Many a fire extended to the church from the monastic buildings which as yet were mostly built of timber. No Norman cloister remains, because Norman monks were content with a timber lean-to. In the contemporary accounts of the building of the monastic quarters, the refectory, locutory (parlour), dormitory, infirmary, kitchens, lavatory, scriptorium (as at St. Albans), the cellarer's building, the bakery, mill-house, " necessarium," granary, brewery, stables and gate-houses, the materials named are generally wood, wooden shingles (*i.e.*, wooden tiles) and lead roofing. Thus at Abingdon, Faricius for his building sent for beams to Wales, and they were brought in wheeled cars drawn by twelve oxen, at great cost, for they took six or seven weeks on the journey going to and from Shrewsbury. At Glastonbury it was the great Henry of Blois who as abbot first planned stone monastic buildings.

The enormous efforts made by the monasteries to raise such sums as 200 or 400 marks (the mark is 13s. 4d.), are the best evidence of the value of these sums. We know not precisely by what number we should multiply to get an idea of their meaning, but even thirty-fold is deemed far from an exaggeration. Anselm, to raise 200 marks, due to Rufus, applied to the convent to find the sum for him, if in return he would give them a manor worth £40 a year. The whole of this manorial income, Eadmer says, was soon used up in building a tower of the cathedral. The monks of Abingdon, to raise 300 marks, stripped the gold and silver off the shrines and reliquaries ; the same method was resorted to when famine oppressed the people, and huge sums were needed by the monasteries to relieve their necessities.

Many records descriptive of the beauty of the church ornaments made in this period have come down to us, but few indeed are the actual relics of the Norman past which can be dated with some pre-cision like the Gloucester candlestick, made in Serlo's time (1072–1104), and early sent over to France, as the inscription testifies. Still grander must have been the seven-branched candlestick for whose gilding Faricius laid £30 of gold on the altar. An abbot gave all his wool of a single year to provide a great " dorser " or tapestry-hanging for the back of a bench. On it was depicted the story of St. Ursula and her virgins. At Abingdon the monks were engaged in making dorsers, embroidered or perhaps painted. All the " obedientiaries " or monks holding offices made a dorser of the Apocalypse. The cathedrals had fine painted ceilings, and at Rochester it is recorded that there were stained windows and a mosaic pavement. At Durham, Flambard filled the windows round the altar with marvellous figures in glass. His castle windows were likewise of glass.

4. Another art on which the Norman Conquest had influence was that of writing. The Hiberno-Saxon hand of the English gave way at last before the continental Roman hand, taught perhaps in the first instance by Lanfranc. His kinsman when he started a " scriptorium " at St. Alban's found it necessary to fill it with hired scribes brought from a distance, who set to work upon texts provided by Lanfranc. The pope when he needed a new Bible sent to the monks of St. Augustine's for one. The bindings prepared at Winchester, of which several specimens remain, are magnificent specimens of the art of leather stamping. Two books prepared for Henry the son of Louis VI. of France before 1146—one was a copy of the letters of Ivo of Chartres—bear some of the same stamps and are thought to have been produced in England. The binding of the " Winton Domesday " which has some stamps identical with those on the Hegesippus (or abridged Josephus), now in Mr. Yates Thompson's possession, may be dated 1148, if, as is likely, it is contemporary with the text. At Durham in the last half of the twelfth century there was an equally important school of binding, with some 114 different stamps. The binding for Hugh Pudsey's Bible has nearly 500 impressions. Scarcely less interesting are the bindings made most likely in London at the end of the twelfth century. One covers an inquest concerning the lands of the Knights Templars. The number of extant twelfth-century

CANDLESTICK MADE FOR ABBOT SERLO OF GLOUCESTER,
NOW IN THE VICTORIA AND ALBERT MUSEUM.

From a pencil drawing.

BINDING OF MR. YATES THOMPSON'S HEGESIPPUS.
From a pencil drawing.

bindings is the more remarkable inasmuch as few of those of the next two centuries can now be identified.

FROM EADWINE'S PSALTER, 1130–1174.

The goldsmith's art went hand in hand with a busy traffic in relics which shocked William of Malmesbury. Long inventories of the human fragments which the monasteries reckoned among their most precious belongings, were entered carefully in their records.   Already to veneration of some of the relics relaxations of penance attached : Richard de Belmes, bishop of London, for instance, conferred privileges upon those venerating St. Osyth's arm.

5. Women of religious character were sometimes attached to the monasteries of men as recluses, till time allowed for the provision of a separate nunnery. This happened at St. Alban's, for instance.   How far the Saxon nunneries underwent in their turn the same revival as the houses for men, after the Norman Conquest, is not clear.   Their history is less familiar, because the Norman period produced no chronicle of a nunnery's inner life.   Certain it is, that well-born English women crowded to those already in existence as the one safeguard from Norman violence.   A letter of Lanfranc's adds a further testimony to the truth of the well-known story of Henry I.'s queen, Matilda. In 1086, while still a child, she entered the famous nunnery of Romsey and wore the veil there, unwillingly, and only to protect herself.   Once in a fit of passion she tore the piece of black cloth from her head and trampled it under foot, for which offence her aunt Christina gave her blows and bad language.

Of the old houses, which were very richly endowed, as Domesday shows, those that held first rank were Wilton, which is named with Romsey as the place of Queen Maltilda's education, Barking, Shaftesbury, St. Mary's, Winchester, and Wherwell, which was burnt in Stephen's reign by William of Yprès, to the horror of his contemporaries, aghast at the sacrilege. Of the new foundations (about a dozen under the first three kings), one of the most interesting is Malling, which Gundulf founded ; while he lived he made himself answerable for its management, and here, in all likelihood, reforms of a Cluniac character were introduced. The first abbess swore an oath of fealty in subjection to the bishop, and vowed to receive no nun without his leave. The nunnery was sufficiently large to bring many merchants to the village, who settled in a long street, and maintained themselves by supplying the needs of the nuns. Hither Robert fitz Hamo, a great baron, sent his daughter, giving with her, as was usual, what would pay for her keep.

A curious story is told of Stephen's daughter, Mary, who in the end was forced to marry at Henry II.'s command ; and this although there was no question in her case, as there may have been in the case of Henry I.'s queen, of the entirety of her vows. She was at first put with some nuns at Stratford, Bow, ladies who had come from Bourges. On account of the severity of their order and " the difference in manners " (between French and English), they packed up their goods and moved off with the princess to Lillechurch, Kent, the manor which Stephen had given them in his daughter's support.

At Kilburn three of the " domicellae " or ladies-in-waiting to Matilda, Henry I.'s queen, retired into religion, probably on her death. The nunnery was subject to Westminster, and Osbert of Clare, at one time prior there, was a friend and correspondent of the nuns.

There is not much evidence relating to the state of learning in the Anglo-Norman nunneries, but the letters addressed to nuns by Anselm, and by Osbert of Clare, go to show that then, as before and after, the nunneries had their merits as " she-schools." Some of the choicest examples of illuminated manuscripts belonging to this period come from the nuns' church or library of Shaftesbury.

6. Of schools for boys, the Norman period shows no dearth. Monastic, cathedral, and parish schools worked side by side. Just as Lanfranc made Christchurch a school for young clerks and monks, so at Norwich bishop Herbert was training boys who were perhaps not all destined for the cloister. Of the secular clerks it is known that at Waltham they had the schoolboys taught in the " Teuton manner." At Sarum, Osmund set an " archiscola " to hear and fix the lessons. At York one of Thomas of Bayeux's first acts was to " establish " the schoolmaster. In London schools were attached to the three great churches, all under a system of ecclesiastical licence. Any school which was started without licence from the bishop or chancellor in charge of the district was quickly put under anathema. There was a licensed school at Thetford, under a certain Dean Bund ; also at St. Alban's, under secular masters selected by the abbot of the monastery ; and at Dunstable, before the house of canons was founded, the schoolmaster Geoffrey of Le Mans got up his miracle-play of St. Katherine's martyrdom. The story is known because he borrowed choir-copes from St. Alban's for the dressing-up. These were burnt while in his

keeping, and his distress was so great that he closed his career as a schoolmaster and became a monk.

The schools of Kirkby and Pontefract were early placed under the collegiate church in Pontefract castle. At Warwick Earl Roger (1123–53) "gave " to the collegiate church its school, that by the presence of the scholars the service of the church might be improved ; the charter which records this may perhaps have been obtained by the church to secure itself against the rival school kept by the collegiate church of All Saints, which was protected by a royal charter.

It was a priest who taught the young Ordericus Vitalis at Shrewsbury, and a parish-school at Norham figures in the story of Godric of Finchale. Theobald of Étampes makes the general statement that there were schools in every town and village, and as many skilled masters as ministers of the royal exchequer. It is impossible then to suppose that the Normans cared nothing for education.

7. Already there were beginnings of teaching of a higher kind at Oxford. Theobald of Étampes before 1092 calls himself " Magister Oxnefordie," and between 1117–21, there were from 60 to 100 scholars there : in 1133 Puleyn lectured there on the scriptures, and in 1149 the Lombard Vacarius taught Roman civil law, but was silenced by king Stephen who represented, it would appear, the opposing forces of Teutonic feudal law.

Theobald, archbishop of Canterbury, had invited Vacarius to teach in his household : and it was in the episcopal palaces that statesmen, princes, lawyers, and historians were reared. The young Londoner Becket was being educated within our period, first by the Austin canons of Merton (who sent him home for his holidays half-yearly), then in the office of a great London burgess, where he was trained to legal business ; then he was sent abroad to Bologna and Auxerre to study law, and finally he entered arch- bishop Theobald's household. Contemporary with him there, during his period of training, was a future archbishop of York. The household of the bishop of Lincoln was an equally good school. Bloet's reputa- tion was kept up by Alexander the Magnificent, who had among his clerks Gilbert of Sempringham, the saintly founder of an order ; and Ralph Gobion (a future abbot of St. Alban's) whilst still a layman, learned to be a book-lover through hearing the lectures of an Italian master, Odo, given presumably in Alexander's household. The said Master Odo was in all likelihood one of John of Salisbury's teachers, and a student of Hebrew. His com- mentaries on the Psalms are extant.

But to get a university education it was usual to go abroad and move from one seat of learning to another ; to go to Paris for the purpose of hearing Abelard or Puleyn on philosophy or theology, to Chartres in order to hear William of Conches teach Latin composition, after a method that holds its own to this day.

Herbert of Norwich has left a vivid account of his own educational method, and tells how he provided the boys with tables prepared with wax (the counter- part of the modern slate), and made them repeat

Latin declensions and conjugations by heart.
"Donatus and Servius[1] I taught you all that year,
sitting on the low form at your elbow," he says,
writing to an old pupil. He was a thorough believer
in Latin verse as the best educational discipline.
Occasionally the children of a knight might be handed
over to the care of a governess, as appears from a
letter of Osbert of Clare.

[1] Interpreter of Donatus and a writer on the rules of metre.

SCHOOL SCENE, *c.* 1150.

VILLAIN WARMING HIS HANDS.

V

TILLERS OF THE SOIL

1. Difficulty of generalisation—2. The position of the serf, the villain, and the freeman—3. The lord's estate worked like a state—4. The open-field farming—5. The manor-court—6. The Peterborough survey—7. The system of weekly "farms"—8. The St. Paul's farm-buildings—9. The knights and the defence of the soil.

1. THE mass of detailed evidence which remains to explain and reveal that system of ranks based on land tenure which was the feudal system, and the nature of the farming which was essential to the maintenance of that system, continually challenges the historian to establish generalisations and as continually frustrates him. The more that is known the less does it appear possible to answer in a few words the leading questions that may be asked concerning

the state of the bulk of the population, the tillers of the soil. It is easy to put questions to the sphinx-like Domesday, but the number of questions Domesday will answer is strictly limited. In her riddles the form of the question is as vital to the solution as the form of the answer. One may easily miss the point. Flashes of inspiration, long and devoted toil, have given the antiquary peeps behind the veil, and it is possible that before long we shall know all that can be wrung from Domesday arithmetic.

And if the vast inquest of 1086 troubles us, it is even more depressing to challenge the many smaller land-surveys which wear the same delusive air of completeness and seem less alarming because less unwieldy, only here again to court rebuff. The surveys of single manors look at first sight capable of ready translation into symbols, into tabular form, and yet as soon as the task is attacked, it is obvious that the sub-groups are indefinitely numerous.

One thing at least is clear, that the Anglo-Norman feudalism was not a very simple social scheme in which the relations of men were governed by a few determinants capable of brief analysis. We are taught to compare this English feudal society to a pyramid ; at its apex the king, for its base the soil ; it is compact of human beings arranged tier upon tier, and the connection between the tiers is land-tenure. Yet such a comparison does not tell the whole truth and may even be misleading, because one man may have a place on one tier in relation to one of his holdings, and on another in relation to another. In every case he is lord to the men who

8

hold, directly or indirectly, of him, and also he is man to the lords of whom he holds, directly or indirectly. The services he owes and the rights he exercises may be of the most various. There are lords occupying the medium or " mesne " rungs of the feudal ladder whose vassality to the lords above is merely symbolic, or they may bear some of the burdens laid upon the soil, apt as a rule to fall on the shoulders of the man who actually tills it. This society compact of lords and men, not one of whom enjoys full and entire ownership in the land he calls his, is a sea in perpetual motion ; for ever vassals are changing suzerains, and lords are making fresh grants on new terms.

The phrase feudal *system* applied to the conditions of Anglo-Norman society under the first four Norman kings is unsatisfactory because no great lawyers had as yet appeared, ready to systematise society and to draw hard and fast lines. English society before the Conquest was in a chaotic state rapidly approaching the verge of anarchy, and the Norman kings restored government but did not immediately revolutionise or systematise society. English society, like every other society in Western Europe, had been trending towards feudalism, looking ever more to the land as the basis of all obligations, the medium of all political relations, but, if the lawyers' feudalism of a later date were unknown to us, we should be utterly at a loss to detect any system in the confused tangle of social relations which the Conqueror found. Throughout there is an admixture of the patriarchal element of an earlier time, but whereas of old the tribal relations

were real, and needed no conversion into terms of
land, here every relationship was so convertible,
either in actuality or as far as half-fanciful analogy
could make it so.

Domesday Book, written in 1086, offers a
statement of the dues owed by the greater part
of England to the king, and apart from the difficulties of language, apart from the fact that we
have not the key to all its expressions, we can safely
say that the society depicted was less capable of
concise legal analysis than at any later date. In one
respect only is there greater simplicity than we shall
meet later ; there has been little sub-infeudation,
and few mesne lords separate the tillers of the soil
from the supreme lord of England. The ladder of
lords erected over a given piece of land is a short
one. The king has a great number of tenants-in-
chief holding their land from him, and he has more
such tenants than he will have later on. His lesser
tenants will think it no discredit to enter knightly
service and become the followers of the great. The
pyramidal form becomes more pronounced as the top
tier narrows. •

2. The bulk of the population maintained its existence by agriculture, and not only its existence but
the existence of the sovereign and of the lords who
lived on the fruits, if by fighting they protected the
fruits, of their tenants' labours. The harvest of grain,
the flocks and herds, the forests, the fisheries, the mills,
bore the whole weight of national taxation. The nation
knew no unit of taxation other than the land, and the
plough that measured the land as it tilled it. The

farmers and agricultural labourers occupied a pre-
eminently important place in such a society.   It was
as to the number of these persons that William I.
inquired when his writ asked how many serfs, cottars,
villains, how many sokemen and freemen are there?
Of sokemen and freemen he asked further how
much land do they hold?   The serfs, numbering
some 25,000 in all, so far at least as Domesday
statistics are complete, must be treated at this
date as a class in every way inferior to the
villains.   Although if we try to put this slave-
class through strict examination as to what it is
in their status that makes them slave we are checked
at many points, inasmuch as the legal tests which
civilised races have invented to decide these matters
were unknown, nevertheless there is plenty to prove
that their slavish status was an acknowledged fact,
and that to cancel it, definite forms had to be gone
through.   We cannot say that their work is given
wholly to the lord's farm, that they possess none of
the implements of tillage, and do no work on their
own account, on land any part of the fruits of which
is their own ; or even that all their food and clothing
is the provision of their lord, for the lord can make
what arrangement he chooses, and can at his will
equip his " servi " with all those things which his free
tenants enjoy.   Some are menials but not all : it is
certain that many serfs occupied cottages and tilled
lands whose fruits were in part for their own use : but
to all " servi " who were known for such, the law
would bring home the general rightlessness of their
condition.   One at least of the legal characters which

to modern eyes make a slave a " chattel " and not a
" person," was conspicuously present, early in our
period : a man might kill his serf and no one could
bring him to justice. Early too in this period there
was a trade in slaves, against which bishops preached
and William I. legislated.

On the lord's farm the duties of the serf were such
as many men freer than himself were rendering, but
in the main the humblest offices of agriculture were
his ; his " arms " were a bill-hook and hedger's
gloves.

Probably in a slightly better position, just above
the serfs, tied to the soil, but not, like the serf, without the greater number of legal rights in the courts,
came a class of boors, *buri,* men who as English
geburs had been in a more favourable situation ; but
their state had been reduced by the processes of the
Conquest, and perhaps even before the Conquest, by
the exigencies of the ruinous Danegeld. About 900
only are named in Domesday, but as they were not
asked for in every writ, probably there were many
more. An account of the classes of men, written it is
believed shortly before the Conquest, records that
the gebur's services vary from place to place ; in
most places he works for his lord two days a week
(three days a week in harvest time), not counting the
ploughing which he does for his lord. His lord
provides him with 2 plough-oxen, 1 cow, 6
sheep, and seed for 7 acres out of his " yardland "
of 30 acres ; that is to say, with seed for about half
his arable, if he is letting 15 acres of it lie fallow
each year, as is not improbably the case. In return

he pays some rent in money, barley, sheep and poultry, but he never clears himself of his lord's debt, and at his death all that he has, down to his pots and pans, reverts to his lord. It seems to be this indebtedness that ties him to the land, and to his lord, not his unfreedom in the eye of the law, for before the law he has rights. Above this class of which Domesday names few, comes the great genus of *villani*, with whom are classed the bordarii, cotarii, coscets. The totals generally given from Domesday statistics are 108,500 villains, 82,600 bordarii, 6,800 cotarii and coscets. The *borde* is French, the *cot* English, and the shades of difference in the meaning of these terms are unknown. The French term " bordier " did not come to stay, and for this reason its meaning is lost.

The work that has been done of late years in analysing the position of the villains has gone to differentiate the villain of the Conquest period from the villain of a later time, who, in the systematising hands of the feudal lawyers, was dragged down to a low level. From the legal side, from the economic side, we run the risk of getting both yes and no as the answer to the questions which naturally suggest themselves, and, that we may not merely juggle with words, we are driven to take refuge in vague ideas. We have to see these "villani" as the English peasantry who occupy the places their forefathers had made for themselves, places that have been shaped gradually by circumstance, and not with any regard to system. Poverty has driven one peasant to the verge of slavery, success has kept another independent. But the tribal character of the original village settlement and the uniformity of the burdens fixed upon the villagers tend to give a common character to each group of villagers.

At the Conquest, the soil of England, or almost all of it, was distributed among Frenchmen : with the men tilling their soil they established varying relations, each according to his own idea of his best advantage. The king dealt very liberally with the peasantry upon his soil, so liberally that in the end the "villani" of the king's lands form a variety of great importance in the evolution of the whole class. At an early date the Abingdon Chronicle notes the reluctance of the "rustics" (or "villani") of a king's vill to be sold into the hands of an abbey. But the tendency for the English peasant to fall in the social scale was incontrovertible. The very language of the French conspired to reduce the Englishman's freedom. To a French law-writer of Henry I.'s day, a man who well understood both the English and their law, the *Francigenæ* or Frenchmen were free without any qualifying word. The Englishman who is not unfree and deserves to be ranked with a Frank is " Anglicus liber " ; he needs the qualifying word. In this society all the "barones," the lords, the "domini," or almost all, are French, or the children of Frenchmen ; the villagers or "villani" are the English natives.

The normal villager's holding, as the new lords found it, was no longer the "hide" once deemed necessary for the support of a family, but a yardland, virgate or quarter-hide, believed to amount under

normal conditions to about 30 acres. The villagers
had been bound for generations in the meshes of
a social institution as fixed as the family. They had
co-operated with their fellows in agriculture and in
meeting every national or seignorial demand, and from
this social force, this co-operation, Norman feudalism
had to draw its strength. In the relative equality of
their economic position, in their fellowship of feeling,
in the state's recognition of the " vill " as the unit
of taxation and of police, there lay the explanation
of the independence and dependence of villenage.
Above the " vill " was the " hundred " and above the
" hundred " was the shire, units in the scheme of
government which like the " vills " had an ancient
history. The outcome of a past whose social scheme
was not based on land tenure, these territorial units
of a tribal civilisation were maintained by the
conquerors, and inasmuch as hundred and shire were
both equipped with courts, where men of all the
feudal tenures met side by side, in a way which the
feudal system forbade, a great force was maintained
to prevent " feudalism " of the purer sort. All jurisdiction would not belong to the lords of lands unless
by a special royal grant. The place held by the
villagers or " minuti homines " or " smallemanni " in
the courts of the hundred and the shire was, for a
time at least, strong to maintain the peasantry in
a condition of relative independence. " Villani "
were summoned to give answers when the Domesday
commission of enquiry was made ; the villages which
were under no lord, or whose lord or his steward was
absent, were accounted for in the hundred or shire

court, for each such village sent its reeve and four men
to answer for or " acquit " the " suit " of the village, to
discharge the duty of regular attendance,—provided
no specific franchises enabled the lord to claim every
sort of jurisdiction over his tenants. But the same
record which is our authority for this system of
village representation, as it may fairly be called, tells
us that these men occupied a very inferior position in
the court. They had lost their old right as " suitors "
of the court, to speak " right," to pronounce judgments ; they had fallen from their rank as freemen in
that they might no longer be the judges of others
who were once their fellow " ceorls." Their oath
is worth so little compared with the oaths of greater
men, and the oath is still a measure of value, that by
Henry I.'s time they are deemed " viles et inopes
personæ," not fit to be numbered among the *barones*
of the county, who are the king's " judges " there.
Even Domesday once boldly contrasts the " elder
and better " men with villains and their reeves, " vile
plebeians."

But throughout Domesday the gulf between the
great class " villani " and the freemen, the " liberi
homines " and " sokemen " is set deep. Both " liberi
homines " and " sokemanni " are to be asked what
lands they hold, and although their dependence upon
the lord seems to vary with the special agreements
they have made, particularly in respect of the depen-
dant's power to alienate his land or to go to some
court of law which is not his lord's manor-court, theirs
is taken to be a dependence free from any humiliating
circumstance. They are taxpayers of position in the

national economy and are not humble people in the courts where they appear. Of the two classes, freemen and socagers, the name of the latter class alone was destined to stay as a distinctive term of tenure and status. So far as the difference between the "freeman" and the "sokeman" of Domesday submits itself to analysis, it is believed that the service which gives the sokeman his character is that he has committed himself to suit of court. All sokemen owe this suit, and they may owe other services besides, services which in amount and in kind cannot yet be classed as wholly distinct in character from the services of a villain of the more fortunate kind. Very different is this from the socage tenure of a later time, the freeman's rental which was ultimately to prevail in England and the colonies.

A lord's serfs had to do what he told them; but with his freemen and sokemen he bargained one by one. With his villagers he did not bargain, but taking the "villani" of each vill as a group, he required at least all that his predecessor had required, at least all that he had been accustomed to get from his villains in his Norman home. If he found that his estate was large enough to require a competent land-agent at a salary, he would get one, but if he could not do this, one of the peasantry was chosen as "reeve" or "prepositus" and authorised to see that the work was done which produced the lord's necessaries.

3. Each manorial estate was worked not as a slave plantation with gangs of oppressed villains under the lash of a superintendent, nor in farms occupied by

tenants at a money rent, tilled with hired labour, but rather as a little state. The lord's dominion over his land is of the nature of sovereignty as much as of ownership, and his relation to his tenants and their holdings is that rather of a ruler than of an owner. It is this perhaps that more than aught else explains the particular form which his exactions take, explains why they are not greater, explains why they are so evenly proportioned among his subjects. Harsh and mean as many of the lord's requirements may now sound, it was this equal and unalterable distribution of them among the groups of his men that took away the sting. In feudal lordship and villain subjection there lay a sense of right secured by custom that gave dignity to the system, a dignity too often absent from the modern relation of employer and employed, of capital and labour.

Evidence relating to the actual services rendered by villains on a given property is provided even in the Norman period, not only from the statements of Domesday, but from the minute account of a Peterborough estate drawn up in 1125–1128, and other passages from cartularies. The Peter-borough survey, penned by Walter the Archdeacon of Oxford (whose connection with the historical studies of the time has already been noted), shows how the agricultural work of an estate was distributed; there is evidence to show how the daily food of a great household was supplied by its several farms, and in this matter no doubt the monastic lords were doing only what there is reason to suppose that the secular lords were also doing;

a St. Paul's record further tells in detail what buildings were erected upon the farms.

4. The normal state of affairs was that in each vill (the Anglo-Saxon " tun ") or manor (and vill and manor as a rule coincide), a certain portion of land was reserved for the lord's home-farm or " demesne." This farm was not as a rule a group of more or less rectangular fields of arable, meadow or pasture, hedged or walled as we now see them, lying round a central farmstead, but consisted, like the holding of the mere villain, of half-acre or acre strips lying scattered in the two or three great arable areas of the village system of agriculture, with rights in meadow and pasture appurtenant to these strips. The lord in some cases had succeeded in securing a compact portion of the most precious land, meadow-land, which he called his croft or close, and it was worth some care in fencing : if not, he might have, like his own villains, " lays " in the village meadow, lying in acre or half-acre strips like-wise, if, as often happened, it had once been arable. But meadow and hay crop were rarely abundant, and for the bulk of the food of the live-stock, the lord looked, with his villains, to the rough pasture of the fallow-lands and wastes.

On a farm of this kind the lord as a rule kept a few ploughs and plough-beasts, to do some of his own work, but he generally had fewer in proportion to the size of his estate than his humble tenants, the villains, for it was to these tenants and their ploughs and plough-beasts that he looked to do the main work of his estate.

The quotas of work rendered by his tenants and
their wives in ploughing, harrowing, sowing, hoeing,
reaping, threshing, ditching, hedging, were fixed at so
many days in the week, so many at certain specially
busy seasons, with or without food at the lord's

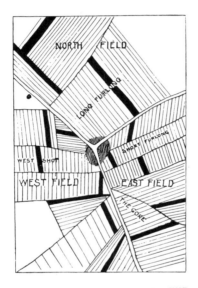

VILLAGE WITH THREE FIELDS. THE
BLACK STRIPS REPRESENT ONE
MAN'S HOLDING.

expense. The size of the " demesne," the number
of villains, the former system of working the
demesne, the amount of stock upon it, and many
other considerations, make these quotas vary from
place to place. But once fixed they were not easily
to be altered.

His quota of service rendered, the residue of the villain's time is his own to work upon the "yard-land" of some 30 acres that supports his own family and likewise yields a certain amount of produce to the lord. This amount was generally fixed in proportion to the grand total rendered by the whole village, and if the lord was lord of many villages, he distributed the necessities of his household among them. One village or group of villages supplied his grain, another his bacon, beef, or mutton, another his bread, beer or honey, lard, poultry, eggs, cheeses, or raiment. These quotas too the lord would find it hard to increase. But the lord's object in the first instance, whether he be secular or religious, was merely to maintain himself and his household in that state of comfort to which he had been accustomed. It had not yet become an object with him to lay up stores of wealth for the purchase of luxuries as yet unheard of. But his lands were heavily taxed by the king for the national defence and for the king's own necessities, and he must have money regularly to defray his "geld." For this he looked to his money rents. When the land could not well yield rent, as in the case of the humble cottager who had but five acres, then the lord charged him a penny for his goat or a halfpenny for his she-goat or pig. Nothing capable of yielding supplies was overlooked, yet no source of supply was taxed to a point of dangerous pressure. The villain must be left with land, stock, and time for labour, sufficient to enable him to live as he had hitherto lived. Individual success was not crushed by individual pressure, for the system was

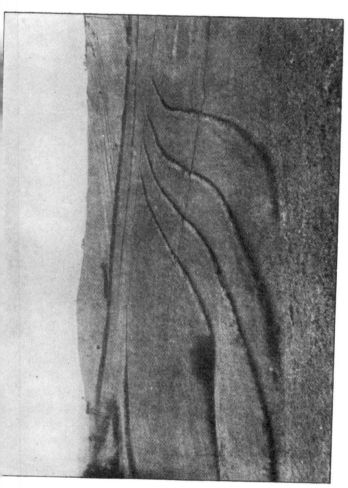

THE ROOD STRIPS AND BALKS IN THE OPEN FIELD OF BYGRAVE, HERTS.
From a photograph by Miss Leonard.

rigid. But under the pressure of the estate taxation, as nowadays under the pressure of national taxation, there might be cases of individual failure, and the villain who had lost his land might have to become a labourer working on the land of the successful villain. At Peterborough for instance there were the "undersets" who did no service save to the "husbands" or villains on whose land they "sat." There may be a class too of "semi-villani," those who reach a rank betwixt and between, who till, maybe, a half-virgate, a half-yardland, while full villains have their whole yardland apiece. The Conqueror's taxation when it stood at 6s. on the hide fell very heavily upon the villain, for if the villain's average be taken, as it reasonably may be taken, at 30 acres, worked by two oxen, he paid 1s. 6d. at a time when an ox cost 2s. 6d.

The "liberi homines" and "sokemanni" rendered similar "customs," but the varieties between individuals were much more numerous and there is less evidence that either class bore a share in the burden of supporting the demesne and household of the lord. Sometimes the lord might bargain with a group for certain services, more often perhaps for service on exceptional occasions, in times of extra pressure, for a "boon-day" done at the lord's request, rather than for the regular weekly service rendered by the "villani." The freedoms which Domesday explicitly leaves to the higher class seem to be the result of individual agreement, not of an ordered system for supplying the lord's primary necessities.

5. The idea that the manorial estate is politically

as well as economically a whole is carried out in the days when every lord of a manor, as such, had the right to hold a court of and for his tenants.   In the Norman period this may not be laid down as a legal principle, for the scheme of the relations of the manorial court to the hundred and shire courts had not been systematised ; but it soon would be universally true, and already it was true of all manors whose lords had received special "franchises."   To the last however it must be borne in mind that the manor-court, unless specially equipped with " *la haute justice*," was a court where only civil plaints or petty personal injuries could be treated.

In the manor-courts, whatever the range of their jurisdiction, the "villani" and the "liberi homines" met as "suitors," and as suitors they were judges of the causes that came before the court : for manorial law was only the old folk-law of the hundred.   No records of the proceedings of such courts in the Norman period are known to exist, and the consideration of their work must therefore be deferred to a later time.   We are in no position to say with certainty of the Norman period what rights the villain could assert to hereditary succession in his tenement, or to security of tenure if he rendered his services, or what rights he had to the control of his moveables and money, and to the liberty of his person.   One of the few generalisations comes from Abingdon, where it is stated that the abbot thought it desirable to win the goodwill of his "rustics" in order to get their aid in his building operations.   The "plebs" suffered from the arbitrary

9

exercise of the reeves' power, inasmuch as through malice or bribery, some were expelled from their dwellings. A villain died, having paid his just dues, but no grace was extended to his wife and children. The stranger who would pay for the land was brought in. Such was the villains' grievance. But the abbey complained on the other hand that the villains were unduly chary of rendering tithe. The abbot summoned his peasantry, offered them merciful treatment, promised " the remedy of freedom " so long as they would pay tithes in aid of the restoration of the abbey. Perhaps " the remedy of freedom " was not intended to bear a very precise meaning, but to the English " villani " it would be a useful phrase to conjure with. To them it would mean the enjoyment of all they had been accustomed to enjoy before the Normans came into the land. But a lord's needs could not often be used as a lever as in this case. A king could move the " churlish folk " from one part of the country to another, and to make a colony in Carlisle he could send a band of villagers whose consent may never have been asked.

6. The Black Book of Peterborough is the only Norman survey which goes systematically through a group of vills and describes the labours of the tenants and their rents in money and provender. The work is planned, like Domesday, to be primarily a " rate-book." The writer's first object is to show who is responsible for the royal " geld." The " demesne " of the monastery was in large part free from the burden : almost the whole charge was fixed on the

tenants. At the end of the survey of each manor,
the writer records the amount of stock which the
abbey has on its "demesne" or home-farm.

The first entry takes Kettering. Here there are
10 hides paying the king's geld. Of these 10 hides, 40
villains hold 40 yardlands, that is, apparently, each had
a normal holding of 30 acres apiece. The 40 villains
had among them 22 ploughs. Each villain ploughed
4 acres in spring for the abbey, and the group found
ploughs for the abbey a certain number of times in
the year. Each laboured for the abbey 3 days
weekly. The money rent of each holding was
2s. 1½d. The villagers together were answerable for
finding a provender rent of 50 hens and 640 eggs
each year. The village had a mill, and the miller
paid the abbey £1 a year for it. This sum he would
recoup no doubt from the milling tolls on villains
who were bound to go to that mill with their grain.
Besides the " villani" there were 8 cottars with 5
acres apiece, working one day a week for the abbey
and twice a year making malt for the abbey : they
paid a small tax for goat-keeping. The shepherd
was landless ; the swineherd had 8 acres. In the
abbey "demesne" were 4 ploughs, each with a full
team of 8 oxen ; and 12 cows, 10 calves, 2 "otiose"
animals (*i.e.*, not fit for the plough), 3 mares, 300
sheep, and 50 pigs, and meadow worth 16s. a year.
The church of the vill paid its offerings to the altar
of the abbey, so its priest was presumably ill-
provided. A heavy sacrifice was called for at the
monastery's great feast of St. Peter ; the village gave
4 rams, 2 cows, and 5s. In exchange perhaps there

was the hope of a scuttle of fragments for the paupers. Elsewhere it appears that the monastery systematically boarded out, as it were, not only the keep of its monks, but also its alms-giving. If an abbot had agreed to render certain payments on feast-days to the sick and poor, this, being an annual charge, was distributed upon the abbey's vills. Similarly the abbey's extra food on feast-days was assessed upon the vills.

7. When a great stationary household had to be regularly maintained throughout the year, organisation in the administration of the estates was essential, and the manors placed *ad firmam* were arranged so as to render the daily, weekly, or fortnightly, supplies in some sort of sequence. At the end of the eleventh century the canons of St. Paul's had so divided the manors of their " communa," that their keep for the year of 52 weeks (and one over), was permanently secured. A fortnight's farm was a common fraction for a village to bear. The earliest date to which we may ascribe the scheme of fortnightly farms for Ramsey Abbey, is not certain, but it probably falls within the Norman period. An average payment from a single vill was 12 quarters of flour for the monks' and the guests' bread, the price of the quarter 5s. ; 2,000 of village loaves or 4 quarters, for the servants' use, the price of 1,000 loaves 6s. 8d. For drink, 24 *missae* (messes) of "grut" (malt 32s. and honey 5s. 4d.) ; *ad compadium* (food that was not bread or drink), £4 in money ; 10 weighs of lard at 5s. a weigh ; 10 weighs of cheese at 3s. a weigh ; 10 fat pigs (friskings) of the best, at 6d. each ; 14 lambs

at 1d. each ; 120 hens at 6 a penny ; 2,000 eggs at
2s. a thousand ; 2 *tines* of butter at 40d. each ; 3 *treis*
of beans at 8d. each ; and 24 measures of horse-meat
(bran) at 8d. each. The value of the whole " farm " is
given as £12 15s. 1d., not counting the £4 in money.
In Lenten farms, less lard and less cheese were called
for, and the deficiency (a half) was made up in
money payment. The meat, if the monastic rule
was adhered to, should have gone only to the sick,
the guests, and the servants who were not vowed.
For spices, wines, and similar extras, the monastery
would have to depend on purchases at fairs or from
merchants ; likewise for salt sea-fish, unless it were
fortunate enough to obtain lands on the coast.   Earl
William of Warrenne charged his herring supply on
Brighton and Lewes, as Domesday shows.   At St.
Alban's, the sometime schoolmaster Geoffrey, the
unfortunate stage-manager of the miracle play, found
scope as abbot.   He arranged 53 weekly " farms " to
see the year round with a margin, and fixed with great
precision the relations between the monks' kitchen
department and the kitchen of the " externs."   At
Abingdon the chronicler sets on record with much
relish all the minutiæ of the arrangements for the
monastic cheese supply.   There are many scattered
statements, too, regarding the payments of *corrody*, the
food supply of a single person.   All these *diets* (day's
quotas) were carefully arranged on a somewhat
similar principle.   A Peterborough benefactor agreed
to send a green bough twice a day on condition that
he might have the " diet " of a monk and his four
servants shared the " diet " of a knight of the church.

The supplies of the King of Scots when visiting the King of England were reckoned on the Exchequer roll in corrodies, and later those of the queen, and the king's son. For the monasteries the corrody was a convenient way of guaranteeing to benefactors a sufficient annuity, when men parted with their property during life. Thus a rich Oxford burgess endowed Abingdon in his life-time and in return he was to be allowed to become a monk, or, if he preferred, he might live in Abingdon as a layman and have the food of one monk and one servant.

Besides the scheme of daily, weekly or yearly farms which aided the domestic economy of a great house or monastery, there was also the allotment of particular estates to particular offices of the house, to secure a proper distribution. The Norman Conquest, an age of organisation, was the date at which many monastic and cathedral funds were more systematically divided than of old. There are several indications that the system itself is older than the Conquest.

Besides the burden of rent and provender, there was also the burden of tithe for the villain to meet, a tithe that was still in some sense a voluntary contribution to the needs of his church ; but with the increase of system, with the increased demands of a Church that delighted in magnificent building and ornament, tithe was destined to become one of the heaviest and most regular of taxes upon agricultural produce.

Such records as the Abingdon chronicle bring out abundantly clearly the freedom with which the lords

of vills handed the tithe of the produce of their
vills to the monastery or the church of their own
choosing, or their own building, dictating at the same
time the particular object to which the money should
be devoted.   In return, if they had given the tithe to
a monastery, they looked to be quit of responsibility
for the parish church of that vill, in support of
which the tithe was supposed to be paid.   The lord
gave up his advowson, and the parish churches were
eagerly fastened upon by the rival ecclesiastical
foundations.   To the lord it was an inexpensive
form of benefaction, for it is not probable that he had
ever pocketed the tithes and oblations of his villains,
rendered to the altar of their worship : what he lost
seemed at the moment to be merely patronage.

8. The early twelfth century leases of the manors
of St. Paul's are interesting examples of the methods
employed in high-class farming.   The lessees were
mostly the canons themselves or their relatives, and
the stock and the buildings were evidently of exceptional excellence.   The leases describe the households
of farmers who are persons of importance.   One
lease of 1141 varies the rent from year to year, rising
each year.   The lessee in this case was receiving
stock, which he was to return if he gave up the
manor, *i.e.*, 20 oxen at 3s. each, 1 horse at 3s.
(evidently a poor one), 3 cows with calves, 120 sheep,
6 rams, and 30 pigs.   He received also a great
grange or barn, full at one end of wheat, at the other
of oats ; a second grange similarly stored, measuring
52 feet by 47 ; besides large " coulisses " or side-
rooms, which are also measured.   A third barn con-

tained rye, barley and hay. He found the lands
either sown with wheat, barley, oats, beans, peas, or
in fallow : in like state he must return them. He
must return also on one side of the grange the winter
and on the other the spring-sown corn, and all the
hay of the year. Some manuring was required of
him.

The household was accommodated in quarters
which are minutely described : there are all the
requisites of a first-class manor, the hall and
" camera" (for sleep and retirement), the private
" domus" next the camera, and another in the courtyard ; the separate buildings, grouped about one or
more " curiæ " or yards, are united by " tresences " or
passages, and pent-houses. There are also granary,
kitchen, hay-house and stable near the hall. The
lessee receives furniture, 4 casks, 3 cups, a boiler, a
bench, a stool, 2 tables ; also some well-seasoned
wood. The buildings are all of one story. In a lease
of 1152 the size of the hall is given as 35 feet long,
30 feet broad, 22 feet high, 11 feet under the beams
(supporting the roof), 11 feet above. There is likewise here a " domus" (the private dwelling), 12 feet
long, 17 feet wide, 17 feet high, 10 feet under the
beams, 7 feet above ; and besides the " domus," a
" camera" 22 feet long, 16 feet wide, 18 feet high.
On the same farm the cow-byre was 33 feet long, 12
feet wide, 13 feet high ; the covered sheepfold 39 feet
long, 12 feet wide, 22 feet high ; the lambing-house,
24 feet by 12 feet, and 12 feet high. For the first
year this farm paid a rent of £5, rising by a pound
each successive year. The " firmarius " promised to

treat and keep "the men of the manor" reasonably, for the tenant of a farm of this kind was in the position of the lord of the manor. An undated lease orders that the lessee's agreement with labourers for hire shall stand confirmed. Evidently these canons of St. Paul's were ready to move with and even in front of the times.

9. But the land bears another burden besides rents of provender. The Archbishop of Canterbury owes the king so many knights : such is the phrase characteristic of the feudal as compared with the modern principle. The central government brings home its claims to a comparatively few great people, who may meet them as best they can. Besides the provision of his own household supplies, besides the provision of the king's taxes, the lord had to allocate a provision for the military service which the king had fixed upon his estate. That service the king had fixed upon both religious and temporal estates, leaving at first the method of its provision entirely to the discretion of his tenant. Even abbots kept their quota of knights in their own households and fed them at their own table, so that they were ready to answer the king's summons without delay. In monastic houses this arrangement was destructive of domestic peace, as is recorded in more than one of their chronicles, and there was no reason why this burden should not be distributed, like any other, upon the lord's or the convent's estates. One of Anselm's councils forbade knights to be kept domestically. At Peterborough eighteen of the knights were housed in part of the

town, and for long received their food from the monastery, so that "the food of a knight" became a familiar measure.

The great tenants-in-chief let out their lands here and there to knights, who formed a distinct "order" in society. They were bound to appear duly armed and horsed, to render military service during a certain season at their own charges. So heavy was this burden deemed, that it cancelled every other. Henry I. released the knights from the burden even of his "geld." They "defended" their lands not by money and ploughing and provender like the farmer, but by their spears and coats of mail. The knight, endowed with his "fee" in land, was lord over those who were tilling his soil, and in his turn he made what bargain he could. If his genius were military he would again sub-let his estate so as to provide himself with the necessaries and extra-vagances of a military life. Or the opposite might happen. Already knightly service could be bought off by a payment of a certain sum of "shield" money to the king. Thus it was possible for the knight to turn farmer, to go on crusade, or to earn his 8d. a day with the hired Flemish warrior. It is not likely even in the middle of the twelfth century that there were more than 5,000 knights' "fees" to be answered for in England : and there is reason to think that this body was never called out for service as a whole.

TILING WITH WOODEN SHINGLES.

VI

THE BURGESSES

1. JUST as there was an " order " of knights, orders of religious persons, orders among the tillers of the soil, so likewise there was an order of burgesses. As in all the other orders here too there is an element of caste mixed up with the element of tenure. The difficulty which we have found in putting precise meanings upon terms that seem intentionally technical, and therefore challenge definition, meets us to the full as strongly in the case of the burgess as

in the case of the villain.   The order is made up of
people in most heterogeneous positions, of rich and
poor, independent and dependent, living in walled
towns, living in the country, of tillers of the soil, of
traders, of the men of many lords.   The "borough"
with which they are somehow or other connected, by
residence, by geld, by service, was a technical term ;
certain legal conceptions had attached to the borough
which differentiated it from both vill and manor,
though in origin it might have been a vill, and in
unity of lordship it might be a manor.   These legal
conceptions found their embodiment in the borough
court, which had long ago taken its place among the
legal institutions of the country, side by side with the
hundred and shire.

A French model, that of the great Earl William
Fitzosbern's castle, Breteuil, was freely taken by a
number of lords who desired to locate boroughs of
freemen upon their lands, especially in the Welsh
Marches.   One bait which proved specially attractive in the offer of these customs was that which
prevented the lord from exacting heavy pecuniary
fines for offences of any kind.   The manner in which
these boroughs were established shows that many
were artificially created to meet a need for well-
established markets, and groups of traders ready to
provide the newly-built castle with commodities.
Such traders would not willingly approach the castle
walls unless they were protected by law from
seignorial exactions.   To develop a market, chartered
rights must be conferred, and the lord, instead of
dealing with individual tenants, found himself, in the

case of his burgesses, confronted by a fairly strong community of interest.

Many French burgesses seem to have come over from France and settled down in suburbs side by side with the English, but in a group so compact and under such distinct customs, that the severance of the two races remained more marked here than in any other part of the country.

The effect of the action of the Norman lords in creating boroughs upon their private estates, by legal enactment, was at first to increase the importance of tenure as an element in the burghal character, but in the end the development of boroughs as places of commerce induced a marked change. Instead of being a typical outcome of feudalism, the borough becomes distinctively non-feudal. Any one can take up the franchise of burgess-ship if he will pay for it.

In the Middle Ages towns did not "grow" but were made. A village, just because it was a large one, could not gradually come to be called a borough any more than it can now-a-days. A definite legal act was necessary to sever it from a hundred and give it a hundred-court of its own. Wherever we can go back to the beginning, this formal act of creation can be traced.

For our present period the material for the history of the burgesses is to be sought mainly in the passages of Domesday which relate to the ancient boroughs, in a few scattered references which speak of diminutive new ones, planted upon a tenant in chief's estate, and in the very few charters which date back to Henry I.'s reign. But there are further two detailed surveys, and one fortunately is of Winchester, England's second capital, which are valuable as giving a really minute picture of a Norman town. Also the legal customs of the Londoners are known in some detail, customs which seem to have been written down about 1135, and form a valuable gloss on the chartered rights.

The Domesday statements relating to the customs which prevailed in the county towns, are in many cases statements concerning the past, and relate of course almost exclusively to those matters which concerned the king's treasury. The king was primarily interested to know how much the borough was contributing to his expenses in direct payments, in service, in judicial fines. It is clear that many of the boroughs had been paying regularly large fixed sums of money; that many of the houses were burdened with a small annual rent to the king; that he looked also to certain "customs," which are not always closely defined; and that certain special judicial fines were his in some of the boroughs.

The burgesses like the villains seem thoroughly accustomed to act together for a number of purposes, and whatever the inequalities of their wealth and their burdens, they generally formed a community in a very real sense. Isolated references to single burgesses and groups of burgesses, concerning whose connection with any borough Domesday says no word, may be urged to the contrary. But Domesday's silence never counts for much. In all likelihood these country burgesses, living in villages that never were boroughs, were attached to a borough, attended its

court half-yearly or thrice-yearly, and paid their share
of the borough's farm or quota of service.   The idea
that residence in a borough was essential to burgess-
ship was not an early one.

The unity of the borough again appears much
broken where its geographical area is honeycombed
with manorial "sokes."   Many burgesses seek their
justice at the court of the lord, whose tenants they
are, or to whom they have "commended" themselves.
The borough court loses the fines of these burgesses,
but the franchise of the soke is not wide enough to
save the burgess who inhabits within it from all connection with the borough court.   Perhaps the borough
officer cannot arrest within the soke, but he can lie in
wait to catch the offender when he is off the privileged
ground.   In some of the boroughs, as Domesday
records, certain grave crimes are the king's, that is,
he gets the fines for them and the fines are royally
high.   In some the king has made his peace supersede the claims of all men in certain parts of the
borough or at certain seasons.   At Dover the
herring-fishing season, at Chester Sundays, at
Wallingford the market day, at Canterbury the open
streets had their special peace, and for an infringe-
ment of that peace the penalty went to the king,
though the penalty was exacted by the borough
court.   In London this "close-season" covered the
Rogation Days, and the king's officer could catch
men in the streets though he might not enter their
houses within privileged "sokes."

2. In most of the boroughs a large area of agricultural land was attached to the walled town, for

this area had formed part of the original settlement. Here lay those arable "fields" which were the normal equipment of a Teutonic village settlement. It was to this land that some of the burgesses looked, like the villains elsewhere, as the main source of their support. Upon this agricultural land the king or his deputy had in some places succeeded in fixing certain claims to agricultural service, whenever such service might be profitable to him. Thus at Hereford the burgesses were bound to reap for three days in August and to gather hay on the day in the year when the sheriff ordered it. At Cambridge the burgesses lent their ploughs to the king's sheriff three times a year in Edward the Confessor's time, and they complained that the Norman sheriff had claimed them nine times, together with additional duties in lending carts and teams to draw them. But these services were not often imposed and were never sufficiently large to take up a measurable fraction of the burgess's whole working season, as was the case with those who were sokemen or villains. The same rough-and-ready system, which the lords used in distributing their necessities in quotas upon their vills, had been used in times past when the king required of this borough certain services in the chase because it lay near his forest, of that borough reaping service because he had need of reapers upon a neighbouring farm, of another, services in navigation because it lay on the coast, and was the place from which he or his messengers were in the habit of crossing. Thus Dover was charged with the necessity of setting the horses of the king's messenger across the Channel at a fixed tariff of 3d. in winter, 2d. in summer, the town finding the helmsman ; Torksey on the Trent was bound to arrange free of charge the transit of the king's messengers travelling by water. Shrewsbury, lying on the disturbed Welsh March,

IRON-WORKERS.

was bound to send forth a cavalcade of burgesses to protect the king for a certain fixed distance on his journey. Chester, where the Irish ships brought marten-skins, sent a certain quantity of these skins to the king. Gloucester, the heart of the iron district in those days, was bound to contribute nails for his ships and other iron goods. The same variety characterises his other rights. Here a watchful reeve has secured the king's death-duties or marriage-fines upon one class of men or one class of property, there upon another class ; elsewhere another has been less watchful ; and in the days when remembered precedent was more powerful than written law, on the foresight and watchfulness of individuals everything depended.

3. The king had already had occasion to realise that land was not the only commodity capable of feeding his treasury. The idea of taking a toll on trading transactions was an ancient one ; the law that protected trade was to be paid for by fines and fees, just as the law which defended men's lives was paid for. The English had artificially encouraged by their laws the natural tendency of trade to centre in populous places ; mints were established in the boroughs ; markets and merchants were protected ; and when the collection of toll had become an item of revenue worth considering, freedom from toll became a franchise to be sought for, like every other freedom from geld. The sovereign right in tolls and markets was loaned, given, farmed, like every other sovereign right. Domesday does not say much on the subject of the "octroy," which affected every retail and wholesale trader who had occasion to get his goods to market or away from market. But it does tell of a specially favoured place, a port which it was desirable to encourage, Dover, whose men were quit of toll throughout all England. The same would doubtless

have been said of Londoners if Domesday included London. Evidence of the immense value set on the right to take toll and on the privilege of exemption from toll comes from all parts. The merchants of Beverley, of Dover, of Winchester have in their "hanshus," their "gihalla," their "chapmansele" or merchants' hall, the outward and visible sign of certain powers obtained by the burgesses: his gildhall is for the burgess what the manor-hall is for the lord. London's "gialla" or gildhall mentioned about 1132 measured 52 feet wide and 132 feet long.

The Merchant Gild within our period took a place among the institutions of mediæval law. It is clearly divided from those private associations which have no place among the institutions of government. The Anglo-Saxons had had their clubs and societies, drinking, burial, friendly, religious; London had gone further and had provided an association for the purposes of police which measures the high-water mark reached by the English in municipal development. The Anglo-Saxon had a characteristic aptitude for co-operation, especially in the meeting of financial claims, an aptitude which the strength of the family tie had taught him. As this tie weakened, he turned to his "congildones" to replace it. The very thieves were "gegildan" in their gains. The state had forced upon the borough a sense of taxational unity, but it was the result of the Conquest that the borough developed as a trading unit. Co-operation in trade there was, no doubt, already, and market regulations, but the idea of a sworn association binding the whole group of burgesses to protect a monopoly of toll and trade appears to have come to England from abroad. Even within this period we get no detailed account of a merchant gild, and the analysis of its working must be deferred to the next.

4. Of London in Norman times a good deal can be known. William the Conqueror addressing the bishop, portreeve and all the burghers, French and English, confirmed to them their Saxon law and willed that every child should be his father's heir, heir to his franchises, perhaps he means.

A very large and wealthy town in a very small county, London's position was from the first distinct. As a taxational unit Middlesex was treated as a mere appendage to London ; the farms of county and city were charged together at £300 and London's officer was made answerable for it. He was called "sheriff" or "portreeve" indiscriminately in the early Norman days.

The part the Londoners played in Stephen's reign gives evidence of their great political importance. They are proud to call themselves "barones" rather than citizens or burgesses, and consider that the election of the king is to be determined by them.

In Henry I.'s day the citizens appear to have first of all leased the shrievalty from the king, and then to have obtained the chartered right to elect their own sheriff, and likewise their own justiciar, to answer for the grave crimes, the royal pleas. Another course was adopted at Lincoln, which borough in 1130 paid heavily that the burgesses might hold "as tenants-in-chief of the king"; they succeeded in dissevering their "farm" from that of the county, and themselves became answerable directly to the exchequer, instead of through the sheriff of the county.

The London burgesses were strong enough to obtain, by money or otherwise, a clear written statement of their rights. Their "farm," which the king had been trying to increase, was kept to the old sum. The citizen was confirmed in his enjoyment of the old English system of compurgation as his means of legal defence: if he could find enough friends to swear that they believed his oath, he could clear himself of the gravest charge. No higher sum might be charged to him as a fine than 100s., the English "wergild" or man-price paid by the kin of the slayer to the kin of the slain.

The city kept its folkmoot or primitive assembly, gathered, at the sound of the great bell of St. Paul's three times a year, Michaelmas, Christmas and Midsummer, at a corner of St. Paul's churchyard. There the community acclaimed sheriff and justiciar, or if the king had chosen his officer, heard who was chosen and listened to his charge. Of its old judicial functions the folkmoot had little left save the formal hearing of a decree of outlawry: at the Christmas meeting the watch was arranged ; at Midsummer the risks of fire were dealt with.

The judicial functions of the folkmoot had been delegated almost wholly to the house-assembly or hus-thing, a weekly court of elders of the people sitting at the gildhall. Here the aldermen spoke "right," and no doubt ordered the arrangements for compurgation, deciding whether the gravity of the case required 36, 18 or 6 purging oaths. Much of the procedure of their court has been set on record and it bears many traces of high antiquity in its curious archaisms.

For convenience of watch and ward, to defend walls and gates, the city was divided into wards, each under an officer called an alderman. These were the elders (in many cases hereditary officers) who were judges in the husting.

Within each trade or craft, the same principle is manifest which is manifest in the borough as a whole, an idea of association which sees in the very craft the common property of those who exercise it ; each "brother" has an aliquot share in it, as the merchant has in the borough commerce, as the villager has in the arable fields.

The goldsmiths and the weavers of London had become sufficiently rich and important to form associations or gilds able to pay heavy annual fees to the king in order presumably to obtain a royal licence which enabled them to have some control over their trade which they thought worth paying for. In other towns there were craft gilds equally wealthy. But next to nothing is known of the nature of these organisations at this time, whether for instance any one was permitted to enter a craft without entering the gild, whether there was a distinction drawn between masters and servers or journeymen, or what was the nature of the control of the craft. Weavers, fullers and dyers may have worked for day and piece wages as in the thirteenth century, or, like goldsmiths and shoemakers, weavers may have been independent producers and sellers of the finished commodity.

There are hints already of opposition to such unions as those of weavers, fullers and dyers, later the object of determined hostility in some boroughs. On the fullers of Winchester had been charged the unpleasing task of dismembering outlaws, and they paid a mark of gold to the king to be quit of it.

The pipe-roll of 1130 bears abundant testimony to the range and variety of the Londoners' trade, a constant theme of boasting in the chronicles. The first two-storied stone house of which there is mention is a London house belonging to Ramsey abbey 1114–1130.

5. The Domesday description of Colchester gives so minute an account of the holdings of individuals that it amounts to a survey. But it is altogether surpassed by the surveys of Winchester 1103–1115 and 1148, as also by the surveys of Gloucester and of Winchcomb (c. 1100). At Winchester sworn burgesses surveyed the king's demesne, street by street in regular order, recording the rents of the houses and the sums due to the king as "gafol," marking the houses which owed help to the watch. It offers valuable evidence of the mixing of French and English burgesses, the variety of the trades, the arrangement of booths, stalls and butchers' shambles, and the changes caused by newly-erected buildings. It tells of the prison, to provide food for which is a "custom" charged on a tenement : it tells of the female hermit, the forges, and the field where linen cloth was sold ; it has been reckoned from the whole detailed statement that the population was from six to eight thousand.

6. By way of contrast with the great cities, London and Winchester, we may take a small monastic borough, Bury St. Edmund's, whose charter belongs to 1121–1148. This charter says that it was customary for the Bury men to find eight men a year from the four wards to keep the town by night ; and on St. Edmund's feast (November 20) sixteen men were to be distributed among four gates, two by day and two by night : so also for twelve days at Christmas. At each of the gates the townsmen were yearly to provide one " janitor " : for the fifth gate, one of his own making no doubt, the abbot was responsible. When the gates had to be repaired, the abbey's sacristan found the wood, and the burgesses dressed it. For the repair of the town ditch, the burgesses agreed to work together with the knights and sokemen of the abbey, but they claimed that the work belonged as much to the knights as to them.

By this charter, as by many others, the burgesses were expressly enabled to sell and bequeath their lands " as if they were chattels " : the lord's consent to alienation was not required ; and at a time when other men could bequeath by will only their moveable property, the burgess escaped sometimes both the old tribal and the feudal law. He was given a very short period of prescription, a year, and special facilities for the easy recovery of debt. Whoever was his lord, and even though he had been guilty of wrong-doing outside the borough, he was protected from all outside courts of law. It was in his borough-court that he should answer ; there he was surrounded by all his friends ; and there he had only to get oath-helpers in order to go quit.

7. The Newcastle custumal which comes from Henry I.'s time shows that the burgesses held that they alone had any right to a share in the borough trade. No merchant who was not a burgess might buy wool, hides, or any other merchandise outside the borough, because the burgesses might want all of it ; and what he bought within the borough (where he must pay toll) must be bought from burgesses. Every burgess might have his own oven and hand-mill if he liked, though there was a king's oven to which he must still do a certain amount of "suit," which involved payment for the service rendered.

At Pembroke by the earliest charter, of Henry I.'s time, the burgesses made arrangements for the ward-ship of their orphans, lest there should arise a chance of seignorial interference. Very close then is the burghal brotherhood that stands in the place of tribal kinship.

8. The brotherhood of burgesses must share and share alike in the opportunities that occur for a good bargain. If a ship came with wine or a cart with herring, no one burgess could buy up the stock and then make his own bargain with buyers, but every burgess who wished to buy could claim by borough law his aliquot part in the original bargain. This was one of the advantages of fellowship in the borough. There was a countervailing disadvantage. If a burgess of, for instance, Nottingham had left debts in Newcastle any burgess of Nottingham who

visited Newcastle was legally liable to have his goods
distrained upon for a debt that was none of his
making.   There was, as it were, chronic warfare
between boroughs, and no international law to protect the property of those who would fain be non-
combatants.   Every borough would treat the burgess
of another borough as surety for his fellow-burgess,
and this system went on until the thirteenth century,
and left its traces even longer in some codes of
borough law.

9. Intimately connected with the history of town
life is the history of the Jews, who began to come to
England in appreciable numbers at the Conquest.
From Rouen especially there was a large migration.
In 1130 the London Jews are found paying the
immense fine of £2,000 "for the sick man whom
they killed." Left at the mercy of the king, protected by his special grace, they found their anomalous position for some time a source of strength.
They were in close relation with the king, acted as
his financiers, and were so useful to him that he had
good reason not only to protect them against all
other men, but also to put some restraint upon his
own greed.   A source of profit to him in their direct
payments, they were likewise a means to obtain
money from Christian subjects : many would pay
"for the help which the king gave against the Jews,
concerning a debt." Every time that a case in which
Jews were concerned came before the king's court,
there was a fine paid from the Jew for being allowed
to plead, or a fine from the Christian for being
allowed to implead the Jew.

Nature herself offers no quainter spectacle than the efforts of the feudal organism to adapt itself to the Jewish intruder. Into a society that was bound together by a system of oaths, in which the oath of fealty strung men upon a chain like beads, came an important group of men incapable of taking Christian oaths : to find a place for this new category strained feudal subtlety to the uttermost. It was left to the royal ingenuity to decide what nature of " peace " the law would extend to these anomalous persons. The Jews have been called royal villains, but more apt perhaps it would be to describe them as men " feræ naturæ," protected by a quasi-forest law. Like the roe and deer they form an order apart, are the king's property, and, though protected by him against others, nothing save the uncertain royal prudence protected them from their protector.

WALL OF SOUTHAMPTON.

MACHICOLATION.

PART II

THE LAWYERS' FEUDALISM

(1154–1250)

VII

THE KING AND COURT

1. Henry II.'s empire and its collapse—2. The Court and its increased formality — 3. Character of Henry II.'s expenses—4. John's account-rolls—5. Henry III.'s artistic tastes—6. Evidences of royal literary taste—7. The queens and their education.

1. BY reason of his inheritance, and by reason of his policy, Henry II. ranked among the greatest of European lords. His subjects boasted that his rule extended from the Arctic Ocean to the Pyrenees. If royal marriages could determine the fate of nations, the greater part of Europe might have passed under his dynasty. He was the head of a new line and in personal appearance showed himself a native of

Anjou. As a Frenchman, he preferred his castles on the Loire and on the Seine to those of England, but as a politic and far-seeing statesman he did not neglect his island kingdom. Trained in the law, a lover of the subtleties of law, canon and civil, he and his staff of learned clerks made it their business to smooth away those ragged edges which the first Norman kings had left in the hurried fitting of Norman on to English law. In the process many and great changes were made, changes calculated to strengthen the central as against the feudal power. A lawyer king found further a grand opportunity before him to display his learning and his strength when he engaged in one of the longest and most exciting rounds in the periodic wrestling match between Church and State.

Upon his death followed Richard's crusade, bringing many changes in the ideas of feudal society, opening many new fields for enterprise, bearing weighty fruits, good and evil, for European civilisation. With John's reign came the collapse of that European empire which Henry II. seemed to have built: and a new sorting of the pieces in the game had to follow before it could begin again. John's reign shows the first union of all classes of his subjects against an English king: that union led to the drafting of the greatest of charters. Then for a moment it seemed possible that England might become more French than ever. The French king's son was invited over. But John's sudden death, and the existence of an infant heir, gave an opportunity for the creation of a national party. As subordinate movements come the waning of the monastic force, the waxing of the universities, and the mendicant orders. In architecture men could attain no greater grandeur than had been achieved already : a new development was sought towards refinement and elegance, towards an improvement of architectural science.

2. On a small scale the changes in court-life reflect some of the greater changes in government, in law, in the spirit of feudal society. If we contrast the court of Henry II. with that of the artistically-minded Henry III., a great change is at once obvious. It is not merely a change in the character of the expenses incurred by the two sovereigns, of which we shall have more to say ; there is evidence of a deeper change, in the idea of what a court should be. At the close of the period, the inward meaning of the feudal relation is obscured, and feudalism is tending to express itself in a certain formality. But formalism has not yet completely masked the reality : the feudal scheme was still far from being an empty husk ; nevertheless ideas of precedence, of legalised dignity, of ceremony, may be seen to have acquired an importance hitherto unknown, and this though there is still no peerage.

In court etiquette a new idea of the functions of officials shows itself, running parallel to the great constitutional changes. Just as in the king's council the outline of the earlier conception is more closely defined, and it is no longer left entirely to the king's will to decide who shall give him counsel, for precedent of his own making has come to tie his hands, so in the minor matter of a coronation, the feudal offices had become, even in Richard I.'s time, rather rights than duties, rather honours than services. The Londoners were willing to pay 200 marks to serve in the cellars, "notwithstanding the claim of the citizens of Winchester." By 1236 the feudalists were ready to enter upon an elaborate legal discussion of such matters. Notions of dignity and historic claim had come in to displace the old notion of service rewarded by perquisites. The perquisite system, of course, remains, endowed with an immortality all its own. After the coronation feast the chamberlain gets the basins and napkins, the officer of the "salsary" or sauce department the knives, the almoner the alms-dish and the further satisfaction of burning any leper who at the receipt of alms ventures to raise a knife against a neighbour.

3. The contrast between the rudeness of Henry II.'s court and the artistic refinement of that of his grandson Henry III., marks not merely the difference in the natures of the two men, but a real progress in urbanity. Peter of Blois, Walter Map, Gerald of Wales, all delight in telling stories of the disorder in Henry II.'s court, of the uneatable bread, the bad wine, beer, meat and fish, of the marshals kicking the people about, of the grab for quarters when the court moved through the country : the king's movements could never be anticipated ; only the court-taverners and courtesans could guess what they would be. A mob of "actors, dicers, mimes, barbers, washerwomen" (*i.e.*, courtesans), disturbed the peace of every one ; even those who had let blood, and ex-

pected some consideration in their weakened state, could secure no tranquillity.

Henry II. was lavish only where the royal dignity could be attested by display. When he sent his daughter to Sicily, famed for its wealth, he provided for her a gold table 12 feet long, a silk tent to hold 200 knights, 24 gold cups and plates, 100 galleys; the items are known to us because of a dispute about their return, when the lady was sent home with nothing but her bedclothes. On ordinary occasions the king had no use for display. If he cut his finger, he sewed it up with his own needle, while his courtiers sat round "in modum coronæ." Thus humbly occupied, he could enjoy an episcopal joke on the ancestral skinner who figured in the family tree.

Henry II.'s building was for the most part utilitarian ; Peter of Blois has set it on record that he was splendid in his castle-building, and in his palaces, but probably his greatest achievements were in his French dominions. His favourite English houses were at Clarendon, Kennington, Woodstock, Windsor, Portsmouth and Southampton. The pipe-rolls, on which his sheriffs entered disbursements made by his order, show him ordering marble columns for Clarendon, and getting the lead for the roof of Windsor Castle from Cumberland. The nails for his houses at Winchester came, as usual, from Gloucester. One entry speaks of the clothing due to the painter who painted the doors and windows of the king's houses at Windsor : and Gerald of Wales describes a royal chamber at Winchester, beautifully painted with

figures. Upon a blank space the king ordered an
eagle to be painted and four young ones sitting upon
it, one about to pick out its parent's eyes. The four
young, he said, were his four sons, who would perse-
cute him to the death.   But Henry II.'s chief
agents were not artists but engineers.   One in
particular, Ailnoth, was continually entrusted with
difficult work, with building at the Tower, at Westminster, at Windsor, in Wales, with the throwing
down of the castles of the king's enemies, for example
Framlingham.   The great square keeps of Bamborough, Newcastle-on-Tyne, Dover, rose at Henry's
order in the midst of the castle fortifications already
reared by his predecessors.

The pipe-rolls now give a good general idea of
such expenses of carriage, clothing and feeding as
were of an exceptional sort. Of the normal expenses
of the royal household there is in Henry II.'s time
no record.   Upon the pipe-roll of the exchequer the
carriage of the king's money from place to place is
one of the most frequent items : carrying 5,000 marks
from Salisbury to Southampton costs 8s. 1d., and
there is also to be reckoned the cost of the barrells in
which the silver was packed, and the nails used to
close the barrells.   The precious cartload travelled
under special letters of safe-conduct. The "corrodies"
of the Queen and royal children, and of the court-
visitors are charged upon the pipe-roll, at least when
the households were separated.   The king's son
Henry, crowned in his father's life-time and bound
to keep up a royal state, was an expensive item.   On
the pipe-roll is recorded what wheat, barley and

11

honey went to make beer for the use of a suitor to the king's daughter, what expense was incurred in carting the young couple's clothes from Winchester to London, or on the forty yards of dyed canvas that was for the king's chamber at Winchester, or on the cost of the small "apparatus," probably kitchen utensils, sent with the king's daughter Joanna to Sicily. But the flashes of vivid detail that illuminate the exchequer-roll are comparatively few and far between. The exchequer is more concerned with the gathering in of the king's treasure, than with the classification of his expenditure. From other sources we know that Henry II. was spare in diet, and recommended the monks who were grumbling at their ten courses (cut down from thirteen) to do with three as he did. But then his were of meat. A tithe of the food that came to his table was distributed to the poor.

4. He died enormously rich, but Richard I.'s expensive occupation, crusading, ran away with the money. Richard was too rarely in the country to leave his personal mark very strongly on the accounts. The brilliancy of his coronation may be guessed at from the thousands of cups and dishes, charged on the accounts of various sheriffs. With John's reign, a new and more personal form of account begins, in what are known as liberate-rolls. The orders for money directed to the Treasurer and Chamberlains of the Exchequer begin to be separately enrolled ; the cause of the expenditure is in each case stated under the writ ordering the delivery of the money. Still more interesting as a record of the daily life of

the court are the two "misæ" or charge-rolls of John's reign, which alone remain as a sample of the rest, and of equally close personal interest is the series of "oblate" or receipt-rolls which now begins, showing the king's gains in the form of all sorts of offerings and fines for offences. Here the king appears as the recipient of gifts of food, money, rare hawks and well-bred horses, by way of placating his too variable temper. When John was on terms with his queen it is by a "liberate" writ that he orders the sheriffs of London to cause the Constable of the Tower and Chamberlain (treasurer) of London to have the price of twelve yards of scarlet cloth, three skins of "biss" (deer-skin), a pelisse of "gris" (squirrel or calabar skins) of nine "fessis" (bands), four pair of women's boots, each pair furred with "gris," black burnet for "hose," four white and good wimples, sent for her use to Marlborough. The employment of his niece Eleanor (Arthur of Brittany's sister) may be guessed from the sheriff of London's order to let her have 5 oz. of silk probably for embroidery. The same young lady was provided with a hood for rainy weather at her uncle's wish; it is charged on the roll. The splendour of his apartments appears from entries on the pipe-roll, for cloth of Arras and silk were ordered for his chamber. Thousands of yards of white "halberg" (padding), of dyed cloth and scarlet, were ordered at the same time, probably for household liveries, and for the king himself a "pour-point" or elaborately stitched "wambeson" (padded leather coat). The beginnings of heraldry are seen in the purchase of three "coats armatory," probably

intended to be worn by the king. Here is recorded
the purchase of a special " supertunic " for getting up
at night, black burnet hose for daily wear (the king
is usually figured with his legs in black hose in the
early illuminations), leather hose for hunting, and
furred boots. The " roba " is shown by the accounts
to consist of tunic, supertunic and cloak ; in the next
period the essentials of a suit of clothes were five in
number. The English stuffs took their names from
the place of manufacture ; Lincolnshire, with its
Sempringham and Stamford cloths, then took the
lead.

King John, among his other extravagances, had a
passion for jewels, and the record is preserved which
tells how a man was rewarded who found certain
precious stones " which we are wont to wear round
our neck." The lost stones may have been credited
with miraculous properties, for the reward was liberal,
20s. of rent in the place of the finder's birth.

Like all the kings, John travelled unceasingly, and
all his movements entailed expense in leather-trunks
and packing-cases to carry his dispensary, buttery,
and kitchen utensils. The sheriffs were continually
arranging his transport or providing the necessaries for
his chase. Men must be found to take game for his
use, to carry bream from his vivaries, to make mews
for his hawks. After the hunting and hawking entries
the most numerous are those for the provisioning of
castles. Of building there is comparatively little
record, but the order for the repair of chimneys and
windows at Tewkesbury gives an idea of comfort.

The king seems to have been cleanly in personal

habit, as his waterman received his fee for the bath
regularly, and baths were "made" by the king's
order at most of his resting-places, generally at a
cost of 5d. The wages of his washerwoman are
entered regularly, with her fee for "chaussure."

John sought to make up for his life's irregularities
by regular and liberal alms-giving; if he had irreligious
convictions, he had not the courage of them. Very
steadily did the paupers, by hundreds and even
thousands, reap their penny apiece, because the king,
or his ministers, led astray by him, ate meat twice on
a fast-day. He fed 350 poor men because he had
good sport one day and took seven cranes. Many
were fed "for the souls of his father and his brother
Richard," that the prayers of the beggar who had
dined might release their souls from purgatory. But
many were the disappointed religious, who looked in
vain for a handsome gift from the king to their
church in return for hospitalities received. At
Worcester the sacrist had had to find the "pall"
which the king offered, and the payment for the
"loan," which followed, one may guess was inadequate. Fierce as the king was, his "misæ" show
that his subjects dared to win from him at betting
games. His losses at "tables," a mediæval form of
backgammon, are regularly recorded. Incidentally
we hear that the bearer of the heads of six Welshmen got from him a shilling apiece.

5. It is not merely an accidental coincidence that
the liberate rolls of Henry III. show a great change of
character. His artistic nature is plainly written in entry
after entry. It is noticeable that of England's artistic

kings, Henry III., Richard II. and Charles I., not one was in harmony with his subjects. In several of his palaces Henry III. ordered elaborate wall-paintings, the subjects and sometimes the treatment of which are minutely described in the accounts. The great hall of the Tower was ordered to be painted with the " History of Antioch," and there was an " Antioch chamber" at Westminster (the Queen's room) and at Clarendon, celebrating the feats of Richard I. at the siege. The story of Alexander decorated the Queen's chamber in Nottingham castle. In Dublin castle, the hall was painted with a scene representing the king and queen seated amid the barons (1243). That the themes were sometimes taken from illuminated manuscripts appears from Henry III.'s order to the Master of the Temple that he should lend a French manuscript to the royal painter in order that he may be guided by it in decorating the rooms of the Tower and Westminster. The Old Testament yielded the subjects of the " great history " that figured on the walls of the king's great chamber at Westminster. Covered at a later period by tapestry, many fragments remain to show the dress of the thirteenth century. On the panels below the " great history," Odo the goldsmith was directed to paint a green curtain where there had been lions, birds and beasts. The charge was £30 for painting "the Majesty of the Lord," in Clarendon chapel, with angels on both sides of the Majesty ; for the history of King Edward in the chancel, with an image of that king ; for illuminating and varnishing the

pictures round the king's seat ; for curtaining the
chapel in green (probably the painted curtaining
of which the king was fond) ; and for painting St.
Katherine's history in her chapel, and making an
image of her ; with other repairs.

A favourite form of wall-decoration with Henry III.
was a scroll with a proverb upon it, such as, " Ke ne
dune ke tune, ne prent ke desire," " If you do not give
what you have, you will not get what you want."
The magnificent conception for the royal banner,
to hang in Westminster Abbey, may well have been
the king's own ; in the middle of the banner of red
samite (silk) was a dragon, sparkling all over with
gold, " whose tongue was to be like a burning fire
continually appearing to move," and the eyes were
to shine with sapphires and other precious stones.
Ever on the watch for a good model, he ordered
an imitation of the Lichfield cathedral ceiling for
one of his palaces.

In Henry's reign the records of glazing become
numerous. The coloured glass which the king
ordered for St. John's chapel in the Tower was
no doubt of the favourite pattern for the Early
English lancet windows, and consisted of medallions
containing sacred subjects, painted with all the
minute detail of an illumination, set one above
another and united by delicate scroll-work. In the
Queen's chamber at Windsor Henry ordered a glass-
window with " the root " or stem of Jesse to be put in
the gable, probably in the form of a rose-window. At
Northampton castle the glass was to represent the
story of Dives and Lazarus. Henry was also fond

of the "oriel-window," and ordered oriels to be
inserted in Kenilworth and Hereford castles. But
many entries show that for the rooms of a less
stately character, a wooden shutter, or a piece of
waxed or greased stuff did the work of glass. An

UNGLAZED WINDOW AT COGGS.

increase of domestic comfort is shown in the
numerous orders for plaster chimneys and fire-
places. For the queen's mantel-piece Henry selected
as the subject for decoration "Winter with sad coun-
tenance." Perhaps the finest specimen of a stone

hall of the period is that of Winchester, built before 1240.

Side by side with these entries must be placed others which show that even the royal household was often content with rude buildings, with thatched roofs, a wooden lean-to and penthouses. It was enough if hall and "camera" were of stone : the "domus," the separate "herbours" or lodgings, the connecting "alures," alleys or "tresances," were temporary wooden structures, which might easily be blown down, as happened once at the Oxford palace.

Of course, the king's artistic and luxurious tastes showed themselves not least in the details of his furnishing, his silk and velvet mattresses, cushions and bolsters, his napery, his goblets of mounted cocoa-nut, his glass cup set in crystal. Matthew Paris has described the splendid outfit given to Isabella, the king's sister, on her marriage with the Emperor : the goldsmiths' work, the chess-table and chessmen in an ivory casket, the silver pans and cooking vessels ; the inventory of her wardrobe, the robes of cloth of gold, of Arras (embroidered), of scarlet, of blue, and green cambric, the two beds of Genoese cloth of gold, the 2 napkins and 13 towels. It was Henry's doing again that the model of the great seal was improved by an artist of repute.

6. All the four kings from Henry II. to Henry III. have left evidence, more or less fragmentary, of their literary taste.   Peter of Blois, however much he might contemn the disorder of his master's court, has left a most pleasing description of Henry II.'s interest in intellectual discussions and enjoyment of the conversa-

tion of scholars.   At his court, the king kept "school"
every day, a "schola" that was almost a "studium
generale," an academy of learning.   The account
of his court which Dr. Stubbs has given can only

SEAL OF HENRY III. BEFORE IT WAS REMODELLED.

be rivalled by that of a Medici at the time of the
greatest intellectual revival.   A royal historiographer
was selected to keep the record of public acts, and he
was assisted by access to what must have been a

court library of historical works. It was not out of mere flattery and subservience that the learned writers and the versifiers of history addressed Henry in terms of literary respect. His taste was catholic, and he saw an object in encouraging not only the serious historical undertaking of Roger of Howden, but also the thousands of French verses that Bénoit de Sainte Maure and Wace poured out, mingling historic truth with historic legend. Gerald of Wales cannot praise him enough or dedicate enough works to him; perhaps his affection had been won by Henry's sympathetic and tactful trifling with the Arthurian legend. It is recorded, and there seems reason to believe, that Map did write a Lancelot romance at Henry II.'s order, though some are inclined to doubt the truth of the statement.

Peter of Blois charges Henry with neglecting his children's education, yet he could hardly have done better for his eldest son than he did, for he put him into Becket's household. His illegitimate son Geoffrey was sent to the great school of Tours, then part of the king of England's territory. Richard I. seems to have been educated in the South of France, where doubtless he learned the art of versification which he found useful in later life when called on to reply to scurrilous lampoons. Some of his " sirventes " or satiric lays still survive. That he was well-read in romance is certain, and his companion in arms was the troubadour Bertrand de Born. Bertrand has left a description of the young princes, of the ill-fated Henry, the best jouster and man of arms since Roland, and of his equally gallant brother Richard

"Oc et No." Whether it was Matilda (the child-wife of Henry the Lion of Saxony) or another whose "rose-blushes" inflamed the heart of Bertrand, is not certain. Bertrand it was, the stirrer of strife between Henry II. and his son, whom Dante saw wandering in hell :

> Io feci il padre e'l figlio in sè ribelli.

Another companion chosen for the young princes was Fulk fitz Warin, himself to be the hero of romance. The first place in their education was given to martial sports, and it was partly his skill in these exercises that attracted men to the young crowned Henry, who made up in personal charm what he lacked in principle. It was for him that Gervase of Tilbury, a kinsman of the king, prepared his lost "Liber Facetiarum," and perhaps his extant "Otia Imperialia" was meant for the same young prince.

John has hardly had justice done to him as a book-lender, and therefore possibly a book-lover. The extracts from the close-rolls have long been in print which show him ordering Reginald of Cornhill to send him at once a copy of the Romance of English History. To the Abbot of Reading he acknowledges the receipt of six books, the Old and New Testament, the works of Hugh of St. Victor, the Sentences of Peter Lombard, Augustine's "De Civitate," and his letters, "Valerianus De Moribus," Origen on the Old Testament, no doubt the Latin homilies, Candidus Arianus' "De generatione divina ad Marium," and so acquits the abbot and sacrist of responsibility for the same.   On another occasion the king discharged the same abbot from responsibility for the Pliny which had been lent to him.   That such works were not John's daily reading we may well believe, but the records show the nature of the court library and the orderly arrangements for the loan and return of books.

Henry III. seems to have been well educated by certain "pedagogues" whose names are not known. He was fond of history and could tell Matthew Paris by heart the names of the electors of Germany, the kings of England who had been canonised (not a long list), and (a more difficult task) the titles of the English baronies to the number of 250.   This achievement speaks perhaps less well of his intellect than does the imaginative power which led him to write a paper in praise of his wife's relative Boniface, whom he had appointed to the archbishopric of Canterbury.   A twelfth century copy of Seneca, now at Erfurt, one which was perhaps used at the court by Howden, was given away by Henry.   But neither literature nor politics can be reckoned his strong point, and his ignorance of martial exercises was made a taunt against him, when, as a way out of political quandaries, he talked of going on crusade.   On the other hand he holds a rare position among kings as a patron of the arts, and as a husband pure in his domestic relations.   He alone of the four kings of our period was free from the most common vice of the Middle Ages: Henry II., it was said, made a mistress of the child who was to be his son Richard's wife ; Richard and John were equally

regardless of sexual decency. The happy domesticity of Henry III. certainly had a good effect
in this matter ; none of his successors ventured to
approach John's example in the number of their
bastard children.

7. Among the royal ladies of the period two
fine figures stand forth, the aged Empress Matilda,
Henry II.'s mother, and Eleanor, Henry II.'s wife,
who both blotted out in old age some evil records
of the past. Matilda had committed many blunders
of policy when she was fighting for the crown : her
feudalising charters were dangerous acts of ill-guided
statecraft, as mischievous as any of which Stephen
was guilty, but once her political troubles were over,
she comes out as a woman of striking character, especially in her relation to the papal schism and the Becket
party. " She is a woman girt about with fortitude : do
not fear that she will waver for an instant," was the
verdict sent by the archbishop of Rouen to a cardinal.
In 1167, the year of her death, she mediated peace
between the king of France and her son, and in her
letters to Louis VII. urged him to communicate
directly with her. Becket's supporters at one time
hoped to get her influence on their side, but they
found that she was " mulier de genere tyrannorum,"
and that to their face she dared to approve certain of
her son's ecclesiastical reforms, despite the fact that
the clergy had read these to her in Latin and ex-
pounded them in French. Her interest in literature
may perhaps be witnessed by the fact that William
Herman, the writer of a morality play, addressed
his history of the Sibyls to her.

Letters from all the queens are extant, but whether any of these were of their own penning is very doubtful. As the results of dictation, however, they are still invaluable as showing the character and mental calibre of the sender. A passionate love letter from Eleanor to Henry of Anjou (Henry II.) is extant, but her early passion was not able to sweeten their matrimonial relations. A lover of pleasures of all kinds, Eleanor did not neglect the pleasures of the mind. Confined for the best years of her life in a semi-captivity, when she came forth she took up the reins of government with first-rate skill and exercised great influence on politics till she was nearly eighty. Dr. Stubbs assures us that she must have spent her captivity in " something besides needlework " to enable her to do what she did. It was a critical moment when, Richard I. being in prison and John in rebellion, it rested with her to raise sufficient money to outbid the French king. It was a case of the English pound sterling against the French *livre tournois.* Of the personality of John's neglected queen Isabella there is little to know, but she has left a curious letter in which she explains to her young son Henry III. that she has married her old lover the Comte de la Marche from "reasons of policy." Henry III. found in his wife a person of considerable character, if not of the most pleasing disposition. The populace fully realised that her influence was a main cause of their grievances, and Londoners on one occasion made their opinion known to her by pelting her with rotten eggs when her barge went under London Bridge. It would appear from her letters that she was a woman of good education, and the record has been preserved which shows her borrowing "a great book of French romances," the gests of Antioch, and a history of the crusades. The statement that she herself wrote a Provençal romance is erroneous. To her influence may be ascribed perhaps Edward I.'s excellent education : many affectionate letters between mother and son remain to show her merits.

CHAIN ARMOUR, FOUND IN A GLOUCESTERSHIRE CHURCH.

PISCINA AT LONG WITTENHAM, BERKS.

VIII

THE NOBILITY

1. It is not possible to exaggerate the effect upon
feudal society of those changes which resulted from
the skill of Henry II. and his clerks in the making
and using of new legal weapons intended to break
the jurisdictional sovereignty of the great tenants-
in-chief. So strong a central power did he secure,
that neither the long absence of Richard I. upon
crusade, nor the harsh tyranny of John, nor the
feeble tyranny of Henry III., could shake that

achievement. The government established by
Henry II. and his ministers was carried on by
men trained in his traditions through succeeding
generations, and a new ministerial aristocracy was
raised whose power was not based upon land tenure.
A gulf divides the Norman feudal society from the
feudal society of Henry III., in spite of the fact that
a conscious and determined effort towards reaction
was attempted in Henry III.'s early years. The
opportunity of the king's minority was seized by
William de Fors Earl of Albemarle, Ralph Earl
of Chester, Faukes de Breauté, to try and recover, each for himself, some of his lost local independence and sovereign power. In consequence
the first portion of Henry III.'s reign is full of the
sieges of baronial castles. But in each case the
struggle proved a failure ; the elements of a great
baronial rebellion, such as Henry II. had had to
face, were no longer to be found. The wiser of the
nobility looked rather to the hope of obtaining
control over the central machine than to their
individual aggrandisement in their own lordships.
In Henry III.'s reign the barons, who were compelled to cast in their lot finally with the English
kingdom, found a ground of cohesion in a policy
that was in so far national as it was anti-foreign.
Though at the beginning of Henry II.'s reign it
was impossible, even in the highest ranks of the
baronage, to say whether the Norman or the English
strain prevailed, politicians soon began to watch
whether the king promoted most the subjects who
lived north or south of the Channel. Gerald of Wales,

for instance, complains of favour to "foreigners." Then at the close of John's reign affairs took a critical turn.

The barons hostile to John had summoned the French king to their aid, a step full of significance as the last and greatest testimony that the English nobility were French. Louis at Westminster received the homage of bishops, nobles and burgesses. But John's death changed everything. The Pope was not willing to see the country, which John had agreed to hold of him for tribute, pass into the hands of the French king. His legate rallied a national party to the young Henry's side, and renewed the Great Charter which the Pope had seen reason to quash in John's time. All who fought for Henry were signed with a white cross, and obtained the reward of crusaders. The long minority over, and it was fraught with constitutional consequences as the first minority since Anglo-Saxon times, the king showed his own hand : he married a Provençale, surrounded himself with a Provençal and Poitevin aristocracy, and imitated French manners and methods ; a new anti-alien cry was raised with great effect, and, by the irony of fate, the centre of the national movement was Simon de Montfort, whom some might feel inclined to call an alien. New political forces were thus started, stronger than the disruptive forces of feudalism.

2. The feudalism that remained began to take another form and new ideals were elaborated by the baronage. A taste for dangerous adventure was considered the best evidence of bravery, and instead

of the fierce and rude but purposeful strength of the
Normans, men prized a martial prowess of a more
artificial kind, the result of a long course of instruction. The tournament begins to take a prominent
place in the chronicles. The hostility shown by the
Church to these festivals was powerless to put a stop
to them. In 1179 Alexander III. forbade those
" detestable fairs" vulgarly called "torneamenta" in
which knights were wont to meet and show their
strength and boldness, whereby men were killed and
souls endangered. But in vain it was proposed to
refuse Christian burial to those who died in the
" conflictus gallicus" or tournament, more properly,
as Map puns, called "torment."

According to William of Newburgh Henry II. was
no encourager of the tourney, but his son Henry,
present at a tournament of 3,000 knights, French and
English, gathered from all parts, gave the signal for
the grand "mêlée," when each battle-corps uttered its
own war-cry. It is notorious, says William of
Newburgh, that these conflicts were never held in
England for exercise and the display of valour without some violent quarrel arising.

Richard I. seems to have regarded them as an
essential part of knightly training. Seeing that the
French were better taught than the English, he
selected five country places where the sport was
licensed on payment of heavy fees. Gerald of Wales
lamented that martial exercises and tilting after the
French fashion had sent literary pursuits quite out of
vogue. In 1220 repressive measures were tried again,
and "torneatores," their receivers and abettors, and

persons carrying food and goods to tournaments,
were excommunicated ; but when Henry attained his
majority the barons were again encouraged to make
a fine art of martial sports.   More than one tournament " à outrance " was arranged between leaders of
the English and the alien party, that their quarrel
might be settled in pitched battle.   The finest horses
were sent for from the Continent, and year after year
the chronicles record with full detail the deaths of great
earls and barons by misadventure in the tournament.

Roger of Howden tells that every youth who
desired knighthood must have seen his blood flow
and felt his teeth crack under the fisticuffs, must have
been thrown to the ground and felt the weight of his
enemy on top of him, and twenty times unsaddled,
must twenty times be ready to begin again, more
eager than ever for combat.   Only then can he hope
to enter serious warfare with a chance of victory, to
go tourneying to make captures and get money,
horses and harness.

3. The armour of this period was already trending
away from the slender, close-fitting mail with sleeves
and breeches, such as a thought of the Bayeux
Tapestry calls to mind, towards the more ungainly,
thickly padded, bulky forms that develop later.   The
chronicles of Henry II.'s day describe the knights :—

Their limbs with so much iron, each with so many little folding plates,
Their breasts with so many leathern coats, so many wambesons they
    arm ;

and the use of the padded wambeson, at first worn
by the burgesses and freemen of the non-knightly

class, spread upwards. In its more costly form, of
padded and stitched silk, it became the " pourpoint "
of Henry III.'s time. Henry II.'s Assize of Arms
had required not only those who held by " knight's
service" to have a coat of mail or "lorica," but all
who were worth between £10 and £11 a year ; those
worth between £6 and £7 were to have an
" aubergel" or light sleeveless coat of scale armour.
The practice of sewing on the scales of mail, or
setting rings up edgewise, changed in favour of
the more elaborate smith's work, the chain-mail. The
network of chains being less easily fitted to the body
than leather, the joints of knee and elbow were
sometimes fitted with separate pieces, the beginning
of the later " plates." With the crusades, and, it is
thought, to shield the metal from the blaze of the
eastern sun, came in the surcoat of fine stuff or silk, a
kind of shirt worn over the armour and split up the
sides to free the legs. Upon this fabric a gorgeous
emblazoning might be embroidered. The helmet
now passed from the small conical form with a nasal
to the square flat-headed shape with a visor.

4. John of Salisbury, who, better than any man, by
reason of his learning and wide reading, could detach
himself from the point of view of his contemporaries
and see them as they really were, writes of the
knighthood of Henry II.'s day, what it should be,
what it was. To the martial spirit he commends an
early training in heavy labour, running and carrying
weights, endurance of heat and dust, a sparing diet,
and the regular practice of arms. But too many, he
says, think that military glory consists in elegant

MURDER OF BECKET.

From Mr. Yates Thompson's Carehowe Psalter, c. 1250.

dress, thorough-paced horses, banqueting, the first
places at table, the shunning of labour, the gilding of
shields, the adorning of tents.

That same spirit which found a means to replace
the tribal by artificial bonds, which conceived of
brotherhoods without blood relationship, which made
the admission to holy, knightly or burghal orders, to
the humblest feudal tie, the occasion of a ceremony, a
sacrament, an oath, of course did not fail to dignify
knighthood with the loftiest aims. The knight's
oath according to John of Salisbury was to defend
the church, to attack the perfidious, protect the poor,
keep his country's peace and die for his brethren.

But the knightly order, like every other, contained
good specimens and bad. Gerald of Wales divided
the knights into the hawks and the falcons; the
hawks are the showy birds, loving banquets,
equipages and clothing, studying only earthly things;
but the falcons reject fleshly delights and love pri-
vation. The knights of the court (the hawks) were
attacked by all the satirists of the period for their
affectation of superiority, in manner and voice, for
their love of spectacular shows, their "vain confabu-
lations," their passion for adulation.

With the usual mediæval love of system, the
knightly order was developed through a series of
definite stages by which the final enrolment was
approached. There must be a definite matricula-
tion, noviciate, and process of initiation. At seven
years a boy was set to act as page to a nobleman,
generally more or less closely related to the child;
the network of kinship which united the barons

made it easy to claim a distinguished kinsman's patronage. To give an early example, there is a reference in the life of Godric of Finchale to a knight educated "a puericia" in the "curia" of Adam de Bruis. At fourteen the "puer" became a "domicel," valet, "garcio," groom, or esquire (shield-bearer) attendant on the lord's body, chamber, stable or hall. To become a knight, to enter the "tiro-cinium," he must be provided with lands and money; as a tyro he watches a whole night of prayer in church, before the initiation. If some of these ceremonies came from the church, it is equally noticeable that the church on the other hand loved to link the ecclesiastical order with the military ; both are a "spirituale tirocinium commilitonum."

5. The high reputation of the Templars and Hospitallers was dimmed early in Henry II.'s time by their rivalry and cupidity, on which Map comments severely. Both orders succeeded in amassing wealth, and they became the bankers of the kings of France and England. The Hospitallers, supposed to be bound to poverty, are said by Matthew Paris to have held 19,000 manors in 1244. The Templars had contrived to modify the rule which made them dependent on their own exertions. Each knight-brother (frère chevalier) required at least one esquire for his three horses, and there were also in attendance sergeant-brothers (frères sergeants), marshals to look after the armour, and others, who in their turn needed horses and esquires. The farming brothers (frères casaliers) looked after the estates, and the artisan brothers (frères de métier) worked in the

several departments of the smithy, saddlery, marshal-sea and wardrobe.   The chaplain brothers performed the masses.   The whole system of both orders, the Templars and Hospitallers, centred rather in France than in England, and when in the thirteenth century hostility to France began, both orders were the more critically regarded in England.

6. As yet no charges of immorality were levelled at the Templars, and evidence of the good or bad state of knightly morals is somewhat scanty.   Baldwin, the aged archbishop of Canterbury, once a Cistercian monk, but since that time not without opportunities of knowing and seeing the world, followed Richard I. to the crusade, and it is told that his disgust at the debaucheries of the crusade camp was a cause of his illness and death.   At the close of the period, Louis IX. complained of the establishment of loose women near his tent, kept there by William Long-sword, called earl of Salisbury.   But the men of Henry II.'s time have won the praise of so cautious an historian as Stubbs, who pronounces it on the whole a time of social decency, though all were willing to bring the foulest charges against enemies. The satirical literature is in the main decent, even refined as compared with the satire of a far later period.

Any sudden death or illness was commonly attributed to poisoning; on perfectly frivolous grounds men of high character like Hubert de Burgh were freely charged with this odious crime.   Yet some slight improvement upon the barbaric brutality of the Norman period may be detected in this very fact.

An earlier generation removed its enemies by violence more direct than poison. The shock which
the proposed mutilation of Arthur of Brittany gave
to the feelings of a humane man is an indication of
a change from the days of Henry I., a change that
might at least protect from the extremes of violence
those of very high position. But though Hubert
de Burgh refused to gouge out the eyes of Arthur,
he did not hesitate to subject London citizens to
mutilation. Indeed contact with Eastern forms
of cruelty seems in some directions to have increased men's brutality. The cutting-off of the
heads of enemies, to be sent by the cartload to
the victor, a custom prevalent in Ireland and
Scotland, was according to Guibert de Nogent
borrowed by the crusaders from the Turks. The
author of Richard's Itinerary describes one of his
battle-fields reeking with blood, dismembered corpses
everywhere, arms, hands, feet, heads lopped off and
eyes gouged out. The bodies which they had just
dismembered "caused our men to stumble." The
shaft of King Richard's lance shivered as if rotten
with blood, and then brandishing his sword he
thundered on, "mowing down some, cutting up
others, cleaving men from the top of the head to the
teeth."

But in spite of all this blood-thirstiness in the
battle-field, such cold-heart cruelties as those of John
were deemed a return to barbarous methods. The
"leaden cope" with which he crushed a prisoner,
slowly starving him to death, the awful fate of
Matilda de Braose and her son, provided with a

sheaf of corn and a piece of raw bacon during their confinement " in diro ergastulo," that they might face death the more slowly, the extraction of a Jew's teeth, were deemed events worthy of remark. Henry III. at least kept his prisoners alive : at the end of three years in the Tower Llewelyn complained that during all that time he had had no change of dress or bedding.

Terrible are some of the mediæval descriptions of men's fury. Of John it was said that his whole body became so contorted with rage as to be scarcely recognisable ; and due to the general absence of emotional restraint are the evidences that these fierce people were easily moved to tears. The election of the treasurer of Henry III. to the bishopric of Coventry so deeply affected the staid exchequer officials that they all wept at his departure, and had to be kissed one by one, with promises of continued affection. Kissing, like weeping, was a part of several mediæval ceremonials. The lord must kiss his homager, and the question whether or no the king would kiss an offending minister more than once agitated the public mind. The kiss of peace of ecclesiastical rite was likewise part of formal legal procedure between reconciled laymen. Simon de Montfort and Richard Earl of Cornwall, for example, formally exchanged the kiss.

Characteristic of the knight's conversation, especially, according to Gerald of Wales, that of the English knights, was the oath by a part of God's body used as an expletive. Each king had his favourite oath ; William I.'s by the splendour of God, John's by God's teeth, were each not a little indicative of the speaker's character. Of jests, by far the most pleasing to men of learning, kings and courtiers alike, were puns. Of the good old jest " presents " for " presence " (*e.g.*, in the invitation to a wedding) Becket himself was guilty in its French form.

7. The baronial class still provided a fair share of the statesmen. The earl of Leicester, son of the earl who was Henry I.'s justiciar, was justiciar to Henry II. and evidently a lawyer of note, for John of Salisbury quotes with approval his doctrines on the subject of treason. It was the same earl who used, when the days of his activity were over, to recite Latin verses in praise of monasticism. Of his early education something has already been said, and through life he ranked with the lettered clerks. No less distinguished were the Marshals, father and son, whose history is known in great detail from a long French epic by a poet in their service. Both were men capable of making great sacrifices for the national good ; it is known of the father that he made himself personally responsible for a payment of ten thousand marks rather than that the country should bear the loss on a queen's unpaid dowry.

Prominent too in this list must stand the name of Simon de Montfort, no untaught genius, but something of a scholar, as well as a born statesman ; his scholarship is made manifest by the details of Grosseteste's correspondence, yet of Simon's early education nothing is known, as is too often the case in the story of the learned laity. His elder brother was a pupil of a mathematician whom Roger Bacon praised highly. One of Simon's correspondents was Adam Marsh, a Franciscan, selected by Simon and his wife as their confessor. To his penitents he addressed many Latin letters, evidently not intended for the public ear, scarcely for that even of the domestic clerk. It is notable that in writing to the perhaps less well-educated queen, the confessor generally used French. In Adam Marsh's letters Simon is exhorted to reading, and references are made to books in Simon's possession. Simon de Montfort chose wisely when he selected Grosseteste, bishop of Lincoln, as the teacher and trainer of his children ; their progress in learning and manners is more than once referred to in the Grosseteste correspondence.

Every baron kept his staff of clerks and it is not easy at any time to say how much of the sum total of reading and writing was exclusively clerkly. It is said for instance of Geoffrey de Mandeville (who died 1166, a man of elegant speech and able in secular affairs, so his contemporaries thought), that he did not leave his son a single benefice " to reward his clerks." He had given them away to monasteries with too liberal a hand. William de Braose's staff of scribes is mentioned by Gerald of Wales, who like-wise describes the scene that occurred when the clerk of Earl Raymond read his wife's letter in public, a letter that was meant for the earl's private hearing. The plot of several mediæval romances hinged on an accident of this sort.

That few of the barons who were not court officials knew any language besides Norman French is fairly

certain. William Earl of Arundel, sent on behalf of
the king to the Pope to present the baronial view of
the Becket controversy, made an excellent French
speech at the papal court, in which he explained that
he and his fellow "illiterates" could not understand
the episcopal Latinity. To secure good French,
Gervase of Tilbury says that many nobles sent their
children to France to learn the language.

Whereas in France the names of those troubadours
which have survived can be shown to belong in large
measure to the families of the nobility, in England
the evidence even of a taste for French romance
among the barons is somewhat scrappy. Marie de
France dedicated her French rendering of an English
Æsop which does her much credit, to a certain
Count William, but whether this was William Long-
sword, a bastard son of Henry II., or William Count of
Flanders is uncertain. Yet that Marie's works were
current in England there can be no doubt. Again,
Hugh de Morville carried with him to Germany, when
he was hostage for Richard I., a volume of romances
which had great influence in spreading the Lancelot
cycle : and a certain Luces " de Gast," lord of a castle
near Salisbury, translated into French the Tristan
cycle. Gastard near Corsham, Wilts, may perhaps be
the place in question. Nor were these all who were
at Henry II.'s court encouraged to like work.

8. What may be called the ministerial class occupies
a position midway between the baronial and the ecclesiastical " estate." As Barons of the Exchequer many
entered the ranks of the baronage by another
passage than that of birthright, and many were

rewarded with bishoprics who perhaps owed but a small part of their education to the church. The great school for the training of statesmen, judges and bishops, was the Exchequer. We may well believe that men who could master Exchequer arithmetic could master anything, and the teaching of this school passed from father to son in a chain of unbroken tradition. Nigel, bishop of Ely, himself nephew of Roger of Salisbury, and a pupil of Anselm of Laon, passed the traditions of the treasurership to his son Richard, bishop of London, author of a text-book on the Exchequer system. The Exchequer-trained Richard of Ilchester, judge and bishop of Winchester, who traversed Europe from end to end, used his practical skill as an organiser on the details, for instance, of the provisioning of Joanna of Sicily's household. The fellow to him is Geoffrey Ridel, born of good stock, archdeacon, or "arch-devil," of Thomas of Canterbury, whom he opposed ; a much travelled judge, yet likewise bishop of Ely and remembered there as a great builder. Such another was William of St. Mère Église, rewarded with Richard fitz Nigel's bishopric. Such men could answer an Exchequer question more easily than one on the Canon, as men were wont to point out with grim amusement.

The poet tells of Peter des Roches how skilful he was in counting, how good at revolving the roll of the king's account, how lazy at turning the leaves of the Gospel, loving lucre more than Luke, the mark (of silver) more than Mark, the "libra" of money more than the " Liber " (Bible).

Hubert de Burgh, who appears first as an ambassador, then as king's chamberlain, ought perhaps also to be added to the group of administrators trained in the government offices, and that he proved himself in Henry III.'s day one of the best, is most clearly witnessed by the nature of the charges made against him when he fell.

An equally prolific nursery of public officials was Becket's household, which as the trainer of Glanville passed on the tradition to Hubert Walter, archbishop of Canterbury and to Geoffrey fitz Peter, who like Hubert de Burgh was one of the few self-made men who kept to the secular path. He succeeded in raising himself to the earldom of Essex by means of a politic marriage. To Geoffrey fitz Peter and to Hubert Walter, archbishop, soldier, builder, the country looked for government during much of Richard's and part of John's reign. Against the archbishop, we have from Gerald of Wales accusations of canine Latinity, but the charges, though most explicit, were later withdrawn by that too hasty critic. The same charge however comes from another source, and a trustworthy one, namely William of Newburgh, who relates that when Hubert told Richard I. to say " coram nos " not " nobis," Nonant bishop of Coventry told the king to stick to his own grammar for it was the better. The accusative with " coram " had the sanction of the Assize of Northampton.

This Nonant, an arch-plotter, was another of Becket's pupils. He had been an ambassador to Germany, and is said to have written a universal history now lost. His best remembered writing is a clever onslaught on his enemy Longchamp, who rose to be Richard I.'s viceroy through his connection with the household of the royal bastard Geoffrey, archbishop of York. Geoffrey, until late in life, was a type of the baronial ecclesiastic, devoting his leisure to hunting, hawking and military pursuits. The pope wrote of him that he neither ordained clergy, nor celebrated synods, nor blessed abbots, but used his office to present youths of bad character to benefices, and to wield the weapon of excommunication on his own behalf. Such was the master of Longchamp, bishop of Ely, who, as William of Newburgh says, was better known as the chancellor than as the bishop. Longchamp's fame was injured by his extravagant airs, which sat ill on one whose grand-father, according to his enemy Nonant, had guided the plough. Yet it was he who introduced the foreign custom of serving on the knee, and remem-bering the ploughman's use of the goad, he pricked on with a weapon the sons of nobles who were care-less in serving. He boasted further that he was a despiser of things English, and this won him no favour when he went up and down England with a suite of 1,000 knights, devastating "like a flash of lightning." The monasteries reckoned that a night's visit from him cost them three years' savings. It was his inability to speak English that betrayed him when he disguised himself as a woman, in a green gown, instead of the priests "hyacinth" garb, in a cape with sleeves instead of a chasuble, a hood instead of a mitre, a roll of cloth for sale upon his arm instead of his maniple, and a huckster's wand for a pastoral staff. To serve the table of this bishop-chancellor who often wore a coat of mail, Nonant says all the best beasts, birds and fishes were ordered. Not a churl who longed for a field, a citizen for a lucrative post, a knight for an estate, a clerk for a benefice, a monk for an abbey, but must look to him. He exhausted the kingdom and did not leave to a man his girdle, to a woman her necklace, to a nobleman his ring (things generally excused from the tax on moveables).

Another of the opponents of Longchamp as a *novus homo* was Hugh de Puiset, the great prince-bishop of Durham, a great-grandson of William I., the nephew and pupil of Henry of Blois, bishop of Winchester. He added to the cares of his bishopric a palatinate and the justiciarship of a whole province. The villains of Auckland built, wherever he went hunting, his hunting hall, 60 feet long, with chapel and kitchen to match. He delighted in castle-building, an art he had learnt from his uncle, and likewise he saw means to become a great shipmaster. His court like Henry II.'s was full of men of learning.

Many others of the highest family found reward for their legal talents in the church, and to the judge-bishop it was often hard to decide which professional claim was dearest. It was this conflict of interests which forced every man to find for himself a compromise between the claims of state and church, and made the rivalry less serious than the doctrinaires, who had less at stake, ever sought to make it. The barons who " would not change the laws of England " in favour of the Canon Law of Rome, were some of them judge-bishops, who loved the national law they ministered in the lay courts more dearly than the law they ministered in the Court Christian.

The making of judge-bishops was preferable perhaps to the making of warrior-bishops. Henry III., for all his piety, made plenty of both sorts. When the monks of Winchester objected against the king's relative Aylmer de Valence, their bishop-elect, that he was " a man of blood," and preferred William de Raleigh, the great judge, the king could only urge that the judge had killed more men with his tongue than the elect of Valence with his sword.

Towards the close of the period there is an increase in the number of lawyers rising to a quasi-baronial position through the law alone, without the aid of the church. Martin Pateshull, a judge who wore out his colleagues with his activity, Bracton, the great law-book writer (he was in deacon's orders), Stephen de Segrave, were rewarded by no bishoprics. If there was a measure of truth in the assertion of Gerald of Wales that the unprincipled and covetous attach themselves to the court, and the ambitious to the public offices, yet by the overlapping of the professions, of the several orders of men, the progress of the country was served. Not the church only, but the baronage also, was an " open class," in the great feudal show. One path upwards lay through the law. Judges were barons and barons were judges, a useful thing at a time when a " tempus guerræ " was still all too likely to necessitate the suspension of the courts of law, while some baronial malcontent was besieged and suppressed. There would be efforts to make, and " conjurationes " whenever a separation of interest was felt, but the moment for the recognition of a common interest uniting the nation into a " communa " of many " communæ " was approaching.

9. The strength of the forces required to overcome the elements of disunion in feudalism is best realised when the organisation of a great baron's household is seen in detail. It was not merely such lordly persons as the future King John, count of Mortain and lord of many English counties, who could keep up a household state exactly parallel to that of the king. For his Irish lordship he had his staff of ministers, his justiciar, chancellor, steward, butler, sheriffs, bailiffs, but so also had the lords in the palatinates, which repeated in miniature the model of the kingdom. And on a less regular system other groups of hereditary offices were held ; for instance, the archbishop of York had his hereditary constable, the abbot of Bury his steward, each rewarded originally by a tract of land in return for service. Every great household was thronged with young men in every stage of ripeness for the knightly degree, learning manners and defending the honour of the lord at whose cost they lived, in the field of tournament or of battle. The king it was said could claim for his household the eldest son of a baron to serve till the age of knighthood, the archbishop of Canterbury the second, but the prestige of these schools of manners was so great that no dearth was ever feared. Becket's housekeeping was splendid, both as chancellor and as archbishop. Whilst he was chancellor he ate daily with earls and barons, had daily fresh straw in

winter, fern and rushes in summer, keeping the floors so clean that the fine clothes of the knights might not be soiled. To his care was given the young prince Henry, and it was for him to decide when the youth should be girt with the belt of knighthood. On the chancellor's embassy to France the sons of nobles thronged his suite and the train of horses and carts required to carry his baggage, pet-animals, food and furniture has been described by his biographer in detail.

As archbishop he gathered to his high table twenty " masters in wisdom," setting the knights and courtly persons at a separate table, to have their pleasan-tries together undisturbed. His table was richly furnished with fair and varied dishes, of which he himself ate but sparingly. A tithe of all the goods coming to the palace he sent to the hospital of St. Bartholomew.

Grosseteste, the son of a villain, was not behind Becket, the son of a burgess, in the influence he exercised through his household, which was crowded with " domicelli." Henry III. once asked him how one of such humble birth could teach the young nobility so well, and he answered that he had learned the art in greater courts than that of the king of England, namely, in his books of history.

10. In spite of Henry II.'s new law which allowed no one to build a castle or a " domus defensabilis " without licence, the reigns of all the kings of this period were chronically disturbed by sieges of unruly subjects in their strong towers. But the greatest of the castles were now under the king's castellans, who

BAMBOROUH CASTLE.

CONISBOROUGH CASTLE.

were carefully chosen from his trusted supporters. For the subjugation of Wales some 250 castles and castellets are reckoned to have been in existence by the end of Henry II.'s reign, and, in England, 657 in all by 1189. Many of these had neither square nor shell keep, but consisted of earthworks such as Neckham has admirably described.

If a castle is to be decently built he says, it should be supported by a double foss or ditch. Nature may so strengthen the site that the mote is seated on native rock. If nature fails, a mote made of stone and cement may be raised. On the mote a "fearful hedge" should be erected of squared pales and pungent rushes. Within, the baily should occupy a wide space, and we may picture the three bailies of Ludlow Castle encircled with a double ditch as described in the romance of Fulk fitz Warin. Neckham directs that the foundation of the wall (if there is one —he writes to bring in words and translate them into French, not to explain castle-building) should be wedded to the soil, and the walls should be propped with buttresses. The top of the wall is to be flat and crenellated at regular distances, and brattices or machicolations should strengthen the tower (keep), and on the brattices (wooden galleries) hurdles should be placed whence to throw stones. For a siege he recommends a provision of corn, wine, bacon, salt-meat, spices, puddings, mutton, beef, pork, vegetables, and adds "take care of the well." The necessary munitions of war which he names are lances, catapults, arbalasts and mangenons (used to discharge bolts and stones), knotty clubs or maces, and "machines of war." There should be palfreys and destriers (war-horses) for knights to ride, and rounceys for the serjeants and "ribalds" or hired soldiery. Musical instruments should be added, to excite martial enthusiasm.

The castle prisons should be divided into cells where men can be kept bound with iron manacles. In the granary, there should be necessaries ; in the courtyard, poultry of all sorts ; in the stables, cribs, carts and harness. The account left of the long siege of Bedford castle in Henry III.'s reign describes a castle divided into bailies and provided and protected much as Neckham directs. But not every lord owned a castle, and so great a man as Geoffrey fitz Peter had to sue for leave to strengthen ("firmare") his house. These licences were freely sold by John.

The manor-house is described in detail by Neckham, with its public court (curia) and more private yard (chors) which was used as a poultry-run, and was not entirely enclosed. The principal covered building was the hall, which might be as grand an erection as that of Walkelin de Ferrers now standing at Oakham, built c. 1180, or a much ruder temporary building. The halls that remain are on the plan of our college halls. On the walls of the hall there might already be tapestry, such as Marie de France tells of in her Eliduc romance. Neckham describes too the hall-porch, the columns, the "specularia" (luvers or smoke-openings), the roof of "shingle" (wooden tiles), or of reed-thatch.

For the "camera" or more private rooms Neckham

says there should be curtains on the party walls to avoid flies and spiders ; from columns should hang tapets and shaloons (quilts made at Chalons) ; a chair should be near the bed and a footstool ; the bed is elaborately described, the embroidered quilt with a bolster, then a striped cloth with the pillows, then sheets of silk or bis (fur) or linen ; then a cover of green silk (vert say) edged with fur of cat, beaver, or sable,—a truly royal bed.

In the camera was the inevitable " perch " which served a double purpose as clothes-peg and falcons' sleeping place. On it Neckham would hang both women's and men's clothes. The dormitory " perches " are spoken of in the rule of the canons and nuns of Sempringham.

The prevalent idea of the extreme rudeness of twelfth and thirteenth century life may be somewhat exaggerated. Hot-water heating for the women's apartment is mentioned by Reginald of Durham. Great lords did not as a regular thing sleep in foul straw or without taking their clothes off : there were beds and bedclothes even in poor houses. The law required of every man who had excused himself from appearance in court on account of illness that he should be "in bed and with his breeches off."

Neckham's list of kitchen utensils contains a very complete " batterie de cuisine " ; and it gives a notion of mediæval organisation to observe that the enormous consumption of poultry required a special place for the washing and removing of entrails. For pantry and cellar he has likewise full lists of requisites. His drinks are beer, must (new wine), claret, nectar, piment (spiced drink), mead, ydromel (beer-wort), perry, red wine, Auvergne wine, clove wine. From his list of flowers, fruits and herbs for the garden, no conclusions can be drawn as to the state of horticulture in England c. 1200. It is merely a list of all the plant-names of which he has ever heard. He expects the garden to grow pomegranates, lemons, oranges, dates, figs, and white pepper; more suitable to the climate are his lettuce, cress, peonies, onions, leeks, garlic, pumpkin, shalot, cucumber, poppy, daffodil, beet, sorrel, mallow, mustard, horehound, medlar, quince, warden-tree, peach, and pears of St. Réole.

11. Of the lives of women, outside nunneries and outside courts, there is little recorded. There may however be some significance in the fact that Grosseteste addressed his French rules for the management of a great household and great estate to a widow, and that he seems to make her answerable for much. His small volume of advice on manorial farming was written in 1240–1 for Margaret, widow of John de Lacy, earl of Lincoln, possibly at her request.

He recommends that the king's writ should be bought to enquire by a jury of twelve men into the extent of the " foreign " lands—those not farmed by the countess herself, but let, in return for rents or services. Having ascertained the terms of these leases, she herself should keep one copy of the " extent " roll, her steward another. She should know the acreage of all her manors, and whether they are adequately stocked with ploughs. To calculate the store of grain, the eighth sheaf of each sort should be heaped at the door of the grange, threshed and measured, and from the result the total may be calculated. The most trusty of the household should watch the loading of the corn. The steward decides what measure of grain must be kept for seed-corn ; and what remains is assigned for the household expenses in bread and beer : as against so many quarters of "dispensable" (household) bread, so many should be allotted to alms. In reckoning for the beer brewing, the weekly brewings of the past will be the best guide.

The charge of kitchen, cellar, wardrobe, wages, must be reckoned for and subtracted, if the money-rents will not cover them : but if rent will pay these heavy charges, it is best to keep the corn until it can be sold at the best profit. Clearly it was in the power of few but capitalists and professed corn-dealers to hold up their store of grain. The granges should be locked and sealed till threshing time comes and only opened when the lady's letters give authority. The straw of the corn that has been sold should be kept for strewing the sheepfold daily, and making manure in the courtyard : it is worth half as much as the grain.

At Michaelmas the lady should plan out her sojourns for the year, arranging to spend so many weeks on each estate according to the seasons and the convenience of the country in fish and flesh : nowhere should she stay till the manor is in debt, but always leave a margin for the increase of stock, and to pay for wines, robes, wax, etc. Wines, wax and wardrobe should be bought at two seasons : Boston fair is the

best for the Eastern estates, Southampton fair for the
Winchester, Bristol for the Somerset estates. St. Ives
is the best cloth fair.

Turning to the household, Grosseteste urges the
countess to exhort to religion, to seek out the dis-
loyal servants, the filthy in person, the greedy and
the drunken, and turn them away. She should see
the food that is given in alms faithfully gathered and
distributed, not sent from the table to the grooms, or
carried off by the untrustworthy ; an orderly division
among the poor, with personal supervision is most
to be commended. Monastic charity, it may be
observed, was by no means the only form of
mediæval charity. Every great household was
bound to give alms, and even small households
kept the alms-scuttle, a custom specially urged on
citizens and burgesses by a famous French preacher
visiting England c. 1200.

The countess is urged to watch the manners of
household servants, and see that porters, ushers, and
marshals are courteous towards guests, lay and clerk.
She should require her liveried knights and gentle-
men to be careful of their dress ; at meals and in
her presence they should wear only what is clean and
decent, not old "tabards" (sleeveless coats), dirty
"herigaudz" (cloaks), and "counterfeit courtepies"
(pea-jackets). Her "fraunche mesnee," or free household servants, are to be evenly distributed at meals
among the guests, and when they are seated, the
crowd of grooms or serving-men are to come in in
an orderly way, and sit and rise together, and avoid
quarrelling at meals. Grosseteste recommends that

the household should seldom or never be allowed
to leave and go home for holidays.

The pantler with bread and the butler with the cup
should come before the high table "foot by foot"
before grace ; valets should be assigned to serve the
two side-tables with drink, and vessels with beer
should be under, not on, the table. Wine should
be on the table, except on the daïs, where, just in
front of the countess, it should be under the table.
From her own dish at the high-table she should
help her guests. The household is served with two
" meats," large and full, to increase the alms, and two
" entremets," also full, for all the " fraunche mesnee."
At supper one mess of a lighter kind, entremets, and
cheese suffice ; strangers may have more if necessary.
Suppers and dinners out of hall should be forbidden :
meals in private rooms lead to waste, and do no
honour to lord or lady. The countess should sit in
the middle of the high-table, whence she may best
oversee all, the service and the faults. Her aim
should be to excite fear and reverence.

The masterful men of the twelfth and thirteenth
centuries could not fail to find in their women-
kind some of a kindred spirit. Richenda, the
sister of Longchamp, wife of the constable of
Dover castle, far exceeded her husband's zeal in
command. She is said to have wished "to burn
London if her brother the Chancellor ordered it."
She was skilful enough to direct the capture of
Geoffrey, archbishop of York (that secular archbishop to whom reference has already been made),
and the weapons of excommunication were blunted

when used against her. Such another was Nicholaia
the wife of Gerard de Camvile, whose virile defence of
Lincoln Castle was every one's admiration, in 1191,
and again in 1216 and in 1217, when she was an old
woman.

In Marie de France, who, there can be little doubt,
was Marie de Compiègne mentioned in the " Evangile
as Fames," literature claims a bright particular star,
who shines alone in the firmament as a romance
writer of the early thirteenth century. It is only
by a happy accident that her name and sex are
known, for almost the only record of her existence
is her own works. Such a story as the Eliduc,
told as she tells it, puts her among the immortals.

Dr. Stubbs, the historian, has noticed the increased
interest which women were beginning to take in history at the beginning of the thirteenth century.
The ladies, left at home while their husbands
wandered on crusades or in search of adventure,
passed their leisure, with their households, in song
and anecdote, as is shown by the story of Ela,
Countess of Salisbury (afterwards Abbess of Lacock),
who had been married at the age of eleven to the
bastard half-brother of Richard I., William Long-
sword, aged forty-seven, the patron, as is generally
supposed, of Marie de France.

The correspondence of Adam Marsh with Eleanor,
the wife of De Montfort, and with Senchia, the wife
of Earl Richard of Cornwall, and indeed the whole of
the Franciscan movement, of which this correspondence represents one aspect only, may be taken to
indicate that lay women of the highest rank were

somewhat better educated, and were regarded as of more social importance, than in the Norman period.

Typical no doubt of the feminine qualities valued in feudal times was the example of the Earl of Leicester's prudent wife, whose foresight is commended by a chronicler (1165). By timely gifts of many yards of fine Reims linen sent to the king, to make shirts, she looked to provide better marriages for her numerous children. The object which the Countess of Chester and her mother had in view when they sent to the archbishop cheeses made from the milk of their tame deer is not recorded.

The woman of a studious turn of mind could find satisfaction for her tastes if she entered religion, and in the twelfth century such men as Gilbert of Sempringham and Hugh of Lincoln did something to counteract the teaching of those of the Fathers who saw in every woman Eve the temptress. Gilbert of Sempringham exercised his good influence on behalf of the female religious. Hugh of Lincoln went further ; he admitted widows to his table, taught them, and did not fear to make outward demonstration of his affection for his friends. He loved to say, " For sure, God, who was not ashamed to be born of woman, loved the female sex. The magnificent and truly worthy privilege is theirs, for whereas no man may call himself Father of God, it was given to a woman to be a parent of God." Very different was the tone of the learned John of Salisbury, and the spiteful Gerald of Wales, who cite all the opprobrious language they can find in the Fathers to bring obloquy upon the opposite sex. The horrors of marriage as depicted by John of Salisbury would frighten all men into celibacy. In every bargain, save that of marriage, he urges, you may inspect the goods minutely ; only a wife must be bought as a pig in a poke. A modern critic might comment that the Church, by the facilities which allowed the "nullification" of marriages, did not keep men very strictly to the bargain. Such doctrines as those of John of Salisbury could not of course be promulgated from the pulpit to a mixed congregation. The old English homilist distinguishes, but has most to say of those "yellow frogs" whom he takes as emblems of the women who wear saffron-coloured clothes, and powder their faces with "blaunchet" to seduce men. These are the devil's mouse-trap, their ornaments the treacherous cheese.

SEAL OF AVICIA DE MORVILLA, WIFE OF THE
CONSTABLE OF SCOTLAND, *C.* 1176. SHOWING
HER HANGING SLEEVES AND HAWK.

14

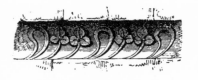

ST. ALBAN'S MOULDING.

IX

THE CHURCH AND THE MONASTERIES

1. Henry II. and Becket—2. Henry III. as a papal ward, and papal abuses—3. Change in the monastic spirit—4. Account-rolls of abbeys—5. Architecture and the arts—6. Nunneries.

1. THE splendid series of records which the biographers of Becket preserved for posterity gives a marvellous insight into certain aspects of mediæval thought, and, though the work of his supporters, in it appear the writings of his enemies. Like Anselm, Becket formed no party of supporters among the English bishops: like Anselm he was no diplomatist, made more extreme claims for the Church than the Pope himself was prepared to back, and neglected to allow for the awkwardness of the Pope's political position; but, unlike Anselm, he was a man of "violent and worldly spirit," to quote the words of Dr. Stubbs, and was judged at times, even by his admiring servants, "a little too sharp." His opponent Foliot, in urging him to climb down from his lofty and impracticable position, said that if Zacchæus had refused to come down from the sycamore, he would never have entertained Christ at his house,

194

and like a good many of Foliot's shafts, this one probably hit the mark.

Henry II. attempted to secure that an accused clerk should be first charged in the temporal court; then, if he pleaded his orders, tried in the ecclesiastical forum; and then, if convicted and degraded from his orders by the church authority, he was to be sentenced to the layman's punishment (death or mutilation) in the lay court. Becket urged that this was to " draw clerks to secular judgments," and to judge a man twice for the same offence, two principles obnoxious to the canon law, as it had by this time been built up on a ricketty structure of texts. But Henry claimed that his scheme was a return to "ancient custom," and as the points at issue were historically disputable, both sides proceeded to manipulate the evidence.

After attempting to give a qualified consent "saving his order," which should not be binding, on any point of ecclesiastical law which could be raised again, Becket ultimately gave a vague verbal agreement. But when the " constitutions " were fully drafted, and he saw more clearly whither he had been led, he repented and did penance, and suspended himself from the office of the altar.

The Pope agreed to absolve him though not in terms that were wholly clear or encouraging, for Henry's alliance was at the moment a political necessity. The king then took up fresh ground, and summoned Becket for trial, as a baron, on a number of charges. Like William I., he sought to make good his hold over his tenants-in-chief, lay or clerk, through their baronies. The church-defenders contended that here a spiritual son was judging a spiritual father, a subject his archbishop, a sheep his shepherd. In the king, says fitzStephen, it is a greater thing that he is God's sheep than that he is king. In Thomas it is greater that he is vicar of Christ than that he is Henry's baron. Again, his "possession," his barony, is not his but the Church's. It *was* secular; but, given to God, it is made ecclesiastical. Its secularity is absorbed by the new title of divine right. Thus neither by reason of his person, nor by reason of his possession, ought he to be adjudged to the judgment of the King's Court. An archbishop can be judged only by the Pope, the Pope only by God. To find a path through this "inextricable labyrinth," as John of Salisbury calls it, was a task that the mediæval mind, having created the labyrinth, was not unfitted to accomplish. The problem was evaded by a series of more or less false analogies, and there was scope for plenty of mental jugglery on both sides. Feudal doctrine was after all as fanciful in its way as the doctrine of the Two Swords. At one moment Becket might take a stand on the doctrine that his Christchurch property was "patrimonium crucifixi," and defy his earthly lord to lay hands upon it. From another point of view it might be of the utmost moment to lay stress on the baronial character of the fee, as many a bishop and abbot found. If on the one hand the archbishop thought well to believe that Christ was judged in his person, on the other he was not prepared to cancel all ties with the state. The archbishop

solemnly did homage when he received his estate.
But Henry likewise was not in a logical position.
He was willing in his turn to get from the Church
what it had to give.   He too made appeals to
Rome, and like Richard I. could use the weapon
of excommunication "as far as a king can."   Gerald
of Wales had heard the term "spiritual baronies"
objected to in the lecture-room, but Henry had no
reason to object to the term or what it signified.
He had the bishops on his side ; and he fully appreciated the advantages of ceremonial religion.   As he
was the strongest power in Europe, the Pope could
not treat him as an enemy, but must accept in him
one of the Church's most loyal sons.   The idea of
pitting   himself   against   the   ecclesiastical   power
wherever it rivalled his own was not in Henry's
mind, neither was it in the mind of any of his
contemporaries.   To desert the Pope was merely to
adhere to the anti-pope.

   To Becket's party the king seemed a tyrannical
Pharaoh, a violator of the rights of the church ; to
the barons Becket seemed a perjurer and a traitor,
continually intriguing with the king's political
enemies.   Becket's flight from England exposed
him to ridicule ; Henry's persecution of Becket's
relatives exposed him to obloquy.   Both sides were
guilty, the one of ecclesiastical, the other of secular
trickery—

> " De la tricherie que curt
>   En l'une e en l'autre curt."

The   pertinacity   of   both   parties   through   many

years excited general interest in the theme, and politically it had great influence on Henry's continental alliances.

Becket was fond of pointing out to his enemies among the English bishops that, in opposing him, they were opposing their own interests. The service of self-interest certainly cannot be laid to the charge of the bishops who opposed Becket, as it could in the case of those who opposed Anselm. What William of Newburgh and Foliot have written proves that their position was the result of conviction. In the joint letter from the English bishops written to Becket in 1166—a letter which Becket was no doubt right in ascribing to Foliot's pen, Foliot argues that Becket, not the king, is the enemy of the church, for he endangers the church's peace by seeking to hinder a king who is " appointed king by the Lord " from making arrangements for its peace. Becket replies that the rights of the monarchy and of the church must not be confounded ; " one of them derives authority from the other." John of Salisbury, writing to praise Becket for this letter, says, however, " I do not place much reliance on the court of Rome whose necessities and conduct I now see through." The Pope is holy, and so is one of the cardinals, but their necessities are so great that the Pope is driven to use his prerogative to obtain what may benefit the State but cannot benefit religion. " Presents will have their weight, and the givers will expect something in return." Becket's opinion of the Roman court, which was the source of all authority in his view, was the same. In the court of Rome the Lord's side is always sacrificed. "Barabbas escapes and Christ is slain ": so he says, and he had every reason to know.

When a compromise was at last suggested, Becket still clung to tacit reservations under the phrase "saving God's honour." At the meeting to settle the terms of peace, which all desired save Becket (so he was plainly told), French, English, Normans, Bretons, Poitevins, nobles and bishops, alike urged him to suppress "that little word " (the aforesaid reservation), and "as a victim before the executioners " he yielded.

Becket's assassination started an enormous cult for his wonder-working relics but none for his ideas. Of him and his two successors in the see of Canterbury it was said, that where Thomas was angry when the Church was wronged, and would avenge the offence, Richard was even more indignant, but sought no vengeance, while Baldwin dared not even make it known that he was angry. All three were archbishops rather than royal ministers, yet it was said that whereas Thomas would first visit the court, Richard first visited the grange, Baldwin the church. Their successors again, Hubert Walter and Stephen Langton, were too much absorbed in the government of the country, too much masters of the machine, to be disturbed by the questions that troubled Becket. The best of the bishops were in their turn too much absorbed in seeking first to remedy the abuses of the Church to seek to aggrandise its power. St. Hugh of Lincoln speaks with no cordiality of St. Thomas, and records that he took money for penances.

A period that begins with Becket and ends with Grosseteste was one of growth and change. In spite of Henry II.'s utter humiliation after Becket's murder, no English ecclesiastic ever contended for the hierarchical position in terms so uncompromising as those used by Becket and John of Salisbury. "Benefit of clergy" becomes indeed a well-established abuse in English law, yet even the humiliated Henry could protect his Forest Law from the encroachments of "benefit." He bids his men lay hands on clerks guilty of forest trespass : " I myself will be your warrant." When King John and the Pope were at loggerheads, an abbot of St. Alban's chose to obey God (the Pope) rather than man (the king), but most men preferred to circumvent the issue by putting it less crudely.

2. In Grosseteste's time England knew what government by the court of Rome involved. The effect of John's feudal subjection to the Pope, not realised at first, was felt when Henry III., a minor, became a papal ward. In Bracton's words, the legate was " quasi tutor domini regis et custos regni."

The new disputes that arose were not over the delimitation of the spiritual and temporal spheres, but disputes between spiritual persons on questions of finance. The cry was raised by clergy, monks and bishops against excessive papal taxation, as the chief among their grievances, and secondly against the policy of " providing " for Italian clerks by means of English benefices. The Pope, with candour, acknowledged " the old scandal and disgrace of the Roman church, its avarice, the root of all evils," and urged that justice would be obtainable in Rome without gifts if only the papal needs were adequately supplied—as they would be if his demands were conceded.   But the necessity for contributing large sums for crusades that did not take place, and for filling the papal exchequer so full as to relieve its ministers from all temptation, was not obvious in England, and the spirit of resistance rose as high as unquestioning acceptance of the papal supremacy would permit.   Grosseteste, bishop of Lincoln, driven by the difficult logic of his position to take refuge in paradox, writes, " fideliter et obedienter non obedio, contradico et rebello," but found it easier to be paradoxical in word than in act.   In vain men pointed out to the Pope that his control of all benefices partook less of the nature of a feudal dominion or proprietorship than of a trusteeship of care and protection ; in vain it was urged that the clerks, who could scarcely provide their daily food, who were threatened with famine if crops failed, who were looked to for help by the poor and by travellers, ought not to be compelled to contribute to papal needs.   Remonstrance was vain, for the only appeal against the Pope lay to the Pope, and, as judge in his own cause, his verdict was a foregone conclusion.

The secularisation of episcopal offices which had had mischievous results on church discipline in Henry II.'s time, when the papacy was politically feeble, was not changed when the papacy's control over the church in England was absolute.   There were of course exceptions to the general principle, in the reign of Henry III., as in that of Henry II. Henry II. selected a Hugh of Lincoln, a Baldwin of

Canterbury, and in Henry III.'s reign the church could boast a Grosseteste, a St. Edmund, a St. Richard.

Personal sanctity was strong as ever to hold its own. Excommunication when uttered by a St. Hugh no one dared to face; uttered by a Herbert bishop of Salisbury (Richard of Ilchester's son) it was disregarded. Hugh could force Richard I. to a reconciliation by simply laying hold of him by his clothes. Herbert had to pay heavily for a return to favour.

3. In the history of monasticism the century 1150–1250 was not one of steady growth; in some respects it is fair to take 1200 as beginning the ebb in the monastic tide. Not that there was a decided check in the number of new houses, though the 157 creations of Henry III.'s long reign are few compared with those of the preceding generation; the change is rather a change in the monastic spirit. The best houses, however well the numbers were kept up (and Christchurch still had its 140, Waverley its 70 monks and 120 *conversi*), now appear less obviously centres of spiritual and learned life, than fine hostelries for the entertainment of guests, places where clever managers of estates were trained, where scribes multiplied copies of books but did not write many new ones. The new Franciscan and Dominican movements drew into other channels the loftier spirits, the most learned men.

The necessity for colleges where secular clergy could be trained pressed urgently, and wherever a bishop whose cathedral chapter consisted of monks tried to divert part of the endowment to this object, he rekindled to the fiercest flame the old hate of the regular for the secular. As the country developed a national and a measure of anti-papal feeling, the monasteries grew more papal, for the papacy had ever looked to the monks to support it against the episcopacy, and by granting exemption from episcopal visitation had brought some of the largest directly under its own management. To the monks every change suggested in aid of the seculars was viewed as a "thin end of the wedge" for a general substitution of seculars for regulars : Roman cardinals it was said were offered the new secular canonries as a bribe for their support. The monks were still sufficiently popular to make their cry heard : but their success only led to a more open litigiousness, to a more habitual forging of charters, a more careless bandying to and fro between ecclesiastics of anathemas and excommunications, a more steady flow of costly appeals to Rome. The abbot of St. Alban's, in so secular a matter as a claim for waste done to a wood, sought first the weapon of ecclesiastical excommunication. The bishop hesitated to use it, and the abbot then looked to the king's court for right. In a dispute with an earl about the cell at Wymondham, the abbot hastily "confugit ad ecclesiasticae justiciae remedium" ; the earl was cited and anathema threatened. Ultimately terms were agreed on, for which the abbot, the plaintiff, it is surprising to hear, was prepared to pay. Far more lengthy were many of the more famous church causes, the suit of Geoffrey archbishop of York against his clergy, the suits of bishops or abbots against their monks. The monastic annals of the thirteenth century, with some notable exceptions, become bulky records of litigation. On the other hand questions of ecclesiastical procedure raised such fierce flames that to settle them, ecclesiastical men more readily resorted to fisticuffs than to the law.

In strangest contrast with this intensely secular spirit are the pretensions to a privileged dominion which, if not founded on and sanctioned by the old ideals, seem baseless indeed. At Waverley a shoe-maker was arrested for homicide whilst on the sacred ground of the monastic shoe-factory. The cry was raised by the monks, " Our places are as free as altars " ; none might be bound and taken in their abbeys, even on their farms, or there would be no distinction between secular and religious places. " Our places will be trodden underfoot like a city market." The peace of the Church and of holy religion had been disturbed by this arrest, and the homicide was restored " to the honour of the order of the abbey ": the bailiff who had arrested him was publicly whipped by a dean and a vicar.

It cannot be established against the followers of the Benedictine rule that they were well-fed and gluttonous in the thirteenth century. Gerald of Wales has given indeed a most appetising descrip-tion of the excellent cookery at St. Augustine's, Canterbury, of the delicate condiments and varied sauces, but it is of courses of *fish* alone that he speaks. To withhold from meat in the English climate is perhaps as much as ought to be required of an

ascetic.   Gerald's list of drinks is also a fairly humble
one as later notions went.   He was shocked at their
having cider, piment (spiced drink), claret, new wine
or " must," mead, mulberry wine, and no beer,
although as he observes, Kentish beer was the best.
The Benedictine rule being drafted for Italians
allowed wine but not flesh-meat.   For northern
climates it might have been better had the rule been
inverted.   Too often some kind visitor taking compassion on the weakness of the convent drink, gave
manors to pay for better ; others would add more for
the same purpose, and the conservatism of the monks,
strong always, and not least strong where drink was
concerned, would prevent any diminution of the
cellarer's swollen fund, with a view to increasing an
almoner's attenuated fund.

   At St. Alban's the diet seems to have been really
severe.   It was an innovation there in the thirteenth
century to allow the sick in the infirmary to have
meat.   It is clear from the detailed custumals of
Abingdon and Evesham that mutton and beef
were not eaten in their refectories, but bacon was
generally consumed, and all kinds of fat.   At
Waverley prior and cellarer were deposed for giving
meat at the dedication feast, as also for allowing the
queen to " pernoctate " there against the rule, when
her eldest son was attacked by sudden illness.   To
the lasting honour of the monks of St. Alban's it is
recorded that for fifteen years they willingly gave up
wine to help the building fund ; in their turn, the
Evesham monks went hungry, cold and thirsty to
carry on their litigation for independence from the

bishop of Worcester's visitation. However, in the twelfth century a suggestion that the Bury monks should drop their " pittances " or extras in food and drink, to aid the monastic funds, was ill-received, and such asceticism as Archbishop Theobald tried to force on the Christchurch monks led to scenes of violence even in his day, and at a later time could never have been suggested. He proposed to exclude all but the poorest guests and to feed the monks on coarse bread and vegetables—one loaf between two. In the thirteenth century the monasteries were as a rule abandoning the sterner asceticism ; if the house were rich, the monks fared well on a liberal diet arranged to compromise the meat difficulty. The decencies of life, order and cleanliness, were observed : of verminous saints, other than poor hermits, Becket was perhaps the last specimen.

To the eye of Richard I., luxury was the leading fault of the Benedictines, and as their frequent guest he may often have had occasion to feel grateful for it. Pride he sets down as the vice of the Templars, and cupidity that of the Cistercians. It was amongst these last especially that the falling off was most per- ceptible ; their very virtues were converted into faults in course of time. Labouring at tillage at first with their own hands, laying special stress on the duty of hospitality, their conscious excellence turned to their own injury. Their passion for " novalia," that is for tilling virgin soil, their care in breeding horses and sheep, their interest in farming improvements, these, the chief interests of their isolated granges, were regarded as meritorious until it was seen that they were in reality traders and farmers rather than spiritual persons, worthy of men's benefactions. The traditions of the order which favoured the strictest simplicity were abandoned, and the Cistercians lavished wealth on their churches and buildings while in the market-place they chaffered for wool and hides, drove hard bargains over their sales of stock, and laid themselves open to satirical comment. It was not on account of their business capacity in managing estates that men had so richly endowed them.

Wireker's typical clerk, who scoffed at the Cistercians for these things, disliked the Hospitallers because they would make him take the cross; the Cluniacs he would avoid on account of their poor diet, floggings, imprisonments, and midnight prayers. It is in their favour that they allow meat on the sixth day, have secret property and wear fur pelisses. The solitude is the chief drawback to the Carthusian order, but they celebrate mass only once a month, and that has attractions. Of the regular canons he thinks the Premonstratensian's is the dress he should prefer, but against that is to be set the allowance of meat enjoyed by the Black or Augustinian canons. When the mendicant orders carried all before them, Matthew Paris declared it was because men regarded the Cistercians as mere farmers (villani), and the Benedictines as epicureans. The order of the Carthusians, characterised by a system of isolation in separate cells, in marked contrast to the other Benedictine orders, alone was free from criticism in England at this period. In St. Hugh of Lincoln

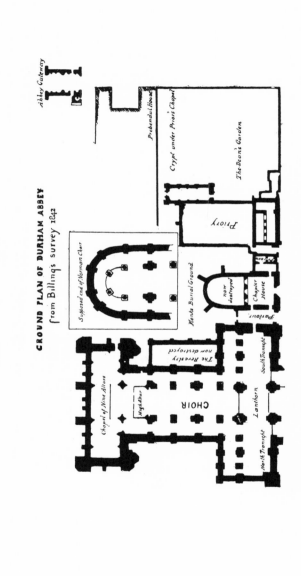

GROUND PLAN OF DURHAM ABBEY
from Billing's survey 1842

Abbey Gateway

Prebendal House

Crypt under Prior's Chapel

The Dean's Garden

Priory

Supposed end of Norman Choir

Monks Burial Ground

now destroyed

Chapter House

Parlour

The Revestry now destroyed

South Transept

Chapel of Nine Altars

High Altar

CHOIR

Lanthorn

North Transept

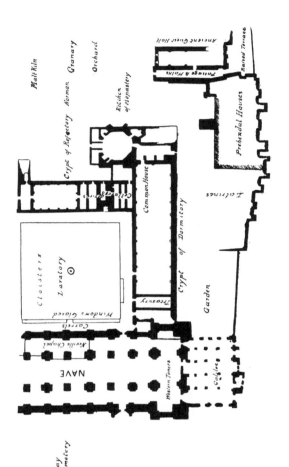

Malt Kiln

Crypt of Refectory Norman Granary

Orchard

Kitchen of Monastery

Cloister Garth

CommonHouse

Cloisters
Lavatory

Crypt of Dormitory

Windows Glazed

Carrels

Neville Chapel

NAVE

Treasury

Garden

Western Towers

Galilee

Lay
Cemetery

Ancient Guest Hall

Passage to Prior's

Prebendal Houses

Raised Terrace

Latrines

15

they produced a man whose charm and originality was felt by all the best of his contemporaries.

A general council in 1237 attempted a reform of the Benedictines. A principal abuse was the demand for a high premium upon the admission of a novice. Gerald of Wales observed that this was commoner in the nunneries than the monasteries. The cartularies of nunneries are full of the conveyances of property made by way of dowry. The council objected likewise to allowances of pocket-money, and to the practice of sending monks to live alone on the monastic farms. With the premium went its counterpart, the corrody system. But if the abbeys were not disinclined to obtain worldly advantages by becoming boarding-houses, it is only fair to add that the kings were equally zealous in using them as such. For instance, John writes : " we order that you cause Philip Russel to 'perhendinate' in some abbey until a prebend of 2d. or $1\frac{1}{2}$d. falls vacant."

The council's orders requiring that all should use the common dormitory and that all should attend the religious offices indicate that abbots had allowed various relaxations. A grave danger in every monastery was the tyrannical exercise of the abbot's powers. Any monkish opponent of his policy could be banished forthwith to a distant cell. Any heated word might be followed by chastisement. Thus at St. Alban's a much valued writer of the abbot's treasury and chancery, who " could write a most elegant letter to the pope, when need was," ventured to think himself indispensable and was rude to the abbot. He was flogged before the chapter till he bled copiously,

ST. LEONARD'S, STAMFORD.
From a photograph by Miss Leonard.

and then, being still not sufficiently humbled, he was kept chained in solitary confinement till he died.   It is not hinted that his arrogance was due to insanity.

On the other hand, a party might sometimes be formed in the convent strong enough to impede a benevolent despotism inclined to direct reform. Schemes for the re-arrangement of the funds, whether good or bad, excited violent resistance. If an abbot ordered stone coffins for the monks, it was done to spite the sacrist, because his fund was to pay; to endow the infirmary with medical comforts meant taking the oblations of an altar, and whatever fund had hitherto had those oblations clamoured for compensation of its vested interests.   The writer of monastic annals in this period rarely treats the spiritual character or mental capacity of an abbot as a point worthy of any notice.   The first, the only, measure of an abbot's fitness for his post was his business capacity: if he was unskilled in the management of landed property, his sanctity or learning would avail him and his monastery little.   Even a very rich monastery needed careful management that there might be savings to meet any sudden and heavy demand; otherwise the "excrustation" of shrines might be necessitated, and who knew when the jewels would be replaced?   An abbot of Bury (who said he would far rather have been a librarian) must be instead a justice, a manager of seven "hundreds," a maker of surveys, of rentals, a president over great feudal courts and councils, where his tenants, his knights and his farmers must meet and find justice.   "In tempore guerræ" Bury abbey must be able to house their lay tenants and protect their chattels, for the tenants' loss is the abbey's loss.

4. A few rolls of the sums of the receipts and expenses of the abbot of Ramsey early in the reign of John give some insight into one part of the financial operations of a great monastery. In 1201 the abbot received from manorial rents £189 odd; from the sale of agricultural produce £113; from judicial fines £58; from fines of knights for exemption from service £30; from a scutage £5 (perhaps a balance kept from the king); in all £395. His balance in his treasury was £200, and his expenses were to meet royal exactions, and corrodies, or the cost of sending horses and dogs to the king, sending monks on messages, keeping up manors, and paying servants and guardians of manors. In 1207 an "aid" or tax imposed on his manors brought in £73; St. Ives' Fair £100; and his income rose to £581. In that year he had to house the legate at the king's order, to support Master Albert the engineer at the king's order, and pay a sum of £97 to the king's treasury. This account does not of course include any of the convent's receipts, or charges for food or clothing and the like. Probably it was upon the abbot's fund that the king, to whom the abbot owed his office, was able to make the largest drafts. It was only rarely that the conventual fund was drained, and that by way of punishment for resistance to the royal will: the saintly Henry III. "lay" in the Winchester monastic manors with a numerous company when the monks rejected his nominee: the most stiff-necked could be brought to submission by punishment so severe.

The system of allowing certain weekly "farms" for the monastic food and clothing went on unchanged, save for such re-allotments as the fear of starvation rendered absolutely necessary. At Bury the great Samson found that his predecessor's system of "farms" only sufficed for a week of five days; with better organisation he arranged for all the days in the year, by finding how many days each manor could be expected to support him with his retinue. He heard the weekly account himself, not by deputy, fixed the number of dishes for his table, and refused to keep any guests, whether magnates, messengers or harpers, for any long season.

The custumal of Abingdon, of Henry II.'s reign, and the customs of Evesham of 1206, are good examples of well-ordered monastic arrangements. At Evesham the priory allotted the tithes of a village to provide parchment and the salaries of copyists, for not all the monastic writing was done by monks. From a fund of rent and tithe the precentor found ink and colours for illuminating and materials for binding, as well as what was needed to maintain the organ. The refectorer's and cellarer's funds are charged very precisely with certain regular expenses. A certain provision of beans and oats goes to provide a Lenten "gruellum." The great treat at festivals was fried cakes, and an improved quality of bread. For those who had been bled or cupped there was special provision, as also for certain monastic servants, not living in the cloister. The servants of the laundry got a monastic loaf when they washed the tablecloths, so too the bathers who bathed the monks at Advent

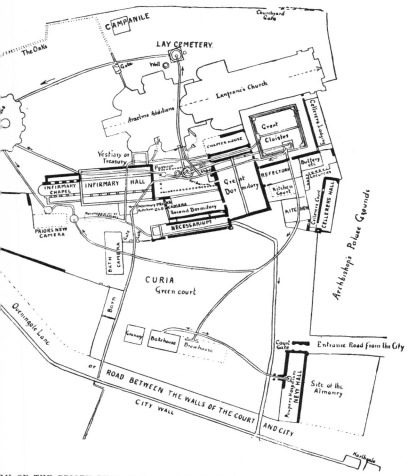

CAMPANILE

Churchyard Gate

The Oaks

LAY CEMETERY

Gate   Well

Lanfranc's Church

Anselms Additions

Cellerers Lodging

Great Cloister

CHAPTER HOUSE

Vestiary or Treasury

Passage

Buttery etc.

REFECTORY

Infirmary Kitchen OLD

Great Dormitory

Kitchen Court

Cellerers Court

INFIRMARY CHAPEL

INFIRMARY HALL

PRIOR'S CAMERA

Second Dormitory

KITCHEN

CELLERERS HALL

Recept. of water or

PRIORS NEW CAMERA

NECESSARIUM

Archbishops Palace Grounds

BATH CAMERA

Gate

CURIA
Green court

Barn

Oveningate Lane

Granary   Bakehouse   Brewhouse

Court Gate

Entrance Road from the City

Aumiry Hospitum NEY HALL

Site of the Almonry

or ROAD BETWEEN THE WALLS OF THE COURT

CITY WALL

AND CITY

Northgate

AN OF THE PRIORY BUILDINGS OF CHRISTCHURCH, CANTERBURY, SHOWING THE
WATER SUPPLY AND DRAINAGE.

From a plan drawn c. 1155, modernised by Professor Willis.

The black lines show existing remains.

(By kind permission of Mr. J. W. Clark.)

and on the three days before Easter. At Abingdon the monks employed among the lay brethren a porter, a dapifer or steward, a larderer, an abbot's and a monks' cook and a servants' cook, servants of the almonry, two infirmary servants, a servant of the refectorer and of the cellarer, of the brewery, of the garden and "hortus" (at Evesham also of the vineyard), of the bakery, a heater of the bakehouse, a treasury-tallier, a shoemaker, a parmenter, or maker of leather-clothing, a carpenter, a mender of gutters, a summoner, a pig-keeper, a stableman, a cowman, four servants of the woodyard, a cooper, a man who saw to the abbot's passage across the river, watchmen, millers, a keeper of the postern gate, a granary man ; and all these had certain fixed "corrodies" in the hall, or wages in the form of "ambers" of ale, bread, a ram or two, or the fruits of certain acres.

The monastic chronicles begin in this period to give longer and longer lists of the works carried out upon the monastic fabric, the granges, the ornaments of the church, and the purchase of books. The Evesham chronicle and that of St. Alban's are fine examples of monastic activity in these directions.

The plan of the arrangements for the water supply of Christchurch, Canterbury, made about 1153, gives a most interesting early example of engineering, and incidentally throws light on all the internal arrangements of a large convent. The Norman shed-roofed cloister is depicted, even the vines trained on the west wall of the kitchen, and the architectural features are clear enough to facilitate a complete restoration of the monastic plan.

5. The noblest architectural monuments that remain testify to a variety of feelings on the part of those who paid for the building. There was a love that amounted, as has been truly said, to an idolising of

NORTH DOOR OF THE CHAPEL OF ST. JOSEPH OF ARIMATHEA
AT GLASTONBURY.

the monastic church, as likewise of the cathedral, the collegiate, and the parish church. There was intense rivalry, passionate *esprit de corps.* Few churches were allowed to remain as they were;

to keep up the honour of the convent or parish, a new piece in the latest style of architecture must be added and only the very best of the older part must be kept. The new style of our period, the Early English, contrasts markedly in its elegance and exquisite proportions with the solid grandeur of the Norman. The introduction of light marble shafts offered an attractive opportunity for development and reconstruction, and after the first great efforts towards a transition had been made at Christchurch, Canterbury (under the architect of Sens Cathedral, William of Sens), at Glastonbury (with Ralph, a bastard son of King Stephen, as director of the works), at Ely and elsewhere, new ideas poured in like a flood. Delicate chiselling displaced the old rough axe-work ; decorative sculpture redoubled its possibilities ; the painted wooden ceilings, where they were not already displaced by plain stone vaulting, could be converted into an exquisite system of ribbed and key-stoned arches, surpassing in grace and solidity all that had gone before. ` At Lincoln under St. Hugh and at Durham under Hugh Pudsey (of Puiset) there was something like a race for priority in the making of the first perfect example of the new style. The extraordinary boldness of Pudsey's Galilee at Durham covering nearly the whole of the west front, rising on rock sheer out of the river bed, rivalled the beauty of the Lincoln choir, at which St. Hugh worked with his own hod ; the rivalry was continued on into the next century, and Bishop Richard Poore, under whom at Salisbury a perfect Early English cathedral had risen from the ground, carried his influence north to plan the building of the Durham "nine altars." The Fountains "nine altars" and the Lincoln choir alone

ROMSEY ABBEY, SHOWING TRANSITION FROM NORMAN
TO EARLY ENGLISH.

could rival his works. The Peterborough west front, the Wells west front, the choirs of Worcester, Beverley, Southwell and Rochester, the east end of Ely, the south transept with its "five sisters" at York, and at Westminster a complete church, were all built or designed before 1250. Opportunities for rebuilding continually occurred, often as the result of an accidental destruction by fire of the thatched cloisters and outbuildings which led to the injury of the church, or through the fall of a central tower, weakly constructed in Norman times; or if no obvious opportunity occurred, one must be created. The efforts made to keep pace with the fashion for building were desperate and sometimes amusing. At St. Alban's a monk having been selected as master of the works, a sheaf of corn from every acre sown was allotted to the fabric; a clerk, very opportunely raised from the dead, made a tour through the country to collect alms; a British barrow was dug up and relics of a most important character were to hand. Yet the annalist groans over the slow progress made; the building scarcely rose two feet in a year. At Winchester the bishop discovered the confraternity system, and got a gild of lay supporters to assist him with funds.

Parallel with the development of the new architecture was the development of the glass painter's, the illuminator's, the goldsmith's, the wall painter's, the herald's, the cartographer's art. Under Benedict at Peterborough the stalls were painted, and it is thought that it was perhaps through his influence that the series of twelve windows at Christchurch, Canterbury, was painted with medallions of types and antitypes. St. Alban's numbered among its monks and lay brethren a family of artists and at least one sculptor, Walter of Colchester. It was Walter of Colchester and Elias of Dereham (Canon of Salisbury) who planned and made the great Becket shrine at Canterbury. Whatever uncertainty there may be as to the works which may be definitely ascribed to Matthew Paris, it is certain that he was a good draughtsman. To Matthew Paris's own hand more has been ascribed than can well have been achieved by a single individual. But what is called his may with certainty be ascribed to the school of St. Alban's, where the style

ROCHESTER CRYPT.

of hand-writing possessed marked characteristics, probably the result of a foreign teacher's influen:e. In the St. Alban's writing-room pupils were taught to level the parchment, rule the lines, rubricate the initials and paint the illuminations. At least three monastic book-catalogues of the late twelfth and early thirteenth century are now printed, those of Bury, Rochester, and Reading, and offer the best possible guide to the literary studies of the time.

Almost all persons who owned books in the Middle Ages, whether monastic or secular, seem to have felt it to be a duty to lend to those who desired to borrow, provided adequate security were given for the return. Several monastic " customs " record the arrangements for lending : at Abingdon books might be lent only to neighbouring churches or to persons of the highest reputation. Early in the thirteenth century arrangements were made for lending Bibles at Oxford. In the monasteries boxes and cupboards were already being found insufficient to hold the literary treasures: the Cistercians at Kirkstall and at Furness, in the second half of the twelfth century, provided rooms.

6. The nunneries were increased in power by the introduction of two new rules which admitted the creation of double monasteries, in which men, under like vows with the women, dwelt in a contiguous cloister and served the nuns' spiritual needs. The order of Fontevrault was popular among the daughters of kings and nobles, and the order of Sempringham with a poorer class. The devotion of Gilbert of Sempringham to the cause of female education was something wholly novel in England, and though it excited plenty of vulgar and cynical comment, such a man as William of Newburgh realised its immense value. The nuns, like most of the monks, devoted more care to multiplying books than to independent authorship. It may be charged to the discredit of the nunneries that they produced no known chronicler. St. Thomas's sister, abbess of Barking, was Garnier's source of information, but wrote nothing herself. There may

have been something of a school at Barking, for Clemence of Barking wrote a life of St. Katherine in French verse, about 1200, a work professing to be derived from a Latin authority. The names of the best artists among the men have rarely been preserved. That of Christina, prioress of Markyate, happens to be handed down as that of a first-rate artist in needlework, through an entry in the St. Alban's chronicle. Sandals and mitres of her "operis mirifici," "admirabilis operis," were sent 1151–66 to the Pope. There are of course many registers, cartularies, and business works coming from nunneries, but these are in their nature anonymous, and it is impossible to say whether the aid of hired clerks or of canons was invoked. Business capacity cannot have gone untrained : the audit of accounts required knowledge of the contemporary methods of arithmetic. In the hospitals women nursed the sick of both sexes, entering some form of the Augustinian order for this purpose.

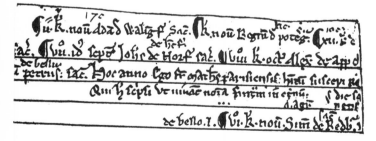

MATTHEW PARIS'S HANDWRITING.

X

THE CHURCH, EDUCATION AND LEARNING

1. Arrival oɪ the friars—2. Deficiencies of the parochial system—3. Types of secular clergy—4. Hermits and anchorites as teachers—5. Schools—6. The Universities—7. New learning—8. Verse—9. Minstrels and players.

1. IN 1224 four clerks and five lay Franciscans were put across the Channel by the charity of the monks of Fécamp ; and the arrival of this small band of penniless persons was fraught with important consequences. They were quartered for a while in the monastery of Christchurch, Canterbury, and finally settled in a house, held by the borough " to their use." This system of trusteeship was arranged in order that the Franciscan vow of poverty might be kept as closely to the letter as possible : it was a system destined to have important consequences in the history of English law. The youngest of the orders, that of the Friars Minor, or Grey Friars (the dress is now brown), was destined to occupy an intermediate position between the parish priests and the monks, and to fill all the gaps still left in the mediæval scheme of religious administration, of education, of charity. Although of monks and

clerks it was probably generally felt that there were more than enough, the desire to do more for the religious life of the laity, once suggested, soon kindled to a great flame. The monks were, by rule at least, secluded ; the regular canons had become almost equally secluded ; the beneficed clerks were either rich and absent from their parishes, or if resident too poor and ill-educated to do much in the way of charity or teaching for those who were poorer still. The story of the spread of the Friars Minor through England is known in great detail from contemporary records. Everywhere they were well received until the monasteries woke up to the fact that dangerous rivals were in the field, that abbots and others were leaving the monasteries to take up the more active life of the new order. As with all the other orders, it was a new and sterner asceticism that offered the initial attraction. To wander barefoot through the country, carrying in the rough woollen hood only flour, salt and a few figs, often to lack a fire, to wait upon lepers, to dwell by the gaol, to reject all comforts, to follow the way that the master Francis had trod, these were ideas that in the thirteenth century set men's hearts on fire with longing, and induced many knights to enter the order. Matthew Paris describes the friars as building schools and little churches in the suburbs of towns, travelling and hearing confessions. Their peripatetic character gave them a certain power : Matthew Paris, with his usual penetration and knowledge of human nature, observes that men were more ready to confess to a friar who left the village next day, than to the

16

priest whom they were certain often to meet again. But many of the friars settled finally in convents, where they opened schools of theology, and read, disputed and preached to the people. It is as educational reformers rather than as philanthropists that the English Franciscans were chiefly conspicuous, and this partly perhaps through Grosseteste's influence. Encouraged by him, the Franciscans led in England the movement towards a new learning, the revival of Greek, the study of experimental physics, the new moral philosophy, the study of the text of the Bible. Building schools where the poorest could be taught, they established "lectors" in country towns, a "university extension" system forestalled. By tact, knowledge of the world and cheerful humour the Franciscans soon obtained great secular influence. As confessors to the king and queen, to bishops and noblemen, they were in control of important consciences : the papacy supported them and found them useful agents. Matthew Paris, hostile to the order throughout, wrote in 1243 of its early degeneracy : a downfall which in the monastic orders, he says, took 300 or 400 years, in theirs took 24. He considers that their degeneracy is proved by their fine buildings, and great wealth ; he charges them with extorting confessions and secret legacies, and his comments were repeated even by their friend and supporter, Henry III., who observed of their preaching that instead of being spiritual as of old, it was all a begging " Da, da, da."

The Dominicans in 1221 established themselves in the Oxford Jewry, with a view to converting the Jews

and preaching to heretics.   But except in Wales,
where they were more numerous than the Franciscans,
the Dominicans played no great part on this side of
the Channel.

2. The Franciscan movement had come to supply
the deficiencies of the existing ecclesiastical powers,
and in the parochial system of the twelfth and
thirteenth centuries there were many deficiencies.
The king and nobility on the one hand, the pope
and the monasteries on the other, could all lay claim
to the disposal of benefices on grounds historical and
legal, and none of the parties gave the religious interests
of the parishioners much thought.   The king issued
his "liberate," "cause A.B., clerk, to have one of the
first churches which falls vacant of our gift," the baron
did the same, the pope did the same, providing for
needy Italians ; the monasteries in their turn, to whom
kings or nobles had given manors and churches,
appropriated the funds that should have supported
the priest with comfort, and put in some one at the
smallest stipend which any clerk could be found to
accept.   The king's system resulted in the showy
courtier-clerk, dressed in military costume or in
scarlet, with jewelled fingers, a haunter of taverns, a
gambler, a hireling in noblemen's halls, "among dogs
and polecats, drunken flunkeys, and ribald minstrels,"
as Grosseteste has described him.   The pope's system
resulted in an estrangement between priest and parish.
If the Italian visited his benefice at all he could not
understand the language of his flock.   Such an one
Grosseteste would put to shame, by going to him as
to a confessor and confessing in English.   Such

priests could neither preach to, nor instruct their parishioners. The monastics on the other hand chose English people, for no foreigner would value their pittance : poverty and ignorance were the chief drawbacks to the priest on the monastic estate. It was more easy, Wireker writes, to find a learned cowman than a lettered clerk. Gerald of Wales, writing for Welshmen, explains that faults in a priest's Latin must not be taken to nullify the sacred rite, and baptism " in nomine patria et filia et spiritus sancta" will be operative. The Welsh clergy no doubt were in need of special leniency, but elsewhere synods ordered archdeacons to instruct the priests in the words of the canon and the rite of baptism, an instruction that must have come somewhat late in the day. A Salisbury visitation of 1222 has set on record some quaint examples of clerical ignorance. A favourite test question was, what case is *te* in " Te igitur clementissime pater," and it proved a stumbling-block to many priests. The greed of the monastery as rector and the grinding poverty of the stipendiary vicar led to every form of financial abuse. Churches, altar-offerings, fees for penance, for mass, for every sacred rite, were farmed, and only a hesitating attempt was made in 1237 to stop the farming system. Grosseteste preached in vain " Si prenderem penderem." Every expedient to augment profits was tried, and in vain Gerald of Wales pointed to the obvious expedient, " fewer churches, fewer altars, fewer ordinations, fewer services."

Gerald has some curious passages on the way in which priests cadged for offerings. The soldiers

CŒNOBIUM OF VERCELLI MONKS AT CHESTERTON, CAMBRIDGE.

From a photograph by Rev. J. G. Forbes.

and laity were accustomed to make oblations at certain gospel passages for which they felt peculiar veneration, in the same way as they would offer at mass. The priests multiplied as far as possible these gospel passages, so that Hugh of Lincoln asked of one, what had he left for to-morrow? The opening of the gospel of St. John was pronounced specially "good physic," capable of driving away ghosts. If the priest found his selection did not draw, "like a minstrel" he would change his piece to suit his audience. If the "song of Lauderic" did not bring the halfpence, he would try the "song of Wacher."

As the pressure of the burden of tithe, of compulsory oblation, of fees for sacred rites, grew ever heavier on the laity, so likewise on to the laity more and more steadily were shifted all the expenses of the church. The maintenance of the fabric, the provision of the church-books and ornaments, the charities to the poor, which tithe and oblations were meant to pay for, were paid for twice over by the laity. The synod of York, 1195, ordered the priests to repair their churches (and not the chancel only): Gerald of Wales taught the law of his day, that if on the death of a clerk the service-books of the church were found to be too few or too bad, or if the roof of the church (the whole church) be ruined, provision for their repairs should be made from the dead man's goods. The service-books, he says, ought not to be left by the clerk to his children unless there be more than one set: the best set belongs to the church.

An institution, a government, which persistently refuses to recognise facts, seeks its main force in figures of speech, issues laws which cannot be executed, masks the truth or divorces the ideal from the real cannot be thought of as organically healthy. In the pretended celibacy of the mediæval clergy there were symptoms of disease. The canonical doctrine that "the Church is the priest's spouse and a man must have but one wife" carried no conviction to the lay or to the clerical mind ; may not a priest move from one benefice of the Church to another? asks Gerald of Wales. The priest's wife was no wife, and yet she was so much a wife that a special word was needed for her. She was a "focaria," and to his fireside companion the priest gave himself and all that he had. Gerald and many others who knew the facts urged that at least the marriages of the minor orders should be legitimatised, but in 1237 a general synod ordered once more the dismissal of all " focariæ."

A few bishops within this period recognised the necessity for a reorganisation of the parochial system : Hugh of Wells and Grosseteste in the vast diocese of Lincoln, De Gray in that of York, prevented the further progress of the appropriation system. Grosseteste and Walter de Cantilupe's visitations were full of homely if conventional teaching, on the over-laying of children ; the profane " feasts of fools " ; the irreverent use of consecrated ground for meetings of courts, for markets and sports ; on the seven deadly sins ; the guilt of usury ; the wickedness of dying intestate, marrying clandestinely or harbouring lodgers for immoral purposes. Already the visitors inquired of the parishioners as to the character of the clergy, the state of the church and its furniture.

3. But to the thirteenth century satirist, the typical bishop was one who loves a cheerful giver, who "dares either right or wrong at the smell of a bribe."

"I do not sell the church," he will say, "I only sell my favour. Why should any one have my favour who has done nothing to earn it?" Under the bishop was his "official," skilled in chicanery, ready to catch the unskilled pleader in his net. Peter of Blois says they break men's contracts, nourish their hates, destroy their marriages, protect adultery, defame the innocent, and all for money. Another describes the Archdeacon as a leech who will not let go till full of the blood of his victim, as one who has no mercy for the needy or the naked ; he is an eagle ever on the swoop for prey. The Rural Dean is born to plotting :—

> "*Decanus* insidias natus ad aeternas,
> Ut exploret symbolum et res subalternas,
> Mutans linguæ modulum et vestes hesternas,
> Migrat in obscuras humili sermone tabernas.
>   *Presbiter* quae mortui quae dant vivi, quaeque
> Refert ad focariam, cui dat sua seque ;
> Ille sacri nominis, ille mentis æquæ
> Legem qui Domini meditatur nocte dieque ! "

St. Hugh's interference, when his men prepared to strip the churches, bears out Gerald's story of the episcopal "official's" claim to perquisites. At its best a visit from the bishop was a severe trial to a needy parish : even if he did not exceed the

canonical allowance, he had thirty horses, his archdeacon seven, not to speak of an uncanonical allowance of dogs and hawks, all billeted on the village.
Men sought to buy off the visitation, but that likewise the canon forbade. Little of course is said
where things went smoothly ; it is the seamy side
that is recorded by the spiteful Gerald, an archdeacon
who could hold his own in any age for learning and
for wit.

The eremitical life still offered charms to lovers of
solitude, and from this period comes the first written
code of directions for a hermit's life. They are
addressed in Latin by Ailred of Rivaulx to a
woman. Fine bread and delicate food he bids her
avoid like the poison of impudicity : she may stave
off hunger but never satisfy appetite. She may have
a dish of vegetables or meal, with a little fat or milk
mixed in to make it eatable, and the Benedictine portion of wine ; for supper a little milk or a " modicum "
of pease. The outfit should be a sheepskin for winter,
a tunic for summer and two stuff chemises, a veil for
the head of black " medium," not of fine cloth, and
hose and shoes. The rapacity of recluses, he observes,
is well known, and their purchases, and sales of
flocks, done under guise of paying for their charities
and hospitalities, are to be no example in her case.
She should live by her handiwork but ought not to
keep a girls-school ; study in silence is to be preferred
to scolding and caressing children, smiling at them
or threatening them.

4. Others who could not achieve the greater sanctity
of the solitary life grouped themselves in twos and

threes as anchorites. To three anchoresses Richard Poore, bishop of Salisbury, addressed his English Ancren Riwle before 1237. A more cheerful life is here depicted, the gossip through the window provided with a stuff shutter, the visit of the pedlar with his soap and needles, the diversion of story-telling with the maids during the season of blood-letting. The ladies are supposed to read English and French, but any Latin texts that occur in the bishop's work are translated. Two meals a day are allowed from Easter to September 14th, except on Fridays, ember-days, procession-days and vigils. In the other half of the year there should be only one daily meal, except on Sundays. No flesh or lard should be given except to the sick. There should be no entertaining as it is not fit for anchoresses to be liberal with other men's alms. From men whom they distrust they had better not accept so much as a root of ginger. They should remember that if they lived in the world they would probably have to be content with less fare and worse. They should not keep cattle as it too often leads to disputes with the villagers about rights of common. The bishop is opposed to harsh inflictions and recommends the sisters not to use iron bands, hair shirts or hedgehog skins, and not to flog themselves with leather thongs, or with holly or briars. They should wear no flax, but "hards" (hemp) and canvas, and they should not have ornaments or gloves. Their leggings should be of haircloth well tied, with strapples reaching to the feet, laced fast. If they have no wimples, they should have warm capes and over them black veils. With Ailred he agrees that the anchoresses should not be school-mistresses, but they may teach little girls if by so doing they can keep girls from being taught with boys; an injunction which shows that the plan was not unusual. On the whole, however, the bishop thinks it is best that the anchoress give her thoughts to God alone.

5. There are many passages in thirteenth century writings which imply that the laity were wholly illiterate, but it is doubtful how far these phrases represent facts. It is recorded for instance of an excellent theologian that he made a vainglorious and blasphemous boast openly in his school, and immediately losing his memory he became "as a layman" and could not read the alphabet or say the Lord's Prayer. A bishop of Durham vouches for it that he saw the poor theologian's son teaching his father his letters as though he had been an illiterate boy of seven years old. A London writer of John's reign, on the other hand, inserted into his collection of "laws" a statement that every freeman who possessed two hides of land was bound to teach his son "letters" till he was fifteen, for the illiterate freeman "pro bruto et cephalo (*sic*) et stulto reputamus." He was perhaps citing as a royal command a law of his own fancy, yet certainly there was no lack of schools. Roger Bacon says there were schools in his time in every town and castle; the cathedrals, ordered in 1179 by a Roman council to have a master to teach poor scholars and others, and not to exact a fee for a licence to teach, were again ordered in 1215 to have a grammar master to teach gratis the clergy of that church and "other poor scholars"; and such

monasteries as Abingdon reared foundlings and taught them letters. Abbot Samson of Bury, who had been a schoolmaster himself, founded a free school for the borough, and the connection between the St. Alban's " villa " school and that of Dunstable remained close, for Neckham (foster-brother of King Richard and King John, reared by that Hodierna, who gave her name to Knoyle Hodierne, Wilts), was master first at Dunstable and then at St. Alban's. In spite of Bacon's contempt for him, it seems that Neckham had a good idea of teaching modern languages, if we may judge from the treatise designed to teach colloquial Latin and French from which I have quoted. His successor as master of St. Alban's school was a brother of the abbot ; he had been to Salerno to learn physic : becoming prior, he was succeeded in the mastership by his nephew, a sound lawyer and decretalist.

The English Pope Hadrian, according to William of Newburgh, was " too poor to go to school," and there is evidence that reformers in the thirteenth century sought to do more for the education of the very poor, in as much as Friar Agnellus opened Franciscan schools for the poor. The first school endowment of which there is record is that of St. Peter's, York, to which Roger de Pont l'Evêque gave 100s. a year (1154–81). London was famous for its schools, especially those of St. Paul's, St. Martin le Grand, Bow and St. Peter's Cornhill. Fitzstephen, Becket's biographer and later a chief justice, has given a lifelike description of the school prize-giving days, as we should call them, when in the churches the scholars displayed their powers in logic and oratory.

6. Although at St. Alban's and in London all the subjects were being taught that were required to bring into existence a university, no "studium generale" received papal recognition there. Oxford obtained that recognition soon after 1167, the result of a migration from Paris. The Cambridge schools are first heard of as the result of an Oxford migration in 1209; recognition from the papacy came in 1233, but the formal grant of the "studium generale" not till 1318. Already in 1231 the king had addressed the sheriff of Cambridgeshire directing that no clerk might dwell in Cambridge who was not under the tuition of some master, and at the same time he addressed the mayor and bailiffs of the boroughs of Oxford and Cambridge on the exorbitant price of lodgings. If a remedy were not found it was feared that the students would leave England, to the damage of those two royal vills, and of the whole realm. The price of lodgings must be "affeered" or assessed "according to the custom of the university" by two masters and two burgesses.

The creation of English universities and the loss of most of the French possessions scarcely changed the peripatetic character of English mediæval scholars. Few were content to have experience only of an English university: for a lawyer a course at Padua or Bologna, for a philosopher a course at Paris was almost essential. Rich and poor students, drunken and sober, well and ill-conducted, streamed to and fro, the poor begging their way, or, if lucky, moving in the train of some wealthy young man. The aristocratic young Thomas Cantilupe, bishop of Hereford to be, took with him chaplains, a Master of Arts as a director, and many poor scholars, when he went to Paris and Orleans to learn his canon and his civil law. In the twelfth century John of Salisbury described how he earned his way by teaching others, " thus fixing his knowledge in his mind."

7. A century which covers both the age of John of Salisbury and the age of Grosseteste covers a great transition in the history of learning. Law was the first non-theological science to become fashionable : at the end of the twelfth century the English passion for legal study excited general notice. The personality of Henry II. and that of Becket, not to speak of the long life and influence of Vacarius, tended to direct the attention of young scholars to the law. While the Becket controversy raged, every man of education must have been called upon to support an opinion. Becket's legal memory was marvellously accurate, and among the " eruditi " round his table, the talk would often be of law, as it was with his successor Richard, himself no lawyer. Two Frisian students spent sleepless nights at Oxford in 1190, copying out Vacarius's abridged Justinian made for the use of poor students. Daniel of Morley, one of the first to collect Greek books and bring tidings of Arabian teaching of philosophy from Toledo to England, says of England at the close of the twelfth century, that it was " wholly given to the study of the law." Even in the monasteries, where canons forbade the study of law, law was the one learned interest

whose practical purpose was unassailable. Evesham monks, with a Thomas of Marlborough pleading their suits in court after court, fainting when he heard the final issue, talked, we may be sure, little else but law.

It had been no fanciful imagining that led John of Salisbury to fear the depreciation of grammar and language studies and made satirists urge that dialectic and logic must become blunt instruments, if they were placed in the hands of children, as, in the scheme of the mediæval curriculum, it was planned that they should be. But what they did not foresee was the opening of fresh sources of knowledge that came in the thirteenth century to save learning from decay, to fill it indeed for a while with new life. John's reign had been comparatively speaking barren, yet even the first quarter of the thirteenth century produced its men of intellect. Theologians place Langton only after Bede for immense theological learning and originality. A great statesman, and closely in touch with his times, from him comes the first French charter, and, it is said, a French morality play on the theme " Righteousness and Peace have kissed each other." When he was studying at Paris he divided the Bible into the chapters we now use. Gerald of Wales was a man of equal verve, original and many-sided. Though he liked to think of himself as one crying in the wilderness, unappreciated, far in advance of his times, he liked equally to boast the splendid reception which he got as a lecturer in Oxford.

By the middle of the thirteenth century a great change in the intellectual point of view of scholars had become an accepted thing. Aristotelian philosophy and natural science displaced in the affections of scholars the grammar and logic of the twelfth century. The restoration to European learning of Aristotle's encyclopædic studies, of the scientific knowledge of the ancients, gave a stimulus to the schools that may almost be compared with the effect of the classical discoveries of the humanists of the Renaissance, but ancient science did not unfold the openings for new development that lay in the wideranging discoveries of the fifteenth century. A few decades sufficed to expose the fact that men had found only a semblance of scientific method, an illusion of precision, and no intellectual emancipation. At the first news of the influx of pagan learning the church indeed had taken fright, and the pope forbade the study of Aristotle's metaphysics and natural philosophy. But in 1231 he was driven to allow a provisional " absolution " till these works might be purged of dangerous elements, and before long the Dominicans, led by the Franciscan Alexander de Hales, were hard at work fitting Aristotle into the frame-work of orthodoxy. In or about 1250 Bacon returned to Oxford and began to show that the merely didactic exposition, which was all the new Aristotelianism was suffered to provide, was leading men down a blind alley.

Medicine stood much where it had stood before. A court doctor, trained in Italy or the South of France, might rise to a bishopric, and the study never lacked its devotees. The efforts to exclude it from the monasteries were for the most part fruitless. The

Cistercians alone expressed strong opposition to it as improper to their spiritual purpose. The Franciscans, partly perhaps in the service of the poor, took to the study of medicine with zest.

If law and medicine were forbidden to the monks, historical study was sanctioned, and history has been their chief contribution to learning. By the irony of providence, men secluded from the world became the chief purveyors of the world's news. Only very strict people like St. Hugh of Lincoln said that monks ought not to hear news. From the days of the Anglo-Saxon chronicle, monasteries had kept historical records. If ever the stream of political tidings failed, there was the monastery's own world to study, and no learning was needed to equip a Jocelin of Brakelond with humour, freshness of style, and keen penetration of human motive. But the lineal descendant of the English official chronicler kept as a rule, in the twelfth century, a professional air of neutrality of judgment; only original minds like William of Newburgh and Matthew Paris admitted the personal point of view.

But it must not be supposed that the monastery had a monopoly of the chronicle : seculars vied with regulars in this as in all else, and Ralph de Diceto, Roger of Howden and Richard fitzNigel, all secular clerks, produced their historical collections, gradually accumulated, corrected, interlined, like those of the monks. Bishops and abbots vied with each other in stimulating literary work; they were rewarded by glowing dedications.

Of the libraries of the seculars, Grosseteste's private

17

collection, bequeathed to the Oxford Franciscans, must have been a fine specimen. St. Paul's, Exeter, and Lincoln, had worthy libraries, and the twelfth century catalogue of Lincoln is preserved : here it was the Chancellor who kept the books and lent them out. The archiepiscopal court at Canterbury had a fine collection, and Becket's Livy (now at Trinity College, Cambridge) was probably there in use. Among the regulars, in addition to the historical and artistic activity already described, men like Robert of Cricklade, the Hebraist, collected for the Oxford canons all the translations of Josephus he could buy ; at the same time he was editing Pliny. At Gloucester a wonderful scholar, Osbern, at his abbot's request, was making an immense etymological Latin dictionary,[1] with citations from classical literature. He opens with a preface in the complicated style of the Hysperica Famina, but casts this off for a simpler method when he explains etymologies. The bulk of his classical references may be traced to Priscian and other late Latin compendia ; but the work is none the less one of great learning, and shows that the secular John of Salisbury had in a Gloucester monk a worthy rival in knowledge of the language of the best classical models.

8. Latin verse was being sedulously cultivated, for instance by Joseph of Exeter, who if he had not aspired to be another Virgil might have earned a more enduring fame. He was attached to the

---

[1] Printed without author's name in Mai's *Novus Thesaurus Lat. Class. Auct.*, viii., and on its authorship see *Rhein. Mus.*, xxix., and Loewe, *Prodomus Corporis Gloss. Lat.*, Leipzig, 1876, p. 240.

archiepiscopal court of Canterbury, where the monk Wireker was also writing not only good verse, but wholesome, well-directed satire. An inexhaustible fount of literary expression was the French epic. Gaimar's work was carried on by Wace, versifying Geoffrey of Monmouth, and the history of the Norman dukes; by his rival Bénoit de Sainte Maure, in Normandy and Touraine ; and in England by such men as Jordan Fantosme, chancellor of Winchester, who put into spirited French verse an account of the capture of William the Lion in 1174. Garnier, a native of Pont Ste. Maxence, wrote his epic on Becket 1172–5, while he was at Canterbury. Ambrose's deeds of Richard I. have only recently come to light : that they were well known in England appears from the Latin rendering which may be the work of Richard, Prior of Holy Trinity, Aldgate. John's reign produced two splendid French epics, the Song of Dermot and the story of the deeds of William Marshal and his son. The historic epic shades off into pure romance through gradations ; the prose French story of fitzWarin is only partly historical ; a poem on the deeds of the Earls of Chester, now lost, was possibly of the same order. Hugh of Rhuddlan's romances of Ipomedon and his son Prothesilaus are specimens of the long - winded romance pure and simple. English stories now begin to pass into French verse, for instance, Havelock, Horn, and the deeds of Waltheof. Marie de France wrote pure romance in her twelve Lays of Brittany, which she had heard, she says, and carefully treasured in her memory. She likewise versified

Æsop's fables and put St. Patrick's Purgatory into verse. The Tristan and the Lancelot cycle were already in vogue among the French-speaking nobility. The Alexander cycle was being vigorously worked at St. Alban's, and popular themes everywhere were the Troy of " Dares Phrygius," visions of Heaven and Hell, the Virgin's Miracles, beast romances, and Eastern legends, such as Barlaam and Josaphat. Christian, Indian and Eastern, Celtic 'and Scandinavian sources, were drawn upon with a catholic taste.

For a circle which could not enjoy French, Layamon was writing his Brut in literary English verse. Side by side, the two languages held their several ways, each affecting the other in grammar, pronunciation and vocabulary. A canon writing French verse at Oxford, 1214, betrays few English traits, but a generation later the French talked in England will cause a Frenchman's smile. Burgesses were writing in French, and clerks who did not keep Latin accounts kept French. There was preaching in French and preaching in English, minstrelsy in French and in English. Samson of Bury preached in the Norfolk dialect, probably extempore, but some of the English sermons of the time are extant. Longchamp, whose inability to speak English betrayed him when he was disguised as a female hawker, found it necessary, so his enemy Hugh of Nonant says, to bring singers over from France when, in the height of his pride, he wished to be sung of in the streets.

9. The minstrel's dramatic power, his skill in

disguise, his feats of dexterity, his lascivious stories, were a common theme, and show that the gleeman sought to entertain the aristocracy, as well as the poor people, with songs less chaste than those which were put in writing. The minstrels are spoken of invariably with contempt as forming one class with the actors, jesters, ribalds, court hangers-on, lechers, dish-lickers, ready for any employ, lost to all sense of shame. Stage-players were refused the rites of the church. Becket, who, as chancellor, had been liberal to "jongleurs," drove them from his court unpaid when he became archbishop ; Samson of Bury most unwillingly entertained harpers at his house ; Godric the hermit "inhorruit societate bufonum." But Gerald of Wales tells how a hermit was cured of his arrogance by meeting a minstrel, "a companion of thieves all his life," who, having overcome one real temptation (the desire to seduce a nun), had obtained a victory worth all the hermit's boasted abstinences. Gerald urges that upon repentance the player should be allowed the sacred rites, but without avail. To turn minstrels and jesters from the door was a merit in a well-conducted monastery, and the begging Franciscans were once driven away as "jesters."

The curious position of these vagabond artists may early have driven them to form a "community" apart, after the favourite mediæval expedient. A curious story is told of the Chester players (histriones) which points to something of the sort. It was due to their aid that the earl was relieved when besieged, and the constable who had obtained their help received the "dominatio" and "advocatio" of the players and the cobblers who had joined them. A "magisterium" of all the lechers and whores of Cheshire would appear to have gone with this privilege, just as it fell to the marshal at the king's court to control these among other hangers-on. The Constable of Chester passed on this curious "advowson" to his steward, in whose family it remained for centuries; the minstrels attended the lords of Dutton at the annual fair with many elaborate ceremonies.

In all likelihood it was not to these professional players, but to amateurs, that the towns looked for their miracle plays. Those which Fitzstephen has described as being performed in London in Henry II.'s day, in which the lives of saints were depicted, were probably in Latin and performed by clerks.

TOMB OF MAURICE DE LONDRES.

SLINGS OF WARFARE.

XI

FARMING

1. THE lords who held dominion over wide lands, in return for their spiritual and military services, were rarely directly interested in the processes of tillage, or in any sense themselves farmers of the land. For the collecting of rents in money and kind, they employed stewards and bailiffs, whose business it was to see after the farms worked by free or villain tenants. But between the tillers of the soil and the lords, tier on tier, who were interested merely in the finance of their lordships, there was an ever-increasing body of men occupied in the superintendence of farming done in their own interest. From the first the Conqueror had urged his followers to subinfeudate upon their baronies men who would render knightly service when called upon to do so. This great class of tenant-knights each holding by military service about £20 worth of land as a single fief or "fee," or some fraction of this amount, tended

247

to become agrarian rather than military in everything but name. The full quota of knights was never summoned ; money could buy off military service, and a definite profession of soldiering developed ; the cohesion of the military tenures was thus destroyed, and the " knight " found occupation on his farm, and in the county and hundred court, where the law called ever more frequently upon him for aid in local administration. Bracton in Henry III.'s time laid it down as a rule that if a tenant owed a single halfpenny to scutage, his tenure was military. But even the knowledge that that halfpenny was due was soon to be obliterated, as scutage ceased to be levied and taxes on moveables were preferred to taxes on land. The line between the socager, or agricultural tenant, and the farming *miles* was becoming a mere technicality : a difference which had been real was about to become one of dignity only. Already by the Assize of Arms, and by Henry III.'s re-enactment, every man who owned a certain amount of property, landed or other, must have the armour of a knight, whatever his tenure. He, like every other freeman, must fight in defence of his country, should an invader appear. But he need not fight in his lord's private war ; at least, it was certain that the king's court would not enforce his service. Even he who held by military tenure could not always be relied on to fight abroad, for the laws and customs of the tenure were vague and uncertain. If the war were acceptable and the king popular, there would be no difficulty ; but political opposition was apt to take form in a refusal to serve, on the ground that the conditions of service did not conform to the customs of the tenure. To meet new circumstances both the army of military tenants and the " exercitus Angliae," which was the old English " fyrd " or national levy, changed their shape. In 1173 Henry II. depended on the fyrd to put down the rebellious barons, but by 1250 the practice of hiring soldiery, the knights at 2s. a day, the less heavily armed at 9d., cross-bowmen at 6d., was already in progress. For castle-ward, the land was still bearing the burden of sending the quota of men for the allotted term ; but in castles too, watchmen were being hired at 2d. a day, to find perhaps a better class than those who held by this tenure would be at the pains to supply.

2. Even at the time when military tenure was a reality, there is in the feudal scheme of service a gradual shading off of the military into the non-military tenures through the group of tenures that took their origin in servantship, and were hence called the " serjeanties." These were neither always military nor always agricultural, but might approach very closely the service of knights or the service of farmers. The original reward of free servantship, as of every other service, was land held " by " that service, and the law in its orderly way gave to the servantships unity of treatment, distinguishing the rules of serjeanty from those of socage and knightly tenure by reason of their non-agrarian and non-military origin. The serjeanty of holding the king's head when he made a rough passage across the Channel, of pulling a rope when his vessel landed, of counting his chessmen on Christmas Day, of

bringing fuel to his castle, of doing his carpentery, of finding his potherbs, of forging his irons for his ploughs, of tending his garden, of nursing the hounds gored and injured in the hunt, of serving as veterinary to his sick falcons, such and many other might be the ceremonial or menial services due from a given serjeanty. Commonest of all was the duty to find "servientes," light-armed soldiers who acted as attendants on the knights and were their esquires, carrying their lord's shield and arms when required. In the "grand" and "petty" serjeanties were the tenures of the highest servants of the king, with those of the humble farmers who superintended the management of his land, and but rarely were called on to send a horse, a truss of hay, an arrow-head or some merely nominal acknowledgment of the lord's dominion and the tenant's servantship. If the service were onerous another could be hired to render it.

3. On the large estates salaried land-agents began to be preferred to the hereditary steward holding land: in every direction there was already a gradual change from a system of which land tenure was the basis to one in which money was the basis.

The episcopal management of an estate, by a highly-qualified steward, is amusingly illustrated by the brisk Latin correspondence carried on between Ralph bishop of Chichester and his agent Simon of Senlis, in the second quarter of the thirteenth century. They discuss the question at what price can a church be advantageously farmed out considering the corn-sales that year. The worldly-wise agent, hearing that the archbishop is travelling and plans to spend a night on the bishop's land, informs him of Chichester that, as it is well known that the archbishop always pays for himself and his retinue, it will be well to propose to pay. The bishop will thus get the credit of offering a civility and run no risk of an acceptance. The agent writes for a writ against a fugitive villain, or to discuss the amount of seed required for sowing ; hounds must be got to chase the wolves which are doing damage ; rights of common are in dispute. The buying of iron and carting it from Gloucester or Bristol to the bishop's lodgings in Winchester, the success of marling at Selsey and how to get carts in order to carry it on, the profits from a new windmill, the state of the crop and the weather for harvesting, these with many legal matters are the themes of the land-agent and the bishop. "Get if you can," says the agent to the bishop, "the custody of a ward from the king, because then I can advantageously provide the manors with stock." "Who is to hear with me the accounts of your reeves in Sussex ? " he asks, or he writes to complain that he cannot sell the old wine in the bishop's Chichester cellars to advantage, because there is too much new wine in the town.

"Can you send your long cart to Aldingburn ? so that on it I can send your venison up to London, with other garnison, and cloth for the poor, as much as you like, for I bought 300 yards at Winchester fair ; I can't send your small carts because the time of sowing is at hand." A foresighted manager, he has stocked plenty of wood for burning, brewing and building ; he has lambskins enough for the winter

use of the household. " Think, please, about getting
mutton in the abbey of Valle Dei (Vaudey) or
elsewhere, and sending it to Sussex." A low offer,
only 15 marks, has been made for two horses ; and
the plans are laid for sending oxen salted for the
larder of the bishop's London house.

4. Within the century 1154–1250 the number of
detailed accounts of estates, describing the nature
of the services and rents rendered by the tenants
multiplies, and in such sources as the Boldon Book
for the north (1182), the two St. Paul's visitations
of manors, 1181 and 1222, the Abingdon customs,
the Worcester rental (1240), and the Ramsey and
Gloucester cartularies, among others, there is an
amount of detail which, however irregular, minute,
and confusing, has charms that tabular statistics
have not. From the economic aspect two leading
generalisations seem in a fair way to be established :
that the "villains" of the preceding period held larger
tracts of land than their successors, the virgaters of
the thirteenth century, and that a tendency to allow
small money payments to buy off agricultural service
was already clearly marked. The lords appear to
have found themselves masters of a larger number
of " works," as the predial services were called, than
they knew how to dispose of, and unforeseeing of
the time that would come when labour would be
scarce and dear, they accepted sums in lieu of
service, which in the long run were to prove greatly
to the villains' advantage. A halfpenny a day was
considered in most cases to be the average value of
the agricultural labourer's service. If the villain

could afford to pay this halfpenny to the lord in
lieu of his service, he could occupy his holding with
the same security as if he were paying merely a
ground-rent. The lords in many cases accepted such
bargains to find themselves a stock of ready money.
To take this course was however still exceptional,
but the greater complexity of the manorial surveys
of the present period seems further to show that the
villagers could not as of old be easily divided into
homogeneous groups, each member of each group
holding the same amount of land and rendering the
same services as the others in that group. The
"extents" periodically made by great landowners
sought, by the process of an "inquest" of sworn
men, to identify in each generation the actual
persons answerable for the services, and more and
more rarely could this be done save by naming
the individual tenants vill by vill, and each individual's services. This lent strength to individual
villains capable of prospering and rising out of their
class, while it weakened the bond that had united
the villains and had enabled them to treat as a body
with their lord.

Of all the many arrangements that might be made
as to the allotment of services, the when and the how
much, the ploughings, harrowings, sowings, weedings,
mowings, cartings, threshings, winnowings, the folding
of beasts, the guarding of flocks and herds, the
making and repairing of hedges, ditches, buildings,
the victuallings, the works "at whatever the lord
wills," of the customs by which the lord gave or did
not give meat, or drink, it is not possible to give

instances here, characteristic of their age though they are. Much can be known of the services rendered to their lords by all ranks of men of every shade of status. As in other societies so in the feudal, the humblest ranks bore the heaviest burden.

Although there is much evidence pointing to stationariness in agriculture, the slowest of the arts to set itself in new courses, evidence pointing also to extraordinary fixity in rents and land values, there are not wanting signs here and there of progress in "assarting" or bringing fresh land into tillage (in all likelihood to the injury of the village commons), in disposing of the lord's excess of "demesne" to rent-paying tenants, signs too of better estate management, of an increase in the amount and an improvement in the quality of the live-stock. Many of the monastic stock-farms were famous for their horses and cattle : whenever the king was in need, it was here that he looked for his levies of war-horses, rounceys, sumpter-horses, palfreys, and plough-horses.

On some of the St. Paul's estates there is a great increase in the number of *liberi tenentes*, and nothing like a proportionate increase in the amount of land they held. There is evidence too that while the total of dues exacted grew heavier, the amounts of labour exacted from individuals in some places were lighter. Here and there, however, there are cases in which the services of one generation can be compared with those of a later, on the same vill, and it will be found that the later generation is doing an extra day's work a week, in spite of all the fixity of the "customs of the manor."

ADAM AND EVE AS PEASANTS OF C. 1250.
From Mr. Yates Thompson's Carehowe Psalter.

In the legal position of the lowest class of men, the "villani," "rustici," "nativi," under all their divers names, there are many marks of change. The villain under the pressure of legal systematisation had fallen in one respect and had risen in another. Although it is said by a high authority that English feudal law was the hardest in Europe in its treatment of the villain, by reason of the Norman invasion, the same writer has shown how many evidences there are of a relative freedom in the position of villains even in the thirteenth century, when legal systematisation had done its worst. In pleas of the crown, before the criminal law, the status of the parties was matter of no account, but in regard to his land, the villain was at the mercy of the manorial court; from it he could not appeal. Yet in the manor court he got the judgment, not of its president, the lord or his bailiff, but of his fellow-tenants, the "suitors" of the court. The lord's power might affect the finding where the interests of an individual "suitor" were at stake, but not where the interests of a body of his tenants united them against their lord.

Though the idea of the serf's inseparable attachment to his "nest," his tenement, was very deeply rooted in the law, there are evidences that the peasants were on rare occasions "cleared" from certain tracts of land, and likewise that serfs were sold independently of the land even in the thirteenth century. The Canons of Osney bought a man for 20s., another for four pounds and a horse, at the end of the twelfth century. When St. Hugh's Charterhouse was founded at Witham, the necessity of providing an absolutely solitary spot for the Carthusian monks led to the compulsory removal of a village ; in this case the peasants were compensated, for they were told that they might go to the royal manors—where villenage had some alleviations—or they might be free, and, presumably, landless. We hear of more than one master of evil reputation, whose contemporaries called him " excoriator rusticorum," and for an excoriation which touches not a man's actual skin, the law then, as now, offered no remedy. We hear also of men of another type, of St. Hugh of Lincoln and St. Edmund of Canterbury, who shocked their stewards by their mildness. St. Hugh, remitting " heriot " to a distressed poor widow, refusing to take the " best chattel " from her sorrowful poor household and asking no " relief" from the orphaned son of a knight, was warned that he ran the risk of losing the lands of these tenants, free and servile, if he gave up these, the legal evidences of the nature of the tenure.

But few managers of estates, lay or clerk, perceived the force of such practical applications of Gospel teaching. The nobleman's flatterer, who told him that the churl, like the willow, sprouts the better for cropping, had the educated opinion of his time with him, if we may judge from the contemptuous expressions heaped upon the " rustics " in contemporary literature. St. Francis's rule forbade the admission of villains to the brotherhood, and this though the friars wore the villain's dress and were mocked at for resembling the " fatuus nativus." By the Assize of Clarendon the " minuti homines " were

18

excluded from entering religion, under ordinary conditions.

On the other hand Henry II. required of them the oath of fealty and an equipment of arms, and Walter Map and Glanville noted their love of education. The "generosi," Map says, were careless in urging their children to study, while the "servi," whom we call "rustici," strive to raise themselves "ignominosos et *de*generes," even in those arts, the *liberal* arts, that are the monopoly of freemen, as their name implies. It is hardly open to doubt that Grosseteste, the greatest figure in the thirteenth century church, was the son of a villain. When good fortune smiled, the villain might graft his degeneracy on a generous stock.

A curious account of a villain's possessions is given by Alexander Neckham in that amusing treatise *De Utensilibus* written with the object of teaching the names of common objects in Latin and French, from which quotation has been made above. He describes the carter dressed in his cowl, with his "capucium" trimmed with *gris* or graywork, a common sort of fur; and his sleeved "frog" or "colobium," which left his hands free; and his hose to protect him from mud. His villain is depicted as having all the equipment of a fisherman, a cheese-maker, a poultry-keeper, and beer-brewer; all the tools of a farm labourer, all kinds of sticks, staves, palings, and hedging materials, and wood-cutter's tools; he has a byre, and a sheepfold (berchery) for fear of wolves; he is aware of the value of his beast's manure; he has stabling and, if fortune smiles, an ass and mule. Of course his plough and its parts are described, and then the kinds of soil it may have to drive through. Neckham teaches the necessity of manuring and marling, of twice-ploughing the fallows or "novalia."

Far inferior is the position of the wretched household servant. Bartholomew the Englishman has described the state of the female servant, "ordained to learn the goodwife's rule," put to offices and work of travail and toiling, who is fed with "gross" meat and simple, clothed with rude clothes and kept under the yoke of thraldom and servage. "If she conceives a child it is thrall ere it is born. A bond servant-woman is bought and sold like a beast, suffers many wrongs, and is scarce allowed to rest or to breathe."

TRIAL BY BATTLE.

MOULDING FROM ST. PETER'S,
NORTHAMPTON.

XII

TOWN LIFE

1. THE complex and irregular, half-feudalised
scheme of Anglo-Saxon society had no sooner been
transformed by Norman legists than new social forces
broke down the boundaries set up to divide classes.
Knights entered the clerkly estate ; clerks entered
the burgess's estate ; "servi" upon the king's demesne
rose above their fellows and obtained a special legal
protection which makes them that contradiction in
terms *liberi villani ;* burgesses entered the knightly
and knights the burghal estate. One man might
belong to several "communities."

The feudal system which based all public rights on
land tenure was forced to find some place for the
commercial idea. From the first the feudal seignorage
found it desirable to treat trade tenderly. The lords
were fostering markets, offering franchises to townsmen

with one hand, while with the other they excoriated the tillers of the soil. For while farm labourers were abundant, craftsmen and traders were scarce. Agriculture was in those days reckoned unskilled labour ; the lord desired to have skilled labour at hand, and also to draw to the gate of his castle all those commodities with which his villains could not provide him. The burgess was wary, having ever before his eyes the fate of the rustics who held of the same lord as he did ; the spirit of co-operation within each of the several estates of men was strong, and before the feudal aristocracy realised what was happening, the burgesses had become a power in the land. Socially their rank was deemed barely respectable by those of knightly origin : Becket, the son of a London burgess who held high municipal office, was taunted repeatedly with his humble origin—in terms that have led some writers to call him the son of a villain. The burgess's liability to the sudden loss of all his possessions by fire made his position a precarious one. His want of military zeal and humble equipment of arms exposed him to satire. In the Fulk fitzWarin romance a man dressed in rusty shabby armour " looks like a burgess." At St. Alban's, prior Warin's election as abbot was opposed because he was born of vulgar burgesses, and therefore likely to be terribly keen about money. On the other hand the Londoners were, even in Becket's time, full of zest for the tournament of chivalry, the Troy game. Tyroes came from the king's court and the houses of the great, to mix with the young athletes of the city in their " hastiludia," " behordia," tilts, bourds or jousts. But

the London " barons " were in advance of the provincial boroughs, where no tournaments were allowed.
The licensed seats of the tournament were all in the
open country.

Contempt for trade is through the thirteenth century
a prevalent note in literature, due in part perhaps to
the burgesses' money-lending, and interest-taking.
London had its " fœneratores and fœneratrices " who
were perhaps not Jews; the Dialogue of the Exchequer
speaks with scorn of the knight who quits his dignity
" multiplicandis denariis per publica mercimonia," or
" per fœnus." Contempt too was perhaps excited by
the legal protection given to villains by the boroughs:
residence in a borough for a year made the villain a
burgess if he paid his dues like a burgess. Only
where the towns were fully populated, steps were
taken to prevent such humble persons from taking up
the borough franchise. But at first it was easy
enough for such a man as the future hermit Godric
of Finchale to become from a " rusticus " a merchant,
" se urbanis mercatoribus consociando confederare,"
by entering a merchant gild, or more than one, and
trading to Denmark, Scotland and Flanders.

2. The towns had from the first paid something
towards the national Exchequer, and the borough-
aid was not a small item. But the introduction of
taxes on moveables in Henry II.'s time points to the
realisation at that date of the fact that a land tax
alone did not cover all forms of property. It has
been noted however that when Richard I.'s ransom
was raised, it was to the churches and barons that he
looked for immediate help, not to the burgesses,

though in the end they would bear their share, as tenants of the king, of churches and barons.

3. Whereas in the reign of Henry I. the purchase by the borough of the privilege of paying a fixed composition for its debts to the crown by its own agents

YPRES TOWER AT RYE.

was a rarity, in the reign of Henry II. it became general in the king's county-towns. Again, the activity of the burgesses of the continent in forming themselves into " sworn communes," every member being bound on oath to co-operate on certain lines in seeking the welfare of his town, was emulated

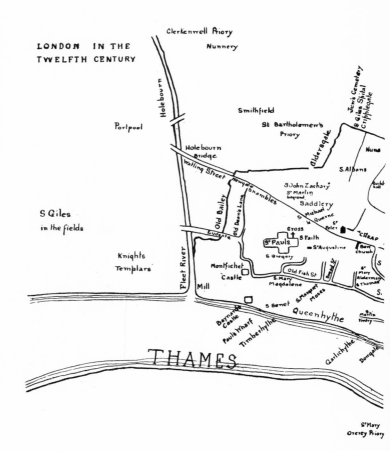

MAP OF LONDON IN THE

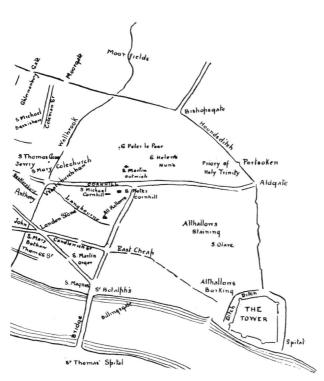

TWELFTH CENTURY.

more or less closely in England, and was not met by active repressive measures. But the fear of repressive measures was kept sufficiently in view by a system of fining for "adulterine" or unlicensed gilds, which helped to fill the Exchequer, gave the central government an acknowledgment of its power to interfere, and satisfied the members of the communities that they would be left to themselves if they caused no general complaint.

The most powerful of these sworn communes were those which included the whole of the burgesses of one town, for instance the commune of London. Next in importance ranks the gild of merchants, the body that monopolised and controlled the trade of the borough, and next the gild that controlled a special craft, or special trade, or the gild of a social character formed for religious, and charitable and convivial purposes. Of these last within the present period we know very little, beyond the fact of their existence. The list of adulterine gilds that paid fines in London in 1170 is instructive: they include four gilds "of the bridge," a gild of pepperers, butchers, cloth-dressers, goldsmiths, pilgrims, and lazars (lepers): others are spoken of merely by the name of their alderman. By a written agreement of about this date, the gild of saddlers, represented by an alderman, chaplain and four "schivini" or échevins were admitted to full participation in the benefits to be obtained by the prayers of the canons of St. Martin's le Grand, in the use of the church-bell, and churchyard, and, in return, rendered alms, wax, soul-scot, and 8d. on the death of each brother.

Evidence of a general hostility among the burgesses to certain gilds of craftsmen, notably fullers, dyers, and weavers, appears in more than one large town: severe borough ordinances were issued to reduce persons of these trades to the level of the foreigner or outsider who did not share the privileges of the borough. London paid heavily to secure the destruction of the weavers' gild. It may be that these prosperous craftsmen had failed to co-operate with the community of burgesses in seeking what the mass of the burgesses regarded as the common welfare.

Gerald of Wales has some comments on the mischiefs resulting from the popular religious drinking gilds. The clergy, he says, get up feastings and potations by subscription, by occasion of which men and women promiscuously assemble and misbehave themselves; such meetings are called speciously "fraternities." Even though the result of such unions be more masses, prayers, and psalms for the living and dead, still, he urges, this does not counterbalance the evil of these gild-potations. It was a fraternity, to which in all likelihood a "scotale" was attached, that helped to build Winchester cathedral.

4. In the time of Henry II. an attempt seems to have been made in London to fix builders' wages—the result perhaps of an early fire that had raised prices. Another scale was fixed in 1212, for the same reason, and by an elaborate ordinance, passed by the London council, no new buildings might be thatched. Tile and wood shingles and lead were alone to be used in roofing; wooden houses that endangered stone houses or the market-place were to be cast

down at the order of mayor and sheriff. All cook-shops on the Thames were to be daubed and plastered inside and out, and divisions removed so that each should contain only "domus" and "thalamus." No brewer or baker might work at night, and rushes and straw might not be used as fuel. The loss of the

SEAL OF THE BARONS OF LONDON.
From Jewitt and Hope's Corporation Plate, by kind permission of Messrs. Bemrose.

bridge built by Isambert, the architect of the great bridges at Saintes and La Rochelle, made the year of the fire of 1212 specially memorable.

In 1212 master carpenters, masons and tilers got 3d., their servers (the journeymen of a later time) 1½d., free-stone carvers 2½d., plasterers and daubers, diggers

and sievers somewhat less, per day ; all received food
in addition or 1½d. in its stead.   A similar attempt
had been made in Henry II.'s time to fix the wages
of bakers' servants, perhaps apprentices.

As in modern times, so in mediæval, the interference of the central government in trade matters

REVERSE OF THE SEAL OF THE BARONS OF LONDON.
From Jewitt and Hope's Corporation Plate (Bemrose).

was somewhat unsystematic.   Much was left to the
decision of members of the trade, but in those of
most widespread importance the central government
spasmodically interfered.   Baking, the wine and beer
trade, weaving and dyeing were the first to be regulated by statute, and in Richard I.'s reign a statute of

measures was enacted which attempted to bring order into the boroughs with their varied and lax customs.

A pipe roll of Richard I. records the purchase of a quantity of standard weights and measures to be sent out into all the counties. To secure inspection

SEAL OF EXETER CITY.
From Jewitt and Hope's Corporation Plate (Bemrose).

and control, some crafts were forbidden to be exercised outside the boroughs.

5. The great extension of the "octroy" duties charged on entering the gates of a town, tolls from which men sought to escape by enrolling themselves as merchant-gild members, is well seen in the quantity of "murage" grants, or royal licences to take certain

specific tolls, levied in order that a fund for the town-walling might be provided. The association between the borough-toll and the borough-wall is probably one of high antiquity. To give a single example, in Henry III.'s grant to Oxford (1235) the Mayor and "good men" were authorised to take once a week for three years $\frac{1}{2}$d. on every cart entering the town loaded with vendibles, if it be one of the county, or 1d. if it comes from outside the county ; $\frac{1}{4}$d. for every horse-load, brushwood excepted ; $\frac{1}{2}$d. on every horse, mare, ox or cow brought to sell ; 1d. for every 10 sheep, goats, or pigs, or $\frac{1}{2}$d. on every 5. There are many longer lists. When there was no murage, a borough might have to depend on the royal charity to find thorns and wood for its paling : Hereford in 1222 depended on the king's forest for its borough-hedge.

6. Although Henry II. had proved a fairly liberal donor of borough franchises (dealing charily only with London, whose powers he probably had seen good reason to check), his successors distributed franchises to the boroughs with a still more lavish hand, always of course for value received in cash. John's confirmations were not sold for a trifle. London paid 3,000 marks for theirs, and many others paid their hundreds. Liberty to manage their own finance, their own judicature, their own trade, freedom from the interference of the king's officers, these were the privileges chiefly sought, and out of them the towns began to develope their councils, their courts, and powers of self-government of every kind. The vague feeling of brotherhood, of fellowship,

expressed in many loose phrases of the early time and answering to a very real sentiment, began to put on legal form. The brotherly feeling between men of like condition was mainly expressed in hostility to all not of like condition, and liberty and franchise meant, as has been aptly said, liberty to oppress some one else. The union of "amici" into a group kept together more by the duties of the bloodfeud than by friendship, still lent a non-Christian character to the burgesses' fraternities, though the old kin-bond had been replaced by the sworn "gildscip."

It would give a false idea of the truth to sing the history of the boroughs throughout in a lofty epic strain; a certain element of unconscious humour must be admitted to give comic relief. Yet here and there in monastic annals there are records which show that upon occasion mediæval burgesses showed themselves worthy to rank with the noblest leaders who have ever lifted from men's shoulders the pressure of a galling yoke. The sturdy spirit of the Dunstable burgesses was not easily to be broken. Rather than be beaten by the prior and convent on the matters in dispute between them, they were prepared to pack and go, yea, to hell itself if need be. That was said in the days when the expression meant more than it does now. Full of unintentional humour is Jocelin of Brakelond's representation of the abbot of Bury's point of view. The cellarer and his men, distraining on the furniture of the poor for certain sums of "reap-silver" paid in lieu of harvest labour, had been met by old women, brandishing their saucepans, threatening and abusing them. So dangerous was

the resistance that at last the abbot found his readiest
means to arrive at a settlement was to make use of
the burgesses' own despised court, the Portmanmoot,
whose orders for distraint alone were deemed by
burgesses to be authoritative. Out of sheer fear of
burghal satire, the abbot was further driven to allow
his country tenants to enjoy a burghal privilege,
compurgation in lieu of the Norman trial by
battle.

The people of Dunstable were among the few who
openly resented the church's exaction of " denarii
Dei " to maintain the church " fabric," whose cost
might have been defrayed from tithe. They cut down
their oblations deliberately, arranging that only two
persons should attend at marriages, burials, purifica-
tions, and as the result of the paltry collections, so the
canons said, the fabric collapsed. Incidents of this kind
showed how needful it was for the monastic lord of
a borough to make concessions in the interests of
peace. In this particular case the canons of Dunstable were after all only reaping in other fields as
they had sown. When in 1220 a carucage was levied
and all religious and their villains were exempt,
the bishops collected a voluntary aid. The priory
of Dunstable had then been triumphant at getting
off with the paltry sum of three marks.

7. More generally characteristic than Dunstable's
rebellious spirit was the profound conservatism of
the burgesses : belief in progress was not a mediæval
doctrine ; the age more golden than the present lay
ever behind not forward. To keep what they had
got was their one constant hope, and as things were

of old, so they would have them now.   Through this
it comes about that the borough custumals embody
antiquarian treasures, that are a joy to the collector,
but were a sore plague to the lawyers of those
days; in the boroughs the old Germanic customs
kept up a flourishing existence, and for many
generations shut out, so far as the burgesses were
concerned, the reforms of the central courts, both in
the criminal and in the civil law.

In London especially the primitive legal customs
that men clung to contrasted curiously with the
rapid development of its constitution, its trade and
its political importance.   For instance, if one of two
witnesses for the defence died while an action was
pending, the survivor, after offering his oath, might
proceed to the grave of the dead witness, and there
offer oath as to what the dead man would have
sworn if he had been alive.   If a foreigner was bound
to make oath for debt or any misdeed, he might
make it with six others, his own oath being the
seventh; but if he could not find six supporters, he
alone might make the oath and take it in the six
nearest churches.   Such rules the Londoners clung
to with an astonishing persistency, from generation
to generation.

8. On the other hand Fitzstephen, Becket's biographer, has given a description of London and
Londoners which, in spite of its would-be classical
Latinity, seems to recall rather the London of
the Tudors than that of the first Plantagenet, so
modern is it in tone.   We seem almost to smell
the viands of the restaurants or cookshops which

he describes with so much feeling.   Again, the building assizes, which dictate the nature of party-walls,
and prepare to meet the dangers from fire, and
prevent litigation between neighbours, show that
London could produce codes of law far more akin
to our ideas of social legislation than Magna
Carta.   The introduction early in Richard I.'s reign
of the sworn " commune," with a Mayor and Council
of twenty-four (who there is reason to think were
Aldermen), a council somewhat after the pattern of
that of Rouen, shows that Londoners were not without the power to adapt a new constitution to their
special needs.   The wards under Aldermen were used
as areas of taxation early in Henry III.'s reign when
they were twenty-four in number ; in John's reign
the . Aldermen were summoning ward-moots, upon
which devolved the duty of arranging for the watch
for protection against fire, and probably also the duty
of assessing taxation within each ward.

Of the rising of William Longbeard, divers views
are given by the chroniclers, according as they saw
or could not see any right on the side of the rebels
For the first time the poor citizens' complaints of an
inequitable assessment were made into a party cry
and politically the rising is therefore full of significance.   But if this short-lived stir was a demagogue's
fiasco, we have the evidence of Matthew Paris, writing
in 1241, that some bitterness underlay the conventional Londoner's outward gaiety.   He tells of the
satisfaction with which men saw the walls fall that
had been built round the Tower at a cost of 12,000
marks.   The citizens knew that if any of them should

dare to contend for the liberty of the city, there were cells in the Tower where they would be confined. Rich and poor alike were insulted when the king took from them a compulsory tallage, treating them like " villani." He should have asked rather for a voluntary aid, remembering their civic dignity.

Londoners however could forget these annoyances in a bout of pleasuring at one of those big ceremonials which it generally fell to their lot to provide. Matthew Paris's thirteenth century account is but a brief epitome of the Tudor descriptions of similar pageants, yet the spirit is the same. He tells of the special cleaning of the streets, the hangings and curtains, garlands and lighted tapers, citizens in holiday garb, mounted on expensive horses, of wonderful street performances by jugglers, actors and gleemen. These episodes, expensive if they were, made the life of London gay and attractive. Nor were the burgesses' interests wholly political, commercial or social. The pleasures of sport were likewise theirs. In common with the rest of the public they might hunt beasts " feræ naturæ " in unenclosed land, which was neither subject to forest law nor protected by royal grants of warren, and the burgesses' chase in the Chilterns, Middlesex, and Surrey, was protected by charter. A hunting clause appears in more than one borough charter, showing that town and country life were not dissevered.

In the boroughs as in every other part of mediæval society, there was movement, a thirst for travel and excitement. A list of the people of a Lincolnshire district who " signed themselves " for the crusade, probably in 1197, bears out the earlier statements of William of Malmesbury as touching the rush of all classes eastwards. The numbers of children in each family are given, and the parent's trade : many of them are described as very poor, some "fere mendices." Again the number of people in every town who took their surname from their native village shows that the villages of the Middle Ages poured forth their young men and women into the stream of a more exciting life : not all the laws of feudal society could fasten the peasantry to the soil.

9. A Jew bids a friend avoid London for its bands of pimps, and crowds of gamesters, its temptations of the theatre and tavern. Its bullies are more numerous than those of France, and it is full of actors, buffoons, eunuchs, "garamanters," flatterers, pages, cowards, effeminates, dancing girls, apothecaries, favourites, witches, vultures, owls, magicians, mimes and mendicants. At Canterbury men risk want of work and want of bread ; at Worcester, Hereford and Chester the risks to life are too great on account of the Welsh ; in Durham, Norwich and Lincoln you will scarce hear any speak the Romance language ; at Bristol all men are soap-boilers. The only place for the Jew to live in is Winchester.

The prominent position of the Jews, 1154–1250, is one of the most striking characters of the century and testifies to a marked change in economic conditions, as well as to the forcefulness and industry of the Jews themselves. The teaching of the Church, based upon certain utterances of the Fathers, that all interest upon capital is of the nature of usury, and

contrary to canon law, left a great void in the arrangements of mediæval society ; as trade developed, and
as the crusades called men to a costly occupation
away from the care of their lands, the necessity for
some sort of banking agency became ever more
urgent. It was filled, in some part, by the monasteries,
sub rosâ (for they acted often as mortgagers), and by
the Templars, more openly ; but the Jewish financial
instinct, coupled with the Jewish freedom from
canonical restrictions, left to the despised and detested
race of the enemies of Christ an almost unrivalled
possession of a great department in the social
economy.

Under Henry II.'s long and firm rule the Jews
flourished apace. The king did not recklessly destroy
his own preserve, and though he, unlike his subjects,
never borrowed from them, but took what he intended
to take without promise of return, he was careful not
to drain the money-giving source. The Jews grew
not only in wealth but likewise in learning. In every
town theirs were the stone houses, the houses of the
rich, strong against fire, strong to protect the in-
dwellers. Aaron of Lincoln boasted that he had
built the shrine of St. Alban and that nine Cistercian
monasteries owed their building funds to him. Bury
owed the Jews £1,200 (without interest) when its
income was only £325 ; Crusaders pledged their
lands ; the parsons gave their promissory notes. If
the king had his screw on the Jew, he knew that the
Jew had his on the nobles and clergy. In 1188, when
a tax was levied on moveables which, by an irony of
fate, was destined for a crusade, the Jewish chattels

yielded £60,000 to the Christians' £70,000.   This was
the moment of their highest prosperity.   With the
reign of Richard they ceased to find strong protection
from the king; the clergy had for some time inflamed
men's hatred of the Jew by circulating stories of
Jewish ritual murders and enrolling the names of
crucified boys among the miracle-working saints.
Only a few of the better sort, such as St. Hugh of
Lincoln, taught otherwise.   The crusading impulse
added fuel to the flames ; and at the beginning of the
new reign a general onslaught was made by Christian
debtors on Jewish creditors.   At York, where the
Jews' banking business of the north had centred, the
object of the Christians was to burn the bonds that
recorded their debts.   The Jews, dwelling in the
constable's bailiwick, as the king's protected, took
refuge with their wives and families in the castle
and, when driven thence, slew their dear ones
rather than suffer the merciless vengeance of their
enemies.

Christian and Jew suffered alike at the hands of
John.   A liberal charter of privileges was of course
easy to buy, but it did not save the miserable Jew
of Bristol from having his teeth drawn.   Under
Henry III., through Dominican influence, attempts
were made to convert them, and here and there
a lord expelled them from a borough.   But as
the percentage on loans was fixed at 43 per cent.
(2d. per pound per week), it was clear that there was,
still plenty of room for their operations.   The chief
danger to the Jews now was that the Christians
would enter the money-lending trade themselves.

Already the Italian merchants had found a way
to become the pope's money-lenders without incurring the charge of usury. Usury was to be
differentiated from interest by some subtle hair-
splitting which sufficed to satisfy uneasy consciences.
It was not mortal sin to agree to pay damages for a
debt that was overdue, though it was mortal sin to
pay for the use of a man's money.

OPEN HEART MOULDING FROM THE JEW'S
HOUSE AT LINCOLN.

GROUP FROM THE PAINTED CHAMBER
AT WESTMINSTER.

PART III

DECADENT FEUDALISM

(1250–1350)

XIII

COURT LIFE

1. Artificiality of later eudalism—2. Conservative forces in the royal household—3. Schemes of reform—4. Edward I.'s expenses—5. Building, painting, and sculpture—6. Furniture, dress—7. Amusements—8. Royal education and literary taste.

1. WHAT may fairly be called the last century of pure English mediævalism closes with the Black Death. The depopulation of England by the ravages of the plague in the middle of the fourteenth century was a principal cause in generating the forces that went to shape society anew, upon non-feudal lines.

By 1350 land-tenure had ceased to be in reality, however much it might still be in idea, the one means for the organisation of society. The life-blood that animated the body of feudalism was ebbing and before very long only its dried-up tissues would remain to show that it had ever been. Already such kings as Henry II. and Edward I. had broken the power of feudalism ; the changes that followed the great plague merely hastened tendencies already manifest.   Traces of fancifulness and artificiality became visible in the last age of feudalism and prove that its organisation no longer satisfied the living and growing needs of humanity.   Within the last age of feudalism a doctrine of kingship which was no wise feudal was shaping—an impersonal doctrine, one of figures of speech, metaphysical, and wholly unlike the feudal doctrine of the dominion that belongs to the lords of lands.   The feudal court of Magna Carta became under Edward I. what Simon de Montfort was prepared to make it, an English Parliament, destined still to bear the marks of its parentage, a parentage that had made it a court of law.   The time had come when men saw a distinction between lawsuit-hearing and other governmental work, could differentiate justices and statesmen, judicial causes and legislative acts.   A doctrine of peerage was shaped, and the privileges of rank were no longer to be associated with tenure.   A House of Lords and House of Commons divide, and do not divide on a question of tenure, for the knight, though he hold of the king, will sit with the burgess, the tenant-in-chief with the tenant of a mesne lord.   Growth of legal theory made possible the peaceful severance of jurisdiction from land tenure. In military matters, too, changed needs had made the old system of knights' fees of no account. Every person no matter of whom he held, must, if he be a man of substance, take up knighthood or compound with the king by a fine. A land-tax was thus converted into a tax on income, and in this way taxation, under the scheme initiated by Edward I. and carried out by his successors, came to be secured upon a purely monetary basis. The church now claimed fewer and fewer of the high places of the state, and the spiritual character of the clerical estate struggled to dissever itself from the temporal, to secure legal differentiation on new lines. The idea that bishops should be judges and go on eyre, long unacceptable to the stricter sort, began to be regarded as scandalous. The quaint prudery that made the clerk save himself from participation in the death penalty by an "et ideo, etc.," a short-hand form which evades the mention of hanging, will now not suffice to enable a bishop to retain his place as a great criminal judge. The new military and clerical professionalism was but part of the manifestation of the professional spirit that was everywhere to displace the old loose bond of fellowship solidified by land tenure.

2. Such were the principal movements of the time, movements that may be seen reflected in the changes that were taking place in the royal household. Here indeed there were conservative forces strong to retain the old perquisites, old abuses, the old confused system of accounts, and the new ideas were less

readily received here than elsewhere. The Constable and Marshal in 1297 made it an excuse for opposing Edward I., who had commanded them to lead an army in one place while he himself led in another, that by reason of their household character they were not bound to serve away from his person. Here the old and new ideas are seen in conflict, but even the household had to yield to reforms, suggested in 1258, begun by Edward I., and continually pressed upon Edward II. Finally Edward II. made a deliberate bid for popular support by propounding an elaborate scheme for the control of his household. In Edward III.'s time again, the wasteful system was attacked, and the writer of the *Speculum Regis* addressed himself with the utmost vigour and outspoken candour to the faults of the royal domestic economy.

3. Edward I.'s scheme of reform (1279) placed the control of the household with one central authority, the treasurer. He with one at least of the two stewards and one of the hall-marshals, inspected nightly the messes served to table, and compared them with the amount remaining in pantry, butlery and kitchen, thus checking the nightly account. He with the stewards had authority to cancel the wages of any servants guilty of misdemeanours not grave enough to require the king's interference. He checked the wine-rolls, the nightly list of wines served, and the great lists of wines received in "prise" (taken by way of toll on the cargo of imported wines). He surveyed the account of the great wardrobe, with one of the stewards and one of the king's council. He was answerable for the appointment of

a man, bound to make purchases at three annual fairs, who was to be called keeper of the wardrobe and sworn in specially for that duty.   The keeper was further checked by an usher of the wardrobe, who witnessed the purchases.   The keeper might not buy or deliver anything without the treasurer's command and the witness of the comptroller.   Even if the king made a special order by word of mouth, the keeper must obtain his warrant from the treasurer and show it to the comptroller.   Wax-lights were dealt with in a separate account, these being one of the heaviest items of mediæval expenditure.   The chandler was to be watched by the usher of the wardrobe who purchased the wax at fairs.   The queen's household was to be similarly ordered.   Her steward was to appear nightly at the account-rendering of the king's household, with her pantler, butler, master-cook, and the marshal of her chamber.   Wasters were to be reprimanded and dismissed by the auditors, unless it were needful to tell the king and queen of the matter.   Special reforms were introduced in the marshal's department, to reduce the number of court hangers-on and the persons claiming "bouche of court" or rations for themselves and their horses. The household was to be cleared of "ribalds" (all loose characters) male and female, and from the horses of those who had no right to hay or oats or wages. These purgings were to take place monthly or oftener if necessary, both in the king's and in the queen's household.   The old system of "liveries" or doles of bread, wine and lights still went on, checked by the treasurer and stewards.   The record concludes with a list of the officers and their fees. The court-surgeon took 12d. a day and 8 marks for robes, the physician took 7½d. a day. Queen Philippa had at one time in her suite a female " surgeon," Cecilia of Oxford.

Edward I., having fixed his servants' and clerks' fees, likewise cut down expense in the carting department, responsible for the removal of the travelling household. Three long carts were allotted to the wardrobe, one to the pantry, one for the household

ROYAL WAGGON.
From the Alexander romance, 1338–1344.

flour, and the trunks of the salsary (salt-cellars and sauce-boats), a long and a short cart for the butlery, one long and two short carts for the kitchen utensils.

Even after Edward's reform the household system was liable every now and again to break down. The king's pantler had to be " put out of wages " for a month, because on a certain occasion he had no proper bread wherewith to serve the knights in the king's hall, so that the knights had to go into town and buy bread and have it brought in by their valets, to the discredit of the king. The pantler's defence was that he could get no money from the wardrobe, but he was told that if it happened again he would be dismissed.

4. From a number of rolls of household expenses of every sort, our means to know the daily life of Edward I. and his successors, their queens and children are extraordinarily ample, so ample that little attempt has ever been made to deal with this evidence as a whole. The daily proceedings of the great departments of state are also extant in unwieldy mass, and make up in part for the inferiority of the work of the English contemporary historians of the period.

If Henry III.'s artistic tastes give a peculiarly interesting character to the detailed accounts of his reign, the accounts of Edward I. are those rather of the great practical administrator ; ways and means were his constant concern, and the regulations of his household which sound mean and parsimonious were typical of the financial shifts to which he was put in the endeavour to make ends meet. The lavishness of Henry III. was in some measure to blame for the drain on the exchequer. The debt incurred on the purchase of the Sicilian crown was immense and the Burton annalist declared that even if gold could be coined from mud, the realm could never bear the burden. Borrowing from Italian merchants had already begun, and in Edward's time was resorted to on a large scale.

The old sources of royal income, the "farms" of shires, had become greatly reduced by the deductions made for the grants of earlier kings. The feudal habit had been to "farm" everything, to accept any ruinous bargain, provided some fixed composition

were yielded. That there would come any change
in the relative values of money and of land no one
suspected, and in the day when the king wanted
money more than land he parted with all that would
have made his successors rich. And while the
streams that should have filled the king's treasury
were thus choked up, those that drained it flowed
ever more steadily. A king could not easily cancel
the benefactions of his predecessor, no matter how
heavily ruinous wars might tax his resources. All
the alms "of old custom," all the old oblations must
be paid, and fresh ones added, if the king or his wife
fell in love with a new Mendicant order, or a new-
fashioned religious house. In Edward I.'s wardrobe
account it becomes clear that the sources on which
he could draw that were uncontrolled by his Exchequer were worth considering: he must keep a
watch on his receipts from fines on markets, fines for
faulty measures, on the pleas of his own private
household court, on the profits from the chattels of
felons, from mint fines, from "pollarded" coins; he
levies petty fines on the masons who do not build his
"peles" carefully enough, subtracts wages from unsatisfactory servants, and does some selling of cloth,
wine, and victuals on his own account. By this
means he secured £10,000 a year over which he had
complete control, apart from the £60,000 of which he
must have an Exchequer audit. But £70,000 was
no large sum to spend on the building and storing
of castles, the transport of troops and supplies, the
thousand and one expenses of peaceful government.
The storing oi castles with provisions that would

GOODRICH CASTLE.

From a photograph by Miss Leonard.

20

keep sound was no easy matter in those days ; often masses of unsound meat had to be got rid of, and were given to the poor in alms.

As the regular expenses of government grew, so grew the expenses of the court : the old rough-and-ready doings, or any form of parsimony, would bring the court into discredit with all classes. Every daughter of the king must have her "capella," "camera," "aula," her ewery, almonry, pantry, butlery, spicery, kitchen, and marshalsea, properly equipped. Men had become so accustomed to the grievance of the " purveyance " or provisioning of the royal household in all its branches, that only some exceptionally severe ravages excited comment. It is known that a visit from the young prince's household to St. Alban's destroyed the markets of all the neighbouring boroughs, for the fact excited a monastic annalist to make an entry : two hundred dishes daily would scarce suffice for the young man's kitchen, his servants scarce gave a wooden tally in return for goods taken, for they thought nothing need be paid for : cheese, eggs, all vendible things were snatched up, even out of the private houses of the burgesses ; if bakers and brewers had no bread and ale, they must make it. A political poet consoles himself with a sarcasm, that it would be better that the great should drink out of wood and pay in silver, than drink out of silver and pay in wood (the wooden tally or " i. o. u.").

5. With the increased desire for out-of-the-way delicacies for the table (Edward I. sent his tailor to Paris to buy Brie cheeses), there went an increase

in household comfort.   Henry III.'s delight in building has already been spoken of, and as time went on
his increasing political difficulties did not restrain
him.   A visit to Paris where he saw houses of several
stories high with beautiful plaster fronts, increased
his zeal to improve domestic architecture.   A full
account of his expenditure on his Guildford palace
exists, and the "French mode" of chimneys and
carved over-mantels, of ground-floors "boarded like
ships" (or laid with painted tiles) necessitated changes
everywhere.

   That comfort was not secured even by royal persons appears from more than one entry : Edward II.
dismissed his Constable of the Tower because he had
so neglected the repairs that rain came in, on to the
bed of his queen when she was confined of her
daughter Joanna (de la Tour).   Henry III. writes
that the "privy chamber of our wardrobe at London
stinks," and a new one must be made in another part
at once, though it cost £100.   But Henry III. sometimes thought of expense : "as you said it would not
be much more costly to cast two brass leopards on
either side of our seat at Westminster than to make
them of marble, let them be of metal."   The figure
of his beautiful infant child, who was deaf and dumb,
was the first brass figure cast in England.   At times
the worries of state entered into poor Henry's artistic
projects, and could not be shaken off.   In the presence
of Master William, a monk of Westminster, (who
painted the gests of Antioch), he ordered a painting
for the wardrobe, "where he was wont to wash his
head," and the subject was to be the story of the

king rescued by his dogs from the plot of seditious
subjects.

Although the mass of painting and building accounts
ends with Henry III.'s death, enough comes from the
time of Edward I. to show that he kept the great
wall-paintings in repair, and encouraged art in sculpture, jewellery, and furniture. From 1285 comes the
detailed account of the building of a hunting lodge
in Wolmer Forest. The " camera " was 72 by 22 feet,
with two chimneys, and six windows of glass ; the
hall was of wood, plastered and painted, with wooden
shutters. The kitchen, two " wardrobes," and a
queen's garden completed the establishment. From
Henry III.'s time come repeated entries ordering the
laying out of " herbaries " and gardens, orders for the
despatch of good fruit trees and other evidences of
care for horticulture.

For the tomb of his father and mother, Edward
employed an Italian artist, but the metal effigies are
English. Peter, a Roman citizen, was employed to
lay the mosaics for the shrine of Edward the Confessor, finished in 1280. On the series of Eleanor
Crosses, the best talent, native and foreign, was
employed, and the names of the workers and their
precise share in the work is in some cases recorded.
Until the fourteenth century, metal and stone work
held the field for the great sepulchral monuments,
of which England has a splendid series. With the
fourteenth century began the fashion for alabaster
monuments and in this substance closer portraiture
could be secured ; above the tombs were wrought
exquisite canopies and tabernacles of light and easily-

carved stone, such for instance as that which covers the tomb of Edward II. at Gloucester.

6. As every article of household furniture was made by special order to the carpenter, we have in some cases a very minute record of the royal orders. Occasionally a description of a glass vessel of exceptional

HALL OF ELTHAM PALACE.

value in the king's collection is given, but that vitreous vessels of a rough sort were also in use is proved by Grandison's comment, made in 1328, that rather than humiliate himself in a certain matter he would drink out of "a glass or wooden vessel," sell his horse and walk on foot. More frequently now

in the inventories of princely collections detailed
descriptions are given of the mountings of cocoa-nuts,
horns and mazers, the vessels of crystal and alabaster,
the enamelling of knife-handles, the "furchetti" of
silver and gold.   Gaveston, Edward II.'s extravagant

TOMB OF GERVASE ALARD, ADMIRAL OF THE
CINQUE PORTS, *C.* 1331.

favourite, had forks for eating pears ; the iron fork of
princess Joan's inventory (1347) was probably a
kitchen implement.

The hangings and "dorsers" and wall-paintings of
banqueting rooms represented stories from history

and romance : Edward III. had on his dorsers the
story of Marculf, the assault of the ladies of a castle,
perhaps that battle of the ladies armed with roses and
the knights with sugar-plums which figures in the
Louttrel psalter. The part of the "demesne" or
private chamber which was partitioned off for the
bed offered scope for rich hangings, and the "bancus
ad lectum regis" for silken mattresses. The great
state chariots for queens and princesses appear likewise in the Louttrel psalter.

In dress Edward I. set an example of simplicity.
He preferred to wear only a "roba" and furred
"collobium" like one of the "plebs," and "cared
nothing for strange dyes, purple or welk-red." Under
Edward III. and Philippa this severity was little to
the court-taste, and elaborate head-gear, quaint gorgets,
dresses of velvet powdered with strange figures (each
dress made in five parts or "garniamenta," namely
mantle, cape, super-tunic, tunic, robe), dresses of
Italian silks, of gold and silver tissue from Lucca, of
fine Flemish cloth, were needed in number for the
royal entertainments, feasts, and tournaments. Besides enormous quantities of fur-lining and fur-trim-
ming, still in vogue perhaps for reasons of chill
necessity, there were feather trimmings, and pearl
embroideries, and over the whole surface of the robe
birds, baboons, squirrels, trees, or perhaps the owner's
coat of arms, were embroidered with splendour and fine
taste. Lace still was wanting. Many of the queen's
garments of ceremony were large and splendid enough
to be cut up into church copes, such as a bishop did
not disdain to accept, as her wardrobe accounts bear

witness. The stuffs used in the making of royal garments and court liveries, for which hundreds of yards were given away as part of every official salary, were very rarely English. The cloth of Candlewick Street (Cannon Street, London), of Sempringham, Coggeshall, Stamford, Lincoln, Winchester and Wilton was rough and unfinished, fit only for men's clothes of the plainer sort. The whole of the court dress-making was done by men, and their bills for "frouncing," lining, padding, tagging, for thread and a score of "extras," show that "as things have been, they remain." Very characteristic of the mediæval court was the habit of attiring hundreds of attendants, male and female, in the same stuff, which must have made fine effect in great ceremonies. In Henry III.'s time one of his wealthy Provençal kinsmen offered to accept a single "roba" at Christmas in lieu of his full "livery" as a means of helping to pay the king's debts. Edward III. provided robes not only for the whole court, but for the judges, for his hangman, for his distinguished prisoners, and for his scholars studying at Cambridge. The variegated patterns which decorated Englishmen's dress excited the contempt of the Scotch, who seeing them "clothed all in coats and hoods, painted with letters and flowers full seemly, and wearing long beards," penned a verse :—

> Long-bearded, heartless,
> Painted hood, witless,
> Gay coat, graceless,
> Makes England thriftless.

7. Edward III. had a strong dramatic instinct, in-herited maybe from his father, who so dearly loved

theatricals that he made his tutor and boon companion Reynolds archbishop of Canterbury, in reward
for his skill as a playwright.

For Edward III.'s Christmas sports (it was the
year before the Black Death) we have the full list of
masks and " visers," a dozen each of lions, elephants,
men's heads with bats' wings, satyrs, virgins, and the
like.[1]

Edward III.'s masks, and craze for "Garter" feasts
were merely another form of the rougher jocularity
of earlier courts.   Matthew Paris describes a scene in
the abbey orchard when Henry III. and his nobles
amused themselves by pelting each other with apples
and dirt, and squeezing the juice of unripe grapes
into each other's eyes.   Even the great Edward I.
was fond of a bit of rough horse-play of this sort as
a relaxation from severer cares.   Yet there is evidence
that society had reached a somewhat gentler stage
in the now numerous stories of pet animals, birds,
monkeys, and their episcopal or princely masters.
Edward I. kept a camel for the amusement of his
children at Langley; Edward II.'s leopard at the
Tower cost 6d. a day, and 1½d. a day for the board of
its keeper.   For the nursing of sick falcons, careful
attendance was provided, and the wax image of the
king's "infirm" gyrfalcon was hung up at a certain
shrine that was likely to work its recovery.

8. With the increased civilisation of the thirteenth
and fourteenth centuries, the evidences of court interest in literature are not scarce.   Henry III. kept a
poet laureate, and his stipend is recorded.   The king's

---

[1] See the tail-piece to this chapter.

books, or some of them, seem to have been kept by the
Master of the Temple, who received the order to lend
the great books on the Gests of Antioch to a painter ;
Henry had also a "custos librorum" (1251). With
Edward I. there came to the throne a man of intellectual power, one whose training in law, language
and literature must have been considerable.   In
earliest youth he had been placed in the care of
Hugh Giffard, the justice, and his bent to the law
seems indicated by the fact that when he passed
through Padua he was there enrolled a member of
the legal faculty.   It may well have been his doing
that Francesco Accursi, son of a famous "glossator"
of law books, himself a professional lawyer, became a
member of his Council, and was provided with lodgings in the king's manor-house at Oxford.   Accursi
is placed by Dante in the Inferno indeed, but in
Priscian's respectable company.   Abroad, Pierre
Dubois, a political philosopher, trained in Aristotle's
politics, to whose charge Edward I. had committed
his ecclesiastical suits, dedicated to him his " De
recuperatione" (on the recovery of the Holy Land).
The Sicilian Guido de Columna is said on the
authority of Boston of Bury to have written his Troy
book at Edward's command, but the work is dedicated to another. In Edward's own library, kept
among his jewels and plate, was a Palladius Rutilius
"De Re Rustica," a book of romance with William the
Conqueror as hero, by Chrétien de Troyes,[1] a "summa"
by the canonist Tancred, and from another source it

---

[1] Printed in Giles, *Script. Gest. Will. I.*, p. 179.

is known that he had a copy of the cycle of Breton
romances abridged by Rustician of Pisa, in French :
a Dutch record tells also of the romances recited
and sung at his Round Table.   Memoranda too are
extant showing the fees paid to men going to London
to find service-books for the king's use, to men who
illuminated the queen's psalter ; and a celebrated
and lovely psalter which was given by Edward and
Eleanor to their son Alphonso still exists.

In preparing his Scottish claim Edward ordered
that the public records should be ransacked for historical evidences, and by placing dependence on such
records he encouraged respect for them.   It is known
that he spoke Latin, French, and English with equal
ease, and it is possible that he knew Spanish.   A
father so well educated naturally bestowed great care
upon the training of his heir, but the results were in
no respect satisfactory.   The future Edward II., to
teach him the conduct of public business, was given a
nominal regency at the age of thirteen.   A curious
roll of his letters, 1304–5, now containing 700, and at
one time more, seems to show that his drilling was
elaborate.   All are in French except those to foreign
ecclesiastics ; many are to his step-mother Margaret,
and concern his money troubles.   It is known that
he could not speak Latin well enough to take the
coronation oath in that tongue, at least he used the
French form provided for such an emergency.   He
was fond of music and as prince of Wales he wrote
to the abbot of Shrewsbury asking that a famous
fiddler in the abbot's household should teach the
prince's rhymer the minstrelsy of the " crowdy," and

that the rhymer might be housed at the convent whilst
he was learning.

His best side was shown in his love of outdoor
pursuits, but unhappily tastes that would now be
considered not unworthy in a sovereign were then
regarded as contemptible in any self-respecting lord.
It was deemed to his discredit that he took pleasure
in digging and fencing with his own hands, in horse
and dog breeding, in smith's work : such occupations
were reckoned part and parcel of his fondness for
low associates, watermen and grooms. If the French
poem said to have been written by him in his imprisonment is really his work it would show that
time and trouble purified his taste.

The good example set by Henry III. and Edward I.
in their happy domesticity was probably not without
social effect ; we hear now next to nothing of royal
bastards till the end of the period. Henry and Edward
kept their children with them more than was usual,
and we have a touching evidence of Edward's care for
the welfare of his infants in the will which he made
in Palestine on the day he received his wound.
Eleanor bore him thirteen children, with a rapidity
that may have caused her regretted death. Of all
Eleanor's family none reached old age ; the nun
Mary lived longest, to the age of 54.

For Mary, the nun of Amesbury, Trivet put his
Latin outline chronicle into French : and for her also
it is said that he wrote his story of Constance in
French, a story which has been familiarised by
Chaucer and Gower and kept its popularity for
generations,

Edward III.'s education was guided by the biblio-grapher Richard of Bury, but it is doubtful whether he stimulated in his pupil his own amiable weakness for book-hunting. Edward's wife Philippa bore him twelve children, and guided their education wisely. The elder children were brought up by William and Elizabeth de St. Omer, whose psalter, illuminated in the best style of the Norfolk school, speaks well of their artistic taste. Mary de St. Pol, who educated a younger daughter, was to be the foundress of Pem-broke College, Cambridge, and was doubtless a wise preceptor. Walter Burley the philosopher educated the Black Prince.

MUMMERS.

A BARBICAN.

XIV

BARONIAL HOUSEHOLDS

1. A VERY curious ordinance of Edward II.'s troubled reign gives an account of the extravagances fashionable in the households of the great, an account as vivid as anything that can be read of the fifteenth century. It was issued at a time of great scarcity; year after year of bad harvests had

led even the barons who formed the government
to seek protection from the demands made on their
hospitality by all and sundry: nominally the order
was issued in the interests of the suffering poor. A
stop is to be put on the claiming of victuals under
colour of minstrelsy and errand-running (messagerie).
In the hostels of prelates, earls, barons, not more
than three or four honourable and genuine minstrels
will be allowed free board, unless the lord invites
them. At the houses of lesser persons none are to
insist on free board against the master's will. On
the first offence the penalty is loss of minstrelsy
(membership), on the second, to foreswear the trade,
and never again to be received as minstrel in any
house. Messengers and runners have no rights
unless they really carry the lord's trunk or have a
genuine errand : of archers and idle people none
shall claim victuals uninvited. Tips and " vails "
are after all nothing to the demands of fourteenth
century conventionality. The order further cuts
down the number of courses upon men's tables :
two courses of flesh of four sorts each should suffice : prelates, earls, barons and magnates may have
an " entremêt of one manner of charge " at their table.

The list of provisions for the feast at an archbishop's enthronement in 1295, gives an idea of the
variety of mediæval diet when flesh was excluded :
300 ling, 600 cod, 7 barrels of salt salmon at 28s. a
barrel, 40 fresh salmon at 7s. each, 14 barrels of white
herring, 20 " cades " [1] of red herring, 5 barrels of salt
sturgeon, 2 of salt eels, 600 fresh eels, 8,000 whelks,

---

[1] The cade held 6 " long " hundreds, of six score each.

100 pike, 400 tench, 100 carp, 800 bream, 2 barrels
of salt lamprey, 80 large fresh lampreys (mostly bred
in the Severn), 1,400 small lampreys, 124 salt conger,
200 large roach ; there are thrown in besides seals
and porpoise and "pophyns." There was olive-oil,
honey, mustard, vinegar, verjuice (an essential in-
gredient of mediæval sauces), £33 worth of spices
and comfits, bread, wafers, and wines, with London,
Canterbury and English beer in proportion. The
London cooks' wages, hired for the occasion, were
£23, the rewards of heralds of arms, trumpeters,
and mimes £20 ; painting the throne and making
"subtleties," huge erections in plaster and wax of
which the edible part was small, or non-existent,
cost £16. The cost may be multiplied some twenty-
fold to get an idea of modern values. It is said to
cost much to become a bishop now-a-days, but perhaps it cost more then. Extravagances of this sort
were not confined to the spiritual peers ; it was
observed of temporal lords, by an archbishop
who was a notably good manager, that the lords
would not keep such big households filled with
"garciones" or grooms if they did not know how
to live by rapine. There are various means to fill
big larders as well as to empty them.

Clerical and lay accounts are in this period fairly
abundant and detailed. There are lists of the expenses incurred by Simon de Montfort's wife, by a
suitor to a royal princess, by the great household
of Lancaster, by the De Lacys, by a bishop of
Hereford. But the departments are numerous and
food and drink and clothes, the items of which we

hear most, do not cover all the sources of expenditure.
The De Montfort account is an account of food and
drink : clothes are entered occasionally on the back
of the roll and tell, it may be, of the cowhide shoes
and russet hose for one of the Earl's sons, or the cost
of the Countess's sheepskin " cruralia " or breeches.
Such entries as the bribes given to secure the friendli-
ness of the burgesses of the Cinque Ports, the cost
of a cat and kittens for the " camera," of the cords to
open and shut the " louver " or smoke-outlet in the
roof of the hall, the fee to a groom keeping the old,
white horse, payments for hot baths, to the barber
for bleeding a household damsel, the Countess's
washing bill (Christmas to the end of May, 15d.),
carry the mind of the reader, back and forward,
between past and present, as an account-book
should. On Wednesday, Friday and Saturday the
diet books of lay and spiritual alike show abstinence
from flesh : the fast days of course meant as a rule
merely a change of diet, an arrangement probably
both agreeable and wholesome in days when there
was little variety. In every big account the feeding
of poor people on bread and beer or cider, sometimes
with the additional luxury of unsound meat, appears
more or less regularly. Three hundred poor men fed
because John of Brabant, and his wife the princess
Margaret, did not hear mass. John of Brabant was in
the habit of losing money at chess, bowls and shoot-
ing matches, and some of his gifts " propter Deum "
to idiots, poor pages, &c., may have had expiatory
intention. His pride in his horses and affection for
them is shown by the record kept of their pet names.

Although such a splendid list of effects as that of the extravagant Gaveston, the king's favourite, may give an impression of lavish furnishing, the entries in the wills of great persons argue the high value set upon a single spoon or kitchen utensil. A bishop bequeathes in 1295 the "spoon which was deputed for my mouth," and gives an abbess his irons to make wafers or galette.

2. The original noble families of the Conquest had by the close of the thirteenth century left few direct representatives, but new families had risen upon the old, and had infused fresh vitality into the "peerage," which now began to claim legal privileges unheard of in older days, privileges which gave a new differentiation to the class thus enfranchised. A House of Lords comes definitely into existence and marks a great break with feudalism. There is much to show that Edward I. went deliberately to work to hasten the killing of what Henry II. had scotched. By what warrant, he asked, did this and this "franchise" exist, the franchise which placed in the hands of a private person, a bishop, a monastery, or a borough, the right to string men up on gallows, to drown women in pits, for such and such offences; to control weights and measures; to hold courts for this purpose or for that, privileges that should be traceable to a direct grant from the king.

Few could answer with any truth, as one or two, it is said, did answer, "here is my warrant" (the rusty sword): "My ancestors came with William the Bastard and won their lands by the sword.

With my sword will I defend them against all usurpers." Edward I.'s great inquest shows in the place of the nascent feudalism of William's Domesday, feudalism decadent : the feudalist might be loud of voice and quick to lay hand on sword perhaps, but the sound and fury signified little and the sword was rusty.

The body by which Edward governed his kingdom, whether we think of it as Parliament or as a King's Council, was no longer a feudal court ; and it was superior to all feudal courts. Yet the inability of the King, in his Council in his Parliament, to do more than indicate the lines of the new policy, showed that the old powers must still be reckoned with. In the usual English way there was to be no revolution, no catastrophic sweeping away of obstacles, but bit by bit the ever busy ants of the law courts removed a huge dead thing from their midst.

3. The lords were ceasing to be sovereigns, kept under only by the iron hand of a superior, the sources and nature of whose strength differed little from their own, but they still were pre-eminently mounted warriors. No peer of the realm could escape the profession of arms or dreamed of desiring to do so. The king's sons, the heir to the throne himself, must engage in hand to hand fighting which was no mere pretence. A failure among monarchs, an Edward II., might fail in the knightly arts, but it would be the surest evidence of his unfitness for office of any kind.

But already the training of the tournament might

vary from a game with blunted swords to the most deadly contest: there was the tourney *à plaisance*, and likewise *à outrance*. Already regulations were being attempted to reduce the danger lest every tournament should become a battlefield, to allow more scope for sport and less for fighting.

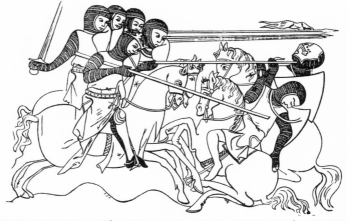

FROM MATTHEW PARIS'S LIVES OF THE OFFAS : SHOWS OFFA'S GREAVES AND KNEE-PIECES, THE BANDED MAIL, THE HOUSING OF THE HORSES ; ONE MAN WEARS A HEAD-PIECE WITH MASK OF STEEL OVER A COIF OF BANDED MAIL.

Statutes were being issued in Edward I.'s time which forbade pointed swords, and reduced the number of esquires and the arming of attendants, and the patent rolls are full of letters forbidding tournaments where there was danger of a " mêlée."

Edward I. made it his object to put down private war ; he refused to allow his lieges to kill each other except in the judicial wager of battle fought on foot, or in the trial of chivalry in vindication of personal honour ; over this last ordeal by duel, the king or his officers must preside in person. When one of his knights challenged another and dared him to encounter with him in France, Edward forbade the challenge to be taken up. A great lord might be driven to no more lordly way of clearing himself than by an appeal to 50 or 500 knights, who would " compurgate " for him ; he might perhaps with such a body overawe the court, but it was to put himself on the same footing as a burgess.

The lords realised the danger of " conjurationes " or sworn bands of "ribalds," especially in towns, and rules which the " chivalry " might think very unfit as yet for their own rank, were thought highly advisable for the humbler sort. Londoners might have their schools of fence and sword-play severely restricted, in the interests of peace ; the royal letters patent would rightly be used to forbid tournaments in provincial towns or in the neighbourhood of the universities, but for the true nobility there must be monthly, even weekly opportunities for the sports which were their education. The descriptions of tournaments found in monastic annals show that the lust for this forbidden fruit troubled not least those dead to the world. The Dunstable chronicler waxes enthusiastic over an Ash Wednesday fight of exceptional severity at which "no ribald or other footman bore aught in his hand but a small shield to resist the onset of the horses." But the gathering of armed crowds in troubled times, such as those of

Edward II., grew ever more dangerous. Edward III., fortunately for his government, offered his subjects in a French war a sterner discipline.

The holding of Round Tables began to be fashionable at least as early as 1252. The proceedings began with a grand dinner at a table arranged round the walls of the room, the guests sitting

SEAL OF ROBERT FITZWALTER, 1298–1304 : SHOWING
SPIKED TESTIERES FOR HORSE'S HEAD.

with their backs to the wall and all facing a central space where minstrels and servers stood. The Round Table dinner might be accompanied with dancing and music, followed by a grand knighting ceremony. If a batch of young men received the honour, as 300 did at the time when young Edward II. was knighted, a scrimmage ensued for the distribution of fine clothes, of splendid horses, which it was part of the entertainment to let loose in the crowd. With Edward III.'s Garter ceremonies, the fun waxed fast and furious, as lords and ladies tripped in the dance "amplexus commiscentes et oscula," while the minstrels or "histriones" made melody.

Such feasts were not given by the king alone : on one occasion (1279) a great lord of the Welsh border, Roger de Mortimer, was "captain" at the round table at Warwick, where were present many noble and powerful lords from foreign countries.

It was the best feature of the tournament that it drew the nobility of all countries together ; to go abroad to a "tourney" was, in a thirteenth century baron's education, the *grand tour* of a more peaceful time. And the elaborate codes of honour, punctilio and etiquette which ruled the gathering, had no small share in framing an accepted system of international courtesy. There was as yet no insularity among the nobles, and very little that was distinctive of national fashion, though a Frenchman would be known for such by his dress in Edward I.'s time.

4. Parisian dwellings set the pattern copied in England. In England as abroad it was becoming more and more usual for the lords to content themselves with manor-houses for dwellings, and those who had money to spend upon them could get the king's licence to "crenellate." Of splendid partly-fortified private buildings, the episcopal palaces of St. David's and of Wells afford the best examples.

Anthony Bek began Eltham and gave it to Eleanor of Castile. But many could do no more than add to the number of buildings round the "curia," join the detached parts by alleys, add plaster and paint, replace "shingles" with tile and add shutters and wooden partitions (interclusoria) for privacy's sake. Hall and stables were still the dormitories of guests and servants.

The elaboration of full-dress armour grew greater as its purpose became less apparent. The "cointises" or streamers from the helmet, the "cyclas" or silk shirt embroidered with the family arms, the varieties in the shape of the moveable helmet-fronts, and, with the fourteenth century, the introduction of plate armour, make every illustration of a fight, every tomb of a knight, a lesson in the technicalities of mediæval armour and heraldry.

5. The elaborate development of a costly suit of armour for man or beast might serve as a type on a small scale of the parallel elaboration of the castle. The concentric castle of the Edwardian period with its lines of defence one within another, each disposed so as to leave no part unsupported, fold within fold, resembled the layers of quilted "pourpoint," mail and plate. The instruments of siege, the scaffolds on wheels, the rams, "sows" and "cats," in all their many forms, had become more and more capable of dealing with the Norman keep. To remain pent up for months in a stone tower was seen to be after all a rather aimless proceeding, for time must play into the hands of the besiegers, whose supplies alone could be increased. By means of the new sally-ports of

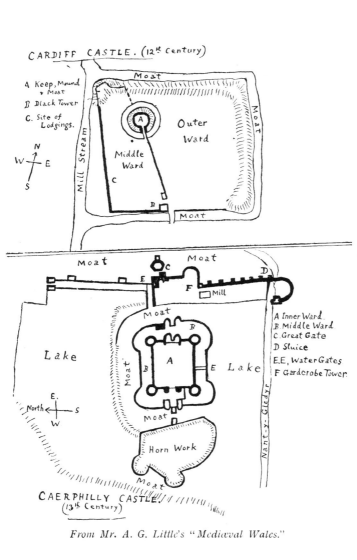

CARDIFF CASTLE. (12ᵗʰ Century)

A Keep, Mound
  ᴠ Moat
B Black Tower
C. Site of
  Lodgings.

N
W — E
S

Moat

Moat

A

Outer
Ward

Moat

Mill Stream

Middle
Ward

C

B

Moat

Moat

Moat

E   c

F   D

Mill

A Inner Ward.
B Middle Ward.
C Great Gate.
D Sluice
E.E. Water Gates
F Garderobe Tower.

Lake

Moat

Moat

B

A

B

E

Lake

Nant-y-Gledyr

E.
North —— S
W

Moat

Horn Work

Moat

CAERPHILLY CASTLE.
  (13ᵗʰ Century)

From Mr. A. G. Little's "Medieval Wales."

the concentric castle, a diversion could be created, supplies perhaps introduced. Mural towers tier on tier, wall above wall, might render impossible the approach of the ram, and the work of sappers and miners. The fall of one wall must not mean the loss of the whole. All these points had been fully apprehended and were put into fullest practice by the young earl of Gloucester at his Welsh castle of Caerphilly. Edward I. made use of the new pattern on a large scale when he issued orders for the building of castle after castle in Wales. The new model covered many acres of ground, for within its wards peasants and their cattle might have to be sheltered, and dwelling houses built. Caerphilly protected its own corn-mill, its own sheets of water. Level ground, rather than the old rock or earthen mound, was best suited to castles of the Edwardian fashion. The London Tower showed itself capable of adaptation and like some hoary veteran armed with the newest weapons, the Conqueror's keep was surrounded with concentric wards.

A good idea of the supplies of food deemed necessary for a castle is given by a list of victuals for Dover castle in war-time, necessary to maintain 1,000 men for 40 days. To make daily 1,000 loaves took 4½ quarters of wheat—180 quarters for 40 days : 600 gallons of wine at a quart per head a day, took 20 tuns : 260 quarters of malt brewed 520 gallons daily, or a quart a head and 20 over. There were for the meat days (18 out of the 40), 104 score carcases of beef, 270 of bacon, 8 score and two of mutton : each carcase of beef made 54 messes, of bacon 24,

of mutton 8; each mess served for two men daily
(this provided 26,784 messes.) For the 22 fish days
there were 18,000 herring, 1,320 cod, 6,000 stock fish
(called middle cod): the herrings were served in
messes of 5 each, each cod made 5 messes, and each
stock fish a quarter mess. Each man should have
daily 5 herrings, a fifth part of cod, or a half of
stock fish. This provided for the 22 fish days 22,000
messes (one mess each and 200 over). There were
six "weighs" of cheese to "amend the kitchen
portion" at the assaults, if there should be any. At
the same time a pottage was allowed of flour and
cabbage. To do the cooking a certain measure of
brushwood was allowed to so many quarters of
wheat, and a limited quantity of firing was provided
for the beer-brewing. The rest of the viands were to
be cooked with "sea-coal." There were 100 quarters
of coarse salt for the meat and for store; there was
beef-fat for candles and 100 lb. of another kind of
fat for lighting purposes; 300 lb. of mutton fat
for knights and others wounded or bruised—the only
medicine: there were to be 2 quarters of mustard,
400 lb. of almonds, 200 lb. of rice, a pipe of vinegar,
2 tuns of "eisell," a sort of vinegar; 40 gallons of
verjuice, some spices and 40 quarters of beans for
store. The garrison can hardly be said to have
enjoyed a plentiful or varied diet during its 40 days
of service. But many an army met a worse fate.
Edward I.'s men fighting against the Welsh were
once cut off from beer and fresh meat, and, being
reduced to honey and water for drink, quickly lost
spirit under such hardships. At the great siege of

Kenilworth, 1266, which lasted six months, 1,200 men of the baronial party were within, with wives and children 53 in number, but they were able to make sorties and levy stores from the surrounding country.

6. The "urbanity" of the castellans of Kenilworth was highly commended by reason of their treatment of a wounded knight belonging to the enemy's party. On his death his body was placed in a shrine, torches were set to burn round it, and with full ceremony the corpse was transferred to the besiegers. Strictly historical sources however do not as a rule tell much of the "courtesy" which was the theme of romance. For the historian there is no harder task than to measure the amount of truth present in the imaginative literature of the past, in so far as society is there depicted : the usual difficulties are multiplied when we cannot even date the romance, and further must make deductions for the antiquity of its plot, for few writers invented new ones. Verisimilitude and realism was no part of the ideal of the romance-writer of the Middle Ages, and his stock-in-trade was limited as a rule to certain conventional themes.

A great French lawyer, who knew England, made something of a new departure in romance-writing when he chose to enrich his story with the ridiculous blunders made by the English nobility and their men in talking a kind of pigeon-French. Writing probably not before 1274, he makes the Earl of Gloucester's men mix their genders and talk bad grammar so as to alter the sense. The earl calls the heroine "mon douce amie," and converts his "belle pucelle" into a "bel pourcel" (pig). There is a touch of exaggeration here no doubt, but in countless little details the story tells the literal truth.   The tale of the love of the French esquire, Jehan, and his English wife Blonde, daughter of the Earl of Oxford, is beautiful, and the delicate treatment of the theme

A CRUSADER IN HOOD AND COAT OF MAIL, WITH SURCOAT.   A HELMET WITH CLOSED GRATING IS BEING OFFERED TO HIM.

does honour to the writer, whose circle of readers would learn nothing but good from him.

The last half of the thirteenth century is a time that may rank high in the history of English morals. Simon de Montfort, the "flower of all chivalry," and

Edward I., on whose grave was written the simple
motto " pactum serva," held up to men a high ideal.
They were alike in faults and virtues, and in some
sense their faults and virtues typify their age.
Excessive violence in temper was in both a fault,
but we must set against it an unbounded resource-
fulness and capacity for thought. Simon's will,
written by the hand of his son Henry, used no
meaningless testamentary form in the phrase that
speaks of his great desire that all his debts should
be paid in full. Love of justice in human relations
was characteristic of both men: so too was temperate
living. Edward's " keep troth " was no canting
phrase; though he might on occasion seek papal
absolution from a promise given.

If we may judge from a political song of the
period, there seems reason to think that the De
Montfort party in their disputes with the court party
1258–64 were inclined to blacken the enemy as evil-
livers : but for all parties the best writers held up a
lofty ideal of knighthood. The girding with the
sword signifies that evil deeds must be eschewed : the
bathing signifies that the knight is to be clean from
unlawful impurities : he must be worthy of all his
attributes. The knight's pride, if in part a cause of
the fashionable vice of violence, might after all help
him up the path toward righteousness. Those of
high " parage" were loth to disgrace all chivalry by
any act that was contrary to the conventional
code, by any act that could be deemed " villain."

The sharp class-divisions, that to our eyes seem
peculiarly characteristic of the age, were regarded by

many as not nearly sharp enough. The Templars required a new member to be the son of a knight and a lady, and the father must also be of knightly descent and of " loyal marriage." This was to meet the trouble described by a political writer:

> " Knightship is icloyd and dolefully idiht,
> Can a boy now break a spear, he shall be made a knight,
> And there been knights gadered of unkind blood
> And envenometh that order that should be so good."

Even the daughter of Edward I., a father whose will was not lightly to be crossed, could choose to marry in " disparage " one who was not even a knight, and the incident had to be accepted and glozed over by the raising of the humble suitor from his dusty estate. And the barons themselves were confounding the issues when in the Provisions of Oxford they sounded the national note as it had never before been sounded, and pronounced it " disparagement " to marry one who was not a native of England. This was the utterance of hate against a particular group of court hangers-on, Savoyards, Poitevins and Provençals. But though strangers in England might be mobbed and despised as strangers, nevertheless the language of the only part of the nation that was reckoned to have any social worth was still French. In 1301 Edward I. caused letters from the Pope to be put into French that they might be read to the whole army. The drafting of Henry III.'s English proclamation giving his adhesion to the Provisions of Oxford in 1258 is of course significant of a certain measure of nationalist force in the political movements of that time, but it must not obscure the fact that generations came and went before the language of the governing class ceased to be French.

The despotism of John and the effeteness of Henry III. had roused a new feeling of political interest, and the songs of the revolutions of 1258 and 1264 both prove this and tell of its nature. The community, they say, should see what sort of men are chosen for the utility of the realm. The king should never set his private interest before that of the community, and its law must rule his dignity. However great the king may be in wisdom, he should consult the magnates. The other side too is represented :—how evil it is that subjects should rule the king, how sad the inversion of the true order of things.

7. Although direct evidence of the literary interests of individual nobles is scanty, the increase in the amount of literature which was intended, as its nature shows, for an audience not consisting of scholars, proves far more than an occasional dedication or hint of personal interest. A man of Simon de Montfort's culture, the friend of Grosseteste and of the Greek scholar John of Basingstoke, a nobleman who was a sound Latinist, was a rarity in the class to which he belonged, but high birth was generally supposed to be accompanied by some claim to "letters." Louis de Beaumont, the ignorant but aristocratic bishop of Durham who could not get through the Latin form of his consecration and asked to have it "taken as read," is

described by Murimuth as being but "mediocriter litteratus" *although* of high birth. The evidence that the nobles possessed books is now more abundant. Edward II.'s favourite the elder Despenser had a library of books ; Earl William de Beauchamp left his daughter a "book of Lancelot," and the ownership of beautiful illuminated psalters and breviaries may often be made out from the armorial bearings figured in the margins. The Howard family gave their lovely psalter to the nuns of Chicksand 1339. The school of Gorleston and other East Anglian centres were producing costly works for the houses of great people, painting the prayer-books with tales from romance, scenes from the chase and other episodes of daily life to beguile the tedium of the service. A Bible in French, containing both Old and New Testament, was illuminated for John of Wells and his wife Maud, before 1361. The possession of a pocket breviary such as that ordered for De Montfort's daughter may be taken to indicate that the owner could read liturgical Latin. To finger with pleasure these beautiful books does not require much education, and the subjects of illustration often show that the reader was expected to feel more interest in the common themes of mediæval romance than in the severer letter-press which the pictures adorned. Yet the multiplication of verse histories such as Langtoft's, the English translations of Robert of Sempringham, the English and French "Bruts," beginning with old-world fables and introducing contemporary events as they approach modern times, all imply a general interest in the literature and events of the fabulous or the recent past. It was an Earl of Hereford who at the close of our period persuaded William of Palermo to translate William and the Werwolf ; an Earl of Salisbury bought for 100 marks a French Petrus Comestor, taken from the French king on the field of Poitiers (1356), and presented it to his countess.

8. A sign of some social movement is seen in the evidences that women of rank were leading a somewhat less narrow life. The heroine of the romance of Guy of Warwick, translated from the French in the fourteenth century, was

> " courteous, free and wise,
> And in the seven arts learned withouten miss."

Her masters were from Toulouse, men white and hoar who taught her astronomy, " ars-metrick," and geometry ; "of sophistry she was also witty, of rhetoric and of other clergy " (clerkly learning). The hero is fitted out with strength, a perfect knowledge of chivalrous exercises, and skill at chess, but not with the accomplishments of learning. This is romance, but the book written to teach French to the lady Dionysia de Mountchesny (she was related to the Valences of Pembroke), by her tutor, Walter of " Bibelesworth," shows that pains were taken at least in the education of a few. The same tutor wrote likewise a dialogue between himself and Henry de Lacy earl of Lincoln, on going to the crusade, and this too may have been designed with educational purpose. In his French verses to Dionysia, glossed with English, he supplies

a vocabulary of all the words required for daily
necessities from the cradle to the grave. Beginning
with the birth of the child, all the apparatus of
nursing is given, and the names of the child's
members. The tutor then clothes the child, naming
the garments, feeds it and describes the food products
after the manner of the latest German pedagogy.
He takes every precaution to prevent such disasters
as befel the Earl of Gloucester's French : all the
possible confusions and synonyms are noted.
Essential to the lady's education was a knowledge
of the terms of the chase and falconry : she must
speak of a herd, flock, covey, bevy, company, in the
right connection ; it is correct to speak of a bevy
of herons, but she must say a crowd of villains
(churls), a company of ladies and of geese, and he
tells her why the same word will do for both these
last. Then there are the words for each animal's
noises, and the words of trades, for household
operations, for setting the table, and he describes
the paring of the bread given in alms, the decking
of the boar's head with flowers, the courses of
eatables. Begin, he says, with venison and frumenty,
then have roast cranes, peacocks, swans, geese, kid ;
at the third course coneys in gravy, and meat done
in Cyprus wine ; quinces and white wine ; then
pheasant, woodcock, partridge, fieldfare, larks,
brawn, fritters, and finally comfits for digestion.

The letters written by women are now natural
in style and show more signs of being in the
writer's own words, if not in her own hand.
Hawisia de Neville writes to her son Hugh,

whilst he is on crusade c. 1266–9, about legal matters and his estate, but the letter breathes throughout the spirit of motherly affection. " If it might be that I could often have good news of you and often comfort you by my letters, there is nothing that could give me more pleasure, if I cannot see you and talk to you " : so runs her simple and natural French.   That the letter deals largely with business is also, we may believe, genuinely characteristic of the writer.

Worthy to number among English heroines was Isabella Countess of Arundel who, with a dignity which, Matthew Paris says, was more than that of woman, reproached Henry III. (1252), when he sought to browbeat her. She made bold to tell the king, " You govern neither us nor yourself well." On this the king, with a sneer and a grin, said with a loud voice, " Ho, ho, my lady countess, have the noblemen of England granted you a charter and struck a bargain with you to become their spokes-woman because of your eloquence ? " She answered, " My liege, the nobles have made no charter, but you and your father have made a charter, and you have sworn to observe it inviolably, and yet many times have you extorted money from your subjects and have not kept your word.   Where are the liberties of England, often reduced to writing, so often granted, so often again denied ? "   It was probably this lady to whom is dedicated a life of St. Richard of Chichester, written by a Dominican, at her request.

But there are not wanting thirteenth century satires to tell the usual story of female levities, and of female

go lactare nūs precibʒ pia memorare

eo grās. D e sčo spiritu. A

benedictum. Et hoc a usqʒ in seculū.

A LADY STAG-HUNTING.
From Mr. Yates Thompson's Book of Hours, c. 1320.

devotion to the needle, to German work and pierced work, Saracen work and combed work, cut-out work and wool-work, and a multitude of other " works " to which the clue seems to be now wholly lost.   Whilst the women are thus engaged, the one who knows most reads to them, the others listen attentively, and do not sleep as they do at mass, " pur la prise de vanité dont ont grant leesce (joy)."   The " opus anglicum " consisted of chain-stitch in circles, with hollows, made by a heated iron rod, to represent shadows. A cope of this work was made by Rose de Burford at Edward II.'s order, and sent to Rome.   One, known as the Syon cope, passed into the possession of the nuns of Syon, Isleworth, and can be seen at the Victoria and Albert Museum.

The tone of literature remains as decent as in the preceding period.   Where the fifteenth century would permit further licence, the thirteenth and fourteenth are restrained.   As an example we may contrast the coarse enquiries made by Henry VII. when he proposed to marry, with the quaint little description of the future Queen Philippa's person, set down by the Bishop of Exeter in his Register, he having been in all likelihood the ambassador deputed to make enquiries.

9. With some signs of increasing urbanity, there is still much barbarity: whether more or less than in more highly civilised epochs it would be hard to guess. Some of the exquisite refine-ments of which cruelty is capable are not there, but there is a universal acceptance of the value-lessness of human life, a doctrine taught by the

Church and the law. The judgment passed on the unfortunate David of Wales in 1282 is a naïve example of the contemporary view with all its mixed feelings. By all the baronage (barnagia) four judgments were passed : because he was traitor to the king who had made him knight, he shall be " drawn " or dragged by horses : because he committed homicide he must be hanged : because the homicide was done at the season of the Passion, for his blasphemy he shall be disembowelled and his bowels shall be burned : and because he plotted the king's death in many parts of England, his members are to be divided and sent out to the four quarters to be a terror to malefactors.

Armies which by royal proclamation and invitation were swelled by criminals and vagrants, like the army with which Edward I. invaded Scotland, were of course scrupulous in no particular. The sickening mutilations of the bodies of much hated men seem to have been specially characteristic of border warfare on the march of Wales and Scotland. The treatment of Simon de Montfort's and Cressingham's body are cases in point.

10. The dissolution of the order of Knights Templars in Edward II.'s reign, a work done at the instance of the Pope and the French king, might, if the evidence had been trustworthy, incline one to take a very gloomy view of the state of morals depicted by the witnesses. That the evidence was utterly untrustworthy is now established, to the lasting disgrace of those concerned in collecting it, but even so, though the order be spared, it darkens the impression of cor-

rupt and tainted thought among the humbler classes. The burden of the shame of it is shifted, but not lifted, if the Templars as an order were innocent of the filthy practices charged to their acccount, for the prurient imaginings of the witnesses remain, and not these only, but the greed, injustice and utter un- scrupulousness of those of all classes who sought to obtain the verdict of "guilty." Hatred of the proud and avaricious Templars, dislike of their secret system, belief that their work was done and their privileges an abuse, are the extenuating circumstances. The story of the dissolution of the Templars runs closely parallel to the story of the greater dissolution carried out by Henry VIII.

Adam of Murimuth says that the Templars when they had to meet the accusations against them confessed the "fama," but not the fact, save for one or two ribalds "in omni statu," black sheep who never would be white. All finally confessed that they could not purge themselves and were adjudged to perpetual penance. Some, he tells us, were put in monasteries where they conducted themselves well. For a time the Knights Hospitallers profited by the fall of their rivals, but soon had to bear alone the charge of avarice and pride hitherto levelled at the Templars. The Hospitallers had always been more favourably thought of because of their charitable works. Their hospitals dedicated to St. John were in every town ; their duty to bury the dead, criminals and suicides, for whom no other church found charity, was one that endeared them to the populace. More than one body cut down as a corpse from the gallows, handed over to them for burial, came to life again. But enriched with Templar wealth, the satirists began to observe their long robes, their elegant shoes and breeches, their splendid horses. It is these things that they contribute to the imaginary order of Bel-ease, which took from each rule the clause which exposed it to the most ridicule.

A BRATTICED BRIDGE.

MONKS' PROCESSION.
From a boss in Norwich Cathedral.

XV

MONASTERIES AND THE CHURCH

1. Monks — 2. Nuns — 3. Mendicants — 4. Relations of Church and State — 5. The bishops as builders.

1. To the " Order of Bel-ease " the anonymous author makes the Benedictines contribute their social drinkings ; the canons their meat three days a week ; the Cistercians their unbreeched legs ; the Carthusians the little comforts of the cell, its plants in the window, its freedom from inspection ; the secular canons, their spiritual attendance on women ; the Franciscans their intimacy with aristocratic families ; the Dominicans their dinner table preaching.

330

The evidence as to the state of the monasteries now pours forth in an abundant stream, and it is possible to know much both of the spirit of the ideal and of the details of the real monastic life of this period. There is evidence that in the large convents the domestic organisation was good : strict attention was paid to the management of what was a business as temporal as any other. That the divorce between the real and the ideal might not become too obvious general councils periodically laid down new rules designed to secure reform. Even if this effort had not been made, the monastic institution had become far too much part of the very being of the mediæval state to be the object of any general criticism. Pretensions to sanctity unsupported by facts might be the theme of some jests, like the human frailties of all self-deceivers. But the self-deceivers after all have endearing qualities, lacking in those who see things as they really are.

To give a new spiritual meaning to monastic vows was not in the power of the united provinces of York and Canterbury, though they were prepared to lay down rules on the question of monastic meat-eating, monastic teaching, learning, pensions, and benefices, rules that should enable the monasteries to move with the times. As touching meat, the English Bene-dictines in 1334 were told that they might eat it at those times when it was lawful for the ordinary Christian to eat it.

It was directed that every monastery should have a paid teacher to teach monks grammar, logic and philosophy, but seculars were not to be taught with monks—a hint that they had been in the past. Had the reformers made concessions in this matter, events might have taken a far different course.   The great concession to the new movement was that one monk in twenty must be sent to the university, and properly provided.   A concession to modern movements was likewise made in the sanction given to the use of cells (musæa) for the purposes of study, after the academic fashion.   Already for the literary monks " carrells " or little wooden shelters, each with one window, had been fitted in the cloister to give some privacy to students.   But as yet the common dormitory was deemed an essential part of Benedictine discipline, a fact not a little significant of the monastic weakness which failed to distinguish the letter and the spirit.   Vowed to obedience, the accepted conventions of the past,—always endowed with a sufficient power to continue their existence after they have become superfluous,—were in the monk's scheme of things furnished with an additional vitality.   A machine so divinely constructed as St. Benedict's rule was expected to keep itself in good order for ever.

The pettiness of spirit which runs through the monastic annals of the time is amusing enough in its naïveté.   The letters of a schoolboy to his parents do not go more straightly to the point than the entries of the annalist.   Money and food are the absorbing topics. The Whitsun beer failed and the convent had five " dolia " (tuns) of wine " which did us a lot of good." An abbot has died who omitted to appoint a day for his anniversary ; thus he, being dead, would miss the prayers for his soul, and the monks, being alive, their extra allowance. In the monk's view the abbot's prayerless future state is most likely a judgment on him for having withdrawn from the convent certain moneys left to celebrate the anniversary of a predecessor. But for what offence the monks' deprivation of drink was a judgment we are not told.

The lists of necessary monkish outfit savour also of the public school. At Ely a novice must bring two pieces of canvas for his bed, a mattress, two pair of blankets, two pair of strayles (thin blanket), two coverlets, one furred coverlet, one serge " blew bed," one cowl with a frock, one black furred tunic, one plain tunic, two white tunics, one amice without fur, a girdle and pouch, with a knife, wax-tablet and comb, thread and needle, a night-girdle, various pairs of breeches and braces (points), hose, socks, day-boots, night-boots, half a dozen kerchiefs, three cushions, one white nightcap, two towels, one dirty-linen-bag, one shaving cloth, one drinking cup, one mazer (mounted cup of wood), one silver spoon. Similar lists are given of a Templar's and an Austin canon's outfit, and describe no doubt the necessaries of a gentleman of the period.

At Christchurch, Canterbury, in the fourteenth century, hospitality had seriously declined : even monks seeking hospitality there were made to lodge outside and got no more than their food. The archbishop orders that they be admitted with horses and servants for one day and night, and the same should be done for secular guests. On the other

hand no doubt there had been gross abuses of
monastic hospitality. In 1275 a royal order limited
the power of the nobility to claim hospitality except

REFECTORY PULPIT AT SHREWSBURY.

in monasteries of their own founding. The Austin
canons of Coxford had to make a rule that women
should not be admitted to the inner offices and
cloister, except great ladies and nobles surrounded

with a great company " who cannot well be repelled
without scandal." Barnwell, after heavy sufferings
when the " Disinherited " of De Montfort's party
were holding out in the Isle of Ely, was "excoriated"
by the burden of entertaining a justiciar and his
wife who had 22 women with her ; and no reward
did the canons get, for the judge amerced the prior !

The Christchurch rules for the " deportum " or
place of monkish disport show that indulgences were
allowed to those who submitted to the full tedium of
the cathedral services, but for such persons little time
remained for "idle tales and wanton jollity." It
was Christchurch too that was driven to look for
a theological teacher among the Franciscans, a
novelty productive of discord, discord due to what
was no novelty, prolonged litigation, on which the
whole thought of the convent centred to the neglect
of every other.

Bury, Winchester, Gloucester, Abingdon, to name
only a few of the printed records, yield for this
period very full details as to the nature of monastic
business arrangements, systems of account, domestic
service, provisioning, farming, alms-giving, building.
The one source of expenditure for which it is rare to
find any permanent arrangement made is the maintenance of the fabric of the church. No regular
" farms " like those for the kitchen, were set aside
for a purpose, which might always be conveniently
adduced as an incitement of the faithful to alms.

The intense conservatism of the monasteries came
out more strongly, of course, in money matters than
in anything else ; every reform touched some vested

interest, and raised a hurricane of murmurs : the consequence was that long before the Black Death even great houses such as St. Swithin's, Winchester, were continually battling with deficits. All the heads of offices had to be able to render account, but each office was and remained distinct ; the monastic exchequer could not be treated by some wise financier as a whole, save on the rare occasions when all the "obedientiaries" felt alike the need for reform. More commonly the need for a loan pressed on all alike, and to bring in ready money the house might be charged with burdensome debts ; for cash down "corrodies" were sold, by which, for so much immediate payment, the house had to provide the donor with his victuals daily, for life. The nuns of St. Rhadegund, Cambridge, paid their butcher's bill by taking in the butcher's daughter. Burdens on posterity were increased that the monks of the present might live at ease. Posterity was likewise to bear the whole strain of the readjustment of agricultural conditions, and went bankrupt under the double burden. The king of course did not scruple to use the convents as they used themselves : bishops too used them to pension off their old servants. A frequent, heavy charge that repeatedly threw the monastery into debt was a visit to Rome or Avignon on a legal quest. St. Alban's spent £1,000 on one of these journeys. In this case an abbot who could not speak Latin was obliged to purchase a favourable reception by extra munificence.

The temptation in time of stress was to cut down the alms-giving. In a well managed house, as at

Evesham, the almoner's duty was to visit the sick poor (sick women by his servant), but abuses are heard of incidentally when the annalist records that an attempt was made to reinforce the earlier system. It must be remembered that the rent-rolls which seem splendid were often heavily encumbered, and while rents remained stationary the standard of living rose within the monastery. Bury was keeping 22 servants in its kitchen ; the Christchurch cellarer had 38 servants, tailors, laundresses, etc., and a like staff was attached to all the departments. The competition between houses was great, and it was generally supposed then, as now, that to keep up the appearance of success leads to success. At Gloucester however economy was attempted ; the abbot's servants were cut down to five squires, "enough for an ordinary gentleman's household " ; that is to say, a steward, marshal and cook, and two to attend his chamber, table and bed. The abbot fought hard for his lost under-chamberlain and finally got the number raised to six. An under-chamberlain, it had been pronounced, was needless, for four palfrey-men, a pantler, butler, undercook (he was to have no sauce-maker), farrier, and foot-messenger should be a sufficient staff to assist the five squires. It was further laid down that when the abbot visited the cells of Gloucester, that is the daughter-houses, 19 horses should suffice and the heads of cells should not be compelled to make gifts. At the abbot's table the scriptures should be read and frivolous chatter eschewed : (the rule that there might be talk *causa eruditionis* was apt to be abused).

Lastly eight sporting dogs and harriers are enough for an abbot and should not be fed in his hall.

Besides the staff of attendants who were performing household services, the abbeys had quaint but tiresome claims to meet from an hereditary constable or butler, who demanded some " serjeanty " in connection with the abbot's enthroning feast, perhaps because his ancestor's sword had been used in the abbey's behalf. In reward he had been given perhaps the goblets on the table, or free liberty to sojourn with his suite, or some other privilege that might cost more in times of luxurious living than was ever anticipated in the rude days of old. The Abbot of St. Alban's tried various shifty means to get rid of his hereditary butler, and declared that the feast was given in honour of the saint, not of himself, but the claimant took good care to touch the best goblet and put it in his own " seisin." Thereupon the abbey brought a counter-claim against the butler's land for the service of a horse. Thus was the monastery, like the nation, burdened with all the time-worn claims of a dead past, together with all the latest demands of the living present.

In many houses the buildings can be traced out one by one as they were added or changed. The monastic annals rarely fail to name the event that loomed largest in the eyes of the chronicler, to tell of the new barn, the new lavatory, that was being reared as he wrote : the buildings are his abbot's greatest works as a rule, but with them must be noted benefactions in books, ornaments for the church, new copes, reliquaries and the like. Such

lists come to us from Evesham for example, and it is
of such acquisitions that in this period we now hear
most. The fever of land acquisition was over, and
the gifts were becoming rarer. It is not now the
lands of the laity which are mortgaged to the
monastery, but *vice versâ*. The lands which the
monks still showed themselves anxious to acquire
were houses in towns, and shops.

The details of a few visitations have been preserved which belong to this period. That of Wig-
more for instance shows how a house might become
thoroughly corrupted by bad influences. There is
secular trading, and the goods of the house are used
to maintain the sons, nephews, and cousins of monks :
the sick go unprovided : there is a gossiping brother
who stirs strife and lets out the secrets to seculars :
books are not studied in the cloister because the
seats are uncomfortable. Brethren in the infirmary
should not be put in charge of a hired secular unless
there is one who has grown old in the monastery's
service and means to stick to the duty permanently.
Conversation at the monks' dinner is to be allowed
in moderation, and there is to be no loud wrangling.
The sending away of refractory monks to isolated
cells on the monastic estates must be put under new
order. All monks playing at chess, dice, or archery
are to be deprived of their *solatium* or extra allowance
of food and drink. The allowance of new clothes
is fixed, a frock and cowl once a year ; travelling-
shoes, once in 18 months ; a pair of nailed boots
every 5 years : the cutting and stitching of the cloaks
must be uniform throughout the monastery and no

dressy girdles or purses or showy knives are allowed.
The honour of the monastery must however be con-
sulted in the distribution of garments ; the monks
are not to be sent out in things that do not fit : and
they in their turn must not ruin the clothes by rough
wear. Monks may have clothes given by their
friends but must see that they are of the monastic
pattern. The rest of the 21 orders are all equally
sensible and to the point, and are a good guide to the
abuses which men thought it most desirable to check.

Everywhere monks were inclined to " strike "

SACRISTAN AND WOMAN IN THE STOCKS.

against the long services which their predecessors
had endured. Such and such items may be cut
short for a " sublatio tedii " : somehow or other the
prevailing tendency to gallop through the liturgy
must be stopped. It is such matters rather than
carnal lapses, though these are named occasionally,
that caused the "visitor" most anxiety. But whether
the offence were small or great, the visitation resulted
continually in mere warnings. The removal of bad
characters in high places was a risky business to
attempt. There might be an appeal to a rival

authority, and endless litigation would ensue. A bishop of Worcester deposed the prior of a cell in his diocese for gross crime, and the Abbey of Westminster took up the cudgels in the criminous prior's defence, simply because he was prior of a cell subject to Westminster.

The litigiousness of rival orders, of the monastery against the secular college, of the convent against its bishop is as great as ever; and a new trouble becomes prominent in this period in the conflicts between the convent and the town which had sprung up around the market-place that supplied its needs. Perhaps in old days the coming conflict between the abbatial "seignory" and the community which lived under that lordship had not been foreseen; an abbot had granted dangerously much; or the burgesses had let a chartered franchise grow rusty by disuse. Some new development of commerce might raise the unsettled question and the flames of controversy rose. Some of the monks might be related to the townspeople, and form a dangerous element, sowing anti-monastic opinions in the convent itself. It had perhaps been acknowledged as a burghal franchise that burgesses only might be on the jury when burgesses were tried: if tried for killing conventual servants in an attempt to resist a conventual claim, burgesses would certainly be acquitted. Force would be met with force. Few towns were so united as Bury, where 3,000 of the burgesses made the abbot sign their charter in the market-place in the presence of an axe and a block.

Elsewhere a more peace-loving abbot might stave

off dangerous explosions by judicious social courtesies. At Dunstable the prior, contrary to monastic custom, dined in town at a feast. It was "excusabilis" because he owed the feast-giver a large sum and dared not offend him.

2. Among the nunneries there was, as in the monasteries, dissimilarity between houses large and houses small, rich and poor, well and ill-managed, with or without libraries, between houses frequented by queens and princesses or high-born ladies, and houses used by the humbler ranks. The evidence goes to show that in knowledge of Latin the nuns had greatly fallen behind. Their visitations, rules, accounts, are more often French than Latin, and some could not even speak French. A case is known in which special application was made to admit one " non litterata nec in gallica lingua erudita." The mystical works which Richard Rolle of Hampole translated from Latin for nuns were all put into English. At Amesbury (which sheltered the Dowager Queen Eleanor of Provence, Edward I.'s daughter Mary, and a company of wealthy ladies), everything that money could buy, in teaching, books, artistic materials, and the comforts of life, was to be had. So too at Shaftesbury, Dartford, St. Clement's, York, and perhaps Sempringham, where one of the Welsh princesses was confined. From a nun of Amesbury Edward III. bought in 1331 a book of romance for £66 13s. 4d., a work of such interest that he kept it in his own room.

A French visitation of a Devonshire nunnery gives a good idea of the life of an ordinary house. The talk should be low, if possible in Latin, and slips of grammar may be overlooked.   Secular women living with the nuns ought also to keep silence.   Sick nuns ought not to be allowed separate chambers but should keep together in the "farmery" so that one waitress does for them all.   The rules for visiting away from the nunnery are minute and show that regular holidays were part of the scheme.   When nuns go home, once a year, a religious companion must go too, and not the same one twice over. Arrangements are made for them to spend the night at Exeter, and they must not go wandering from inn to inn looking for lodgings.   A month must suffice for visits to distant relations ; longer leave will only be given in case of illness.   If the furlough be exceeded, that of the following year will be cancelled. Minute arrangements are made for the nuns' phlebotomy.   The ladies of religion may not each have her own servant as cook, but there is to be only one cook for the house, and this cook is to be a man. Clearly this was a house for the rich ; but at Chester the nuns in 1253 addressed the queen saying that they are compelled to beg their daily bread—such as it is. The nuns of the visitations seem incorrigible in their tendency to attach a number of boarders and children to the house, whether as pupils or otherwise.   Archbishop Peckham, visiting the Barking nuns, speaks of the nuns who turn the feast of the Innocents into a game by having children to perform the office. The Barking nuns were excessively fond of talking and merry-making—in the archbishop's view, which was probably a severe one.   With the nuns, as with the monks, the idea of seclusion from the world was no longer operative as a general rule : ample and pleasant intercourse is desired and acknowledged. All that is required of ordinary vowed men or women is that they travel with companions of like vows, each to keep watch on the other. There were also more strictly "enclosed" orders, but papal licences to visit these with large suites were very freely dispensed.

The prevalent passion for pet animals which infected both sexes, and the lay as well as the religious, was commented upon in visitations of monks and nuns wherever it had become a nuisance to some of the inmates. The abbess of Romsey stinted her nuns to provide for her dogs and monkeys.

Such were the dangers in the houses for the well-to-do. The French rules for the nunnery of Sopwell, in dependence on the monastery of St. Alban's and managed by a monk as "custos," speak of a stricter life, probably in a poorer house. The silence required by the rule in church, cloister, refectory, and dormitory, was to be strictly kept. But the wise institution of the conventual chapter, which gave a form of democratic organisation to the "fellowship" of the house, was to be robbed of its power : the abbot of St. Alban's writes "we do command that in chapter there be 3 voices only, that of the lady-president, that of the sub-prioress or her deputy, and that of the nun charged with offence." The abbot however forbade the punishment which allowed the faulty nuns neither to read, nor sing, nor see the sacrament of the mass.

Relations with seculars were here carefully regulated: a nun speaking with a secular must cover neck and face with a kerchief and have the veil, as pertains to the order of religion. The male tailors and furriers of the house must live in a place near the cloister and must not enter any of the rooms of the house. Female guests, whether secular or regular, must not sleep in the dormitory, and each nun must have a separate bed.

When Sir Osbert "called Giffard" in 1286 abducted Alice Russel and Alice Giffard from Wilton nunnery, the offence was punished by the order that on Ash Wednesday he should come to Salisbury cathedral in mourning, wearing no cloak of lamb's wool, or spurs, or knightly girdle; he was then, and on three holy days, to be flogged round the church, and on three Tuesdays through Salisbury market: he was to go through the same ordeal at Wilton church and in Wilton market, and at Amesbury and Shaftesbury: finally he was to go to the Holy Land for three years. The two sisters were to be readmitted, subject to what penalties we do not hear. Respect for the person of a nun was one of the elementary principles of mediæval morality.

3. The Dominican Kilwardby was succeeded as Archbishop of Canterbury by the Franciscan Peckham; his three successors were all seculars; and these facts show how mendicants and secular clerks were taking up the reins that were slipping from monastic fingers. The steady flow of the people's benefactions begins to be to the " four orders," Carmelite, Augustinian,

Jacobin, (the French name of the Dominicans), Minorite, whose initials spell " Caim," a word beloved or hated according to the measure of men's orthodoxy.   It is they, or the gild attached to some chantry in the parish church, who are remembered in fourteenth century wills : monasteries are out of fashion and supposed to be sufficiently self-supporting.   With success, came the trial of the mendicant character ; living more exposed to the public view than the monastics, bringing their lives into touch with those of the laity, the glass of contemporary criticism was directed very frequently upon their faults.   Their own records, in spite of their good libraries, university education and zeal for learning, happen to be ill preserved in this, the period of their chief activity.   By one of time's often mismanaged revenges we happen to know more of what was said against them than what they said themselves, and with the customary infelicity of the " religious," there was an internecine warfare between Franciscan and Dominican, as deadly as the old war of secular and regular.   The Franciscans tell of the Dominicans' " proud port " : the Dominicans bid men beware of Franciscan pretensions to asceticism : they go barefoot it is true, but they eat meat.

The Mendicants' success in securing the corpses of the great, and therewith all the oblations from crowded funeral congregations, brought down upon their heads the hate of all rival claimants.   The very fact that the friars were beloved of the laity, chosen by them to confess, to absolve, to make the disposal of their property, to bury them, was a crime in the eyes of those who lived by the same means. To the Mendicants, as the papal emissaries, fell the sale of the pope's remissions of enjoined penance, and here was the great opening for scandal.

4. The divisions within the ecclesiastical world became ever more numerous and more obvious : the pope, living at Avignon, the creature of the French king, with whom Edward III. was at war, ceased to

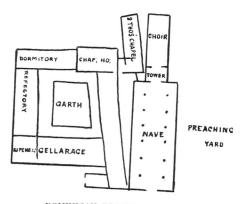

DOMINICAN FRIARY AT NORWICH.

command the same universal respect that of old had been tendered to him. Yet few saw the folly of un-disguised secularity in the use made of ecclesiastical institutions. For default of payments claimed by the papal court of Avignon, Archbishop Meopham was denied Christian burial in his own cathedral. Peck-ham refused burial to Cantilupe because he was excommunicated on a question of jurisdiction. Yet the corpse of the excommunicated bishop began to

work miracles so vigorously that a canonisation was
ultimately effected. Whether for neglect of some
payment, or by reason of a feud for supremacy or
visitatorial rights, the excommunication of bishops
had become fairly common. Though still accursed
in their every act, with bodies (should the curse
operate) infected with every loathsome disease, with
souls extinguished and delivered over to the eternal
company of devils, men did not now shrink from
them and avoid speaking or eating with them as of
old they had done—as witness the case of Hugh de
Puiset, the Bishop of Durham. After all they were
in a position little more distressing than the baker
of Doctors' Commons' fame, excommunicated for
objecting in a vestry to a paving rate. The
episcopal prince palatine and monks of Durham paid
small heed to the periodic thunders of the archbishop
of York : the archbishop of York in his turn was
periodically engaged in a struggle to carry his cross
erect in the diocese of his rival of Canterbury, who
forbade his parochians to sell food to the intruders,
and ordered his servants to smash the elevated cross.
Vainly the pope suggested that this feud should be
settled " to the praise of God."

Internecine warfare of this sort inclined the lay
world to turn a deaf ear to the clerical claim of sacro-
sanctity for every portion of church property. In
vain the Burton annalist points out that he who
" invades " a serf of the church, or brings a counter-
claim to a clerkly cart, is guilty of sacrilege. Setting
out the claims of religion in their most ample form,
he declares the church's right to protect all criminals,

except the public thief and "night walker," exceptions which seem rather to disprove the rule. But the exceptions may be accounted for by the fact that the monastery itself may at times have been in need of police protection.

The discord between the facts and the fictions of the Church's position grew more obvious, and neither pope nor prelate, neither regular nor secular, attempted to induce a greater harmony. Under Edward I. the pope forbade the taxation of clerical property without his consent : when the clergy refused to pay, the king put them "out of his royal protection," out of his "peace." The king's courts of justice would not protect their property, which any man might pilfer without fear of temporal punishment. Fear of ecclesiastical punishment was found inadequate to protect the Church's temporalties, and the clergy made their peace with the king.—

Not all lay persons had this strong weapon to use against rival pretensions ; it was only the king who all along had secured his own hand. Only the king was strong enough to keep hold of his "peculiars," to keep, as endowments for his men, his domestic churches. Time was when any lord might have peculiars : the church which he had reared, and endowed with the tithes of his tenants, was his very own. For good or ill that was no longer generally true.

There were of course great dangers in a system which made the relations of church and state hinge so largely on the relations of a pope and a king.

Edward I. might be an opponent of ecclesiastical pretensions, where these encroached upon a domain which he regarded as his own : he would adopt them where they could be of service to his interest. As it was the habit of kings to use benefices to pay men who had been faithful servants, regardless of spiritual considerations, here lay the papal defence for " provisions " and " reservations " ; but in the pope's case they went to pay needy Italians for services rendered or to fill the papal exchequer by the proceeds of their sale. If the outcry against " provisions " was justified, equally well justified doubtless was Peckham, when he told Edward I. that the royal clerks held " a damnable multitude of benefices." The pious Henry III.'s not very pious servant Maunsel held 700 livings, worth 18,000 marks, according to one chronicle. And the same king pointed out to the bishop of Salisbury that he should know his place : " I raised you from the dust : you were the scribbler of my writs, a justice and a hireling." If Henry III. scrupled not to offend in this matter, his less saintly descendants were not likely to be troubled in conscience : and where kings and popes led the way, the lords followed after, presenting chaplaincies to clerks who could do kitchen accounts or were skilful builders, but were ill-equipped to read the psalter.

5. Very few of the bishops, whatever their moral character or intellectual powers, failed in this period to direct great architectural changes in their cathedrals, changes which entailed careful management of financial resources. Many, whose names are

EXETER.

Photograph by Messrs. Valentine.

honoured by their connection with beautiful buildings would otherwise pass undistinguished.

Into the first half of the period 1250–1300, fall
some of the richest examples of the late Early
English style: at Lincoln the "Angel" choir, 1260–80;
at Wells and Salisbury the chapter houses.   As the

LEOMINSTER : BALL-FLOWER ORNAMENT, *C.* 1320.

beauty of the new Decorated style, lending warmth
and tenderness where the Early English had been
severe and cold, seized the public taste, rebuildings
and additions were undertaken throughout the land.
Only the choicest examples of the earlier styles were
spared.   The stone-masons, co-operating with the

glass-painters, wearied of the lancet window, and, adding light to light, grouped circles, trefoils, quatre-foils and cinquefoils till they spread into a leaf-like tracery. The deep mouldings which are the most lovely characteristic of Early English were lost ; in their place the new school loved to group, in dense clusters, slender shaft by slender shaft, and on the uniting fillets, on the largely massed capitals, could be embroidered the natural flow of foliage, and all that wealth of chiselled ornament which has given the name " Decorated " to the style. The symmetrical dogtooth of the Early English could offer nothing worthy to compare with this. Likewise in its spires and battle-ments, and roofs groined in countless ribs, the new style in certain points gained upon the old in beauty and in knowledge of the building art.

It was Lichfield that Simon Simeon, a Franciscan traveller writing in 1322, singled out for superlative praise, but nowadays the injuries done there incline us to put many another equally high. The fact that it is possible to date the parts of Exeter with accuracy lends to its early Decorated nave a special interest. Elsewhere it is the harmony of Early English and Decorated that most excites admiration, as at Beverley and Ely.

Those who reared the buildings saw to it that the fittings of wood and glass and the books and the vessels and vestments should be worthy. At St. Paul's Simon Simeon selects the singing for his special praise, at Westminster, the bells.

A FRIAR.

XVI

THE CHURCH AND THE NATION

1. Cathedral canons—2. Parish priests—3. Salaries—4. Miracles—5. Mysticism—6. Heresy—7. Education—8. Oxford and Cambridge—9. English historians—10. Minstrelsy—11. Religious plays—12. Jests.

1. THE prelacy still adhered to the old idea of hospitality and charity. A bishop of Lichfield, who was incapable of preaching because he was a foreigner, was told that at least he must provide for the poor. The worldling Drokensford, bishop of Bath and Wells and keeper of the king's wardrobe, ordered his steward to feed 200 poor daily at his manors. It was this burden of hospitality which emptied some of the secular churches of the canons who should have resided and conducted the services. The pecuniary advantages that of old had attached to residence

were severely reduced to provide grants for the hospital, for the vicars choral and choir boys, for the poor (the Dean of York was bound to feed 50 poor people daily). The economy of the secular minster, like the monastery, needed thorough reform. The old idea that all that men needed was bread and beer no longer held, and canons were not content with presents of hot wastells from the cathedral bakery. Residence on the prebendal estate was preferred to a life without employment save in the cathedral services. A certain number of canons were always absent for study if "teachable"; others might claim leave of absence for pilgrimages, three weeks if in England, seven if going to St. Denis, sixteen to Rome, a year to Jerusalem. An English pilgrimage was to be undertaken yearly, the longer ones not more than once in a lifetime.

2. It is from the lower ranks of the church that evidence of a lively spirit of genuine religious zeal chiefly comes, though here too the demoralisation of the higher ranks of the secular clergy had evil effect. The synods wisely and constantly urged priests to the duty of a minimum of simple religious instruction, and the books written for the use of priests, to guide them in teaching their flocks, the contemporary sermons, the evidence of the episcopal registers, all argue that some provision was made. Peckham orders that once a quarter the priest should either personally, or by deputy, instruct his people in the vulgar tongue, without "any fantastical admixture of subtle distinctions" in the Creed, Ten Commandments, evangelical precepts, seven works of mercy,

seven deadly sins and seven sacraments. Whether
this can be deemed wholly adequate instruction in
religion is a matter of opinion : it was probably as
much as the parishioners desired. What they desired
we can know, from the visitations recorded, when the
parishioners, such as were chosen or cared to come,
were examined on oath as to the conduct of their
pastor. The common answer was that the priest
can preach and does teach : there may be criticism
of the quality of the preaching—it drives the
parishioners away, or is not clear enough, not
doctrinal enough, or too doctrinal. The sort of
preaching that seems to have been most popular was
in the form of short moral tales, or fables from Æsop,
legends of saints, or elementary natural history, after
the style made fashionable by the Dominicans. The
peacock complains that he cannot sing like a night-
ingale, and Destiny bids him be thankful for what he
has—his lovely neck and tail. A fish is happy in salt
water ; touched by the rain he pretends to be dying
—and so with many, says the preacher, happy with
their work all the week, finding the world's bitterness
sweet : on Sunday, at the touch of the dew of God's
Word, they hasten away, saying they must to dinner.
Many legal themes, tales of the perjuries of jurymen,
of the lies of bailiffs, are to be found in the French
sermons of Bozon, who addressed an English audience
probably of fair education.

The councils of the church were ever contending
with the clerical love of games, a taste the clerk
shared with the common people. They are repeatedly
forbidden to join in contests at the quintain (arietes

levare), to frequent plays (palestras publicas), or to play at dice. The making of "scotales" in churches —the brewing of a vat of beer of which all devout parishioners must buy—was the parish priest's "bazaar" of the Middle Ages. Vainly the bishops deprecate inter-parochial fights as to precedence, in processions with banners to the mother-church.

In the sworn testimony of the parishioners, the provision of a suitable vicarage is frequently discussed. The priest must have a decent house, where he can entertain visitors, and not sleep "minus honeste" in the church. A vicar who "preaches well" uses the church as a granary. The vicarage like the manor-house should have more than one "domus," and contain hall, camera, wardrobe, cellar, kitchen, dairy, and barn. One pastor, it is complained, has put his door so far from the hall that infirm parishioners can only find him out at their own peril. They cannot be heard calling outside.

3. By more than one regulation the minimum stipend of the vicar on an appropriated benefice had been fixed at 5 marks (£3 6s. 8d.) a year. This was considered enough "to keep hospitality in some measure" and to provide for old age and sickness. Out of his five marks, like the farmer or craftsman, he might be providing for his "focaria" and family: bequests to the "fireside women" were still forbidden by the bishops. According to Quivil, the five marks were to be allowed wherever the benefice was worth 40 marks ; if worth more, then the vicar should have more. A curate's stipend was but 40s. The priest with his income of 5 marks was getting rather more than a Fellow of

a College of the same date, who took 10d. a week and
10s. a year, or £2 13s. 4d. a year; the scholars of
Balliol in 1343 lived "mechanice" on £2 10s. a year.
The monks of Durham College got £4 a year; the
students, 5 marks.   The king's archers with their 2d.
and 3d. a day got (in regular service) their £3 or
£4 10s. a year.   But the food alone of a knight imprisoned in the Tower was reckoned at £3 2s. 6d. a

OPEN-AIR PREACHING.

year (2d. a day).   The lesser prizes of the clerical profession were such offices as the royal chaplaincies of
10 marks: the same sum was paid to the royal nurses.

The orders of synods dealing with sumptuary
offences show that some of the secular clergy could
afford to dress expensively in garments that could
not be distinguished from those of the wealthy laity.
Incomes were being eked out by the (forbidden) sale of

the sacraments, and ecclesiastical offices and clerkly property, once acquired, was peculiarly well protected by the system of ecclesiastical law.

The men who made wills and the very few who did not, risking the danger of an intestate and unconfessed death, were all alike sources of profit to clerks.   The king and lords had been driven out of their claim to the escheat of the intestate's possessions; and these fell to the church as a trust for the dead man's imperilled soul.   But ecclesiastical councils had to remind bishops that the trust must not be regarded as the trustee's personal property.   The lord contending for his heriot, the priest for his mortuary, fought out the battle for the dead man's " best quick good," and the priest won.   In mediæval morals the expiation of sin on the deathbed, by a bequest of goods that have no further value to the testator, was an elementary principle.   If no greedy friar were beforehand with him, it was at the deathbed that the parish priest could secure the claims of his church.

4. We are apt to think of the Middle Ages as more subject to credulity than our own: and yet their volumes of miracles which record how the bone of a saint did everything required of it, from the least to the greatest, from finding a piece of lost property to supplying men with lost members, are scarcely more curious reading than modern advertisements of quack medicine warranted to cure every ill.   The clergy, if they lived by men's superstitions, were as foolish as the rest.   Always too there were men who saw the folly of these things.   St. Hugh of Lincoln snubbed his biographer, anxious for miracles, and

refused to emulate the example of miracle-workers. Edward I., who had a special patron in Our Lady of Walsingham and carried about a complete museum of relics, perhaps as tests of perjury, laughed to scorn the idea that his dead father had miraculously restored a rogue's sight. "He would rather have had such a man blinded."

The wardrobe accounts show Henry III. periodically distributing in alms the weight of his child in gold, or giving clothes to the figure on the Crucifix of the same length in "samite" as that of his sickly babe,—for many and various were the recipes of faith. The dead Becket kept a workman's pork incorrupt for 40 days (whether in summer time we know not), and the dead Simon de Montfort cured with great facility a broken-winded palfrey and the wounds of a child, who lay for half an hour on a fire with four "ribalds" on top of him. Simon seems to have been most successful where a bent penny was offered, or a wax model of the injured part. The risk of a change in fashion, the discovery of something new in wonder-working, no doubt led some to make hay while the sun shone. Annoyance with the stupidity of saints was allowable too even in religious persons. An abbess of Elstow was so vexed at a villainous baron's successes that she put her apostle Paul into temporary disgrace. But these things were merely due to the primitive passion for "sortilegia" which possibly took far more degrading forms in the clerk and lay of less educated instinct. What were the "sortilegia" for which Adam of Stratton, the judge, was convicted? No book exists to set out in writing mediæval superstitions not sweetened with some Christianised flavour.

5. The monstrous regiment of clerks more or less ordained, tonsured in hundreds together, sometimes a thousand at a time, by the hard-worked bishops "in partibus," took in of course many bad characters. A more pleasing aspect of the fourteenth century is given by that school of mystic pietism whose chief representative was Richard Rolle of Hampole. He and others poured out in English verse and prose their passionate longings for a spiritual love which contrast strangely with the reasoner's scholastic logic : doubtless their words had power to set many hearts on fire to seek "the form of perfect living," the true union of the contemplative and the active life. The sweetness of the love of Jesus, His infinite compassion and tender mercy, are the themes of which Hampole and his followers never wearied: seldom he turns to paint the terrors of purgatory and hell, and ever hastens back to his "song of love-longing." It was the work of this group of religious revivalists to translate the Psalms into English, and more and more hands were busy in rendering into English or French certain parts of the Bible.

6. A few heretics were already being burned in England. The chronicle of Meaux (Yorkshire) records the burning of 55 men and 8 women: in 1285 Clapwell, a Dominican, held "only to the canon of the Bible" and denied transubstantiation. On the other hand crusading days were not yet over. "Many shepherds and women of England" started in 1319 for a crusade. Adam of Murimuth records with humorous gravity,

that, finding the distance too great, they took to killing Jews as the enemies of Christ in Toulouse and Aquitaine, and so got hanged themselves.

7. The evidence is gradually accumulating to prove that there were many " free " schools, where teaching was given to a certain number of boys gratis. At Ashburton there was a free school by 1314; at Beverley in 1312 a quarrel was in progress as to how many pupils the schoolmaster must take gratis: it is ordered that the choristers only are to be free, and the succentor is not to make spurious choristers, to defraud the schoolmaster of fees. An agreement dated 1307 is extant by which 7 choristers were boarded and taught for 4s. 8d. a week. From St. Peter's, York, comes the rule that the chancellor may not appoint the same schoolmaster for more than three years except under special conditions. A synod of Exeter, in 1289, required that whenever there was a school within 10 miles of the parish church, one of its scholars was to be chosen as "aque bajulus," or holy-water bearer, in order that the various small church fees might form a provision for him. At St. Alban's early in the fourteenth century a bequest was made to the school to release 16 of the poorest from all payment. This school was also supported in part by funds from the monastic almonry. In connection with many convents, for instance Evesham, Bruton, Bridgewater, Lenton (its school was at Gloucester) there were grammar schools, all presided over by secular clerks, whose stipend was sometimes guaranteed by the convent which made profit of the school.

The elaborate code of rules for the school of St. Alban's, 1309, shows that there was a system of examination and that something like a degree was conferred. Those who wished to become "bachelors" received a theme (proverbium) from the master and must compose in verse thereon, and publicly dispute.

The old jealousy of "adulterine" schools, which injured the licensed school already in possession, showed itself wherever competition was dangerous, but the description in the Philobiblon of the pedagogues who taught raw lads their A B C seems to show that village teaching of a rude sort was easily obtainable. The "schools" to which Peckham was anxious to send the Welsh for education that they might learn "civility" were probably those of Oxford.

8. At Oxford many changes were taking place. In medicine there was something of a revival under the influence of the Franciscans and the leadership of Bacon and Peckham. The text-books that were being written in England combined a vast wealth of quotation from classical and Arabic sources with current notions of practice, some of which were sensible and suggestive enough. Gaddesden recommends a colic belt of sealskin, and his belief that by red hangings he prevented small-pox scars, often cited as a mediæval absurdity, seems likely to obtain confirmation, as the action of red light has been shown by a Danish experimenter to have beneficial effect.

The Aristotelian renaissance of Henry III.'s reign had brought with it new teaching in physics, metaphysics and mathematics, and while some of the greatest minds were devoted to the problem of giving Aristotelian form to church doctrine, others, filled with a new faith in human reason, turned to experimental science. Among the philosophers a mighty conflict raged, in which such giant controversialists as Bacon, Ockham and Duns Scotus engaged. In the attempt to probe to the root of the principles of individuality and of the universe a new technical jargon was developed, of entity, quiddity and haeceity, which served rather to hide the shallowness than to plumb the depths of human thought. The name of the subtlest exponent of mediæval metaphysic has become to us a bye-word, and Bacon's philosophic gospel of the unity of knowledge was scarcely allowed to reach men's ears. His works were nailed, it is said, to the shelves where they lay, and men's critical and reasoning powers were again sacrificed on the altar of convention. The new teaching could only be accepted, provided it could be forced into harmony with the old tradition.

The study of Greek, almost wholly ignored by the twelfth century students, who concentrated their efforts on Latin, began again in England to show faint signs of life, after a sleep of centuries.

Grosseteste, before he knew enough Greek or Hebrew himself to be able to translate, was interested in others who knew more. Bacon reports that he cannot name four men who knew Hebrew, Greek or Arabic grammatically: that he himself wrote grammars of all three is considered certain. What are believed to be his Greek and Hebrew grammars have lately been published, and it is possible that a Greek dictionary, still in manuscript, may be traced to his authorship. Daniel of Morley's efforts, John of

Basingstoke's visit to Athens, the coming of visitors
from the Greek church to England, led to the forma-
tion of a small group of scholars anxious to revive the
study of Greek.   The monastery of St. Alban's was a
centre of the movement, and prior Gregory of Huntingdon (c. 1290) put together a fine Greek and
Hebrew collection at Ramsey abbey ; Greek and
Hebrew were in the Middle Ages often harnessed
together in an awkward fellowship.   The movement
did not die out at once, for in the next century a
bishop of Winchester, Rigaud, who died before 1323,
required every rector in his diocese to pay a farthing
in the pound towards an Oxford professorship for the
study of Greek and Hebrew.   The Franciscans in
particular contributed to the number of the linguistic
students.   But the expulsion of the Jews and the small
provision for Greek teaching left both studies in a very
backward state.   Richard of Bury, Bishop of Durham,
in his Philobiblon, repines at the want of books in
these languages.

In the fourteenth century, though there is an
absence of brilliant stars in the firmament of learn-
ing, there is no lack of names more or less famous.
In Richard of Bury's suite of learned chaplains
(many of them Merton men), there was a school not
unworthy to rank with Becket's.   The Dominican
Holcot, who may have had a share in writing the
Durham bishop's famous book about books : the
Aristotelian student Burley, tutor to the Black
Prince, commentator on the Politics and on the
Ethics, works addressed, one to a bishop who had
been Richard's chaplain, the other to Richard him-

self: Thomas Bradwardine, "doctor profundus," mathematician and moral philosopher : Maudit, an astronomer : and a famous English preacher, the opponent of the mendicants, fitz Ralph, were all chaplains to the Bishop of Durham. Himself a patron of letters he was probably much less learned than the patronised. His biographer calls him " sufficienter litteratus," but says that it was commonly believed that he had more books than all the bishops of England put together. Besides keeping them in his several manors, he had them in his bedroom in such numbers that a visitor could scarcely get in or stand upright, without knocking against them. Richard accuses the monasteries of neglecting their manuscripts, but it is possible that his passion for collection led him into bad ways of using his power. The St. Alban's chronicler notes that the abbot gave Richard a Terence, Virgil, Quintilian, and a Jerome against Rufinus, to promote the advantage of the convent in the king's court, a gift which the writer characterises as abominable, for it deprived the cloister of its chief solace. " No one," says the recipient of the gift sententiously, " can serve books and mammon." The St. Alban's abbot sold 32 books for £50, giving of this sum £15 to the refectory, £10 to the kitchen, and keeping the rest himself. However, it is to be remembered that the same abbot wrote many learned books and made mathematical instruments for the house. Another early fourteenth century bishop left a good library, the "lot" of 80 volumes being marked for probate at £116 14s. 6d ; an Avicenna was marked £5, a Bible £10.

Richard of Bury's library went to Durham College, the rules for the library being more detailed though not unlike those of the Sorbonne. Balliol too was early well provided : its scholars had books of all the faculties, in common, by the grace of William Felton,

ST. PYTHAGORAS SCHOOL, CAMBRIDGE.
From a photograph by Miss Cunningham.

1343. In the statutes of Merton and Oriel, and in the Cambridge statutes of Peterhouse (1344) and Trinity Hall (1350), the library rules are detailed and careful. Some statutes allowed books to be lent out of the college on pledge, others forbade it.

All the learned men named above were trained at Oxford, many of them likewise on the continent. The great names are those of secular clerks, of Franciscans or Dominicans, but the old jealousy of the seculars and regulars was useful in keeping up a wholesome rivalry for power in the Universities. A rule of 1337 required that one monk in every twenty should go to the University, and the foundation of more colleges resulted. It was Walter of Merton who (from 1264 to 1274) compiled the body of rules for a college of secular clerks which was the parent of the English collegiate system. To his house he would admit no " religious " person, neither monk nor friar, and in his seminary of clerks he arranged that all the scholars should be supported by the revenues of the foundation. A "grammaticus" was to teach the younger students, and the necessary books were to be provided. The liberal arts, leading up to theology as the chief, were to form the course of study for those who were destined to be parish priests. Only four or five might study canon law and only canonists might study civil law. The founders of Balliol, University College, Oriel, all looked to the Merton statutes as a model, for Merton was pouring out a stream of archbishops and bishops, and its fame was known everywhere. At Cambridge, where Merton had bought land in the event of a removal, his scheme was the model for Peterhouse and Michael-house (Trinity). By the statutes of Michaelhouse, 1324, the scholars were all to be priests ; and a stipend of 5 marks a year was given, out of which food and habit were to be bought. The cost of the weekly food, at the common table, was not to exceed 1s. a week, " nisi ex causa necessaria et honesta." Two servants were kept, at 10d. a week for food.   The washing and barbering for the whole college was charged at 40s. a year.   In choosing new members all considerations of a personal kind were to be eschewed, and the best only chosen.   Those absent for three months without leave, or neglecting their studies, falling ill, entering religion, or obtaining an income of £5 a year, were to leave, and there were rules for the ejection of all quarrelsome members and persons guilty of crime.   At Stapeldon Hall (Exeter College), Oxford, all favour, fear, claims of kinship, and affection set aside, those only were to be chosen who were best recommended by their capacity, good conduct and poverty.   The Fellowship was to last only for three years.

In 1252 Matthew Paris writes in praise of the "savoir faire" of the Oxford student, his staidness of demeanour, style and address, and of the sternness of Oxford morals, saying that an archbishop was compelled to acknowledge Oxford to be a worthy rival of Paris.   Cambridge was still behind-hand in contributing to the roll of great names : yet it was selected as the place of education for the brother of the Bruce.

9. From 1250–1350 the use of English in speech gradually ceased to be a mark of vulgarity.   Edward III. at the beginning of the war with France found it needful to urge the teaching of French.   In 1258 the first governmental document was issued in English, as well as in Latin and French, no doubt

25

in order to appeal to a humbler class than had as
yet been thought worthy of notice. It was part of
the same movement that led to the summoning of
burgesses to parliament. Not only did English
begin to rise in the scale, but French likewise began
to show signs of displacing Latin as the official
language. By the end of the thirteenth century,
bishops and statesmen, as well as lawyers and town
clerks, used French where fifty years back they
would have used Latin. In the Universities, where
it was assumed that the students had mastered the
elements of Latin, the use of French was allowed by
some college statutes. At Merton the grammar-
master was directed to assist the students in their
Latin speech, but at Peterhouse, French was allowed
for "just and reasonable cause," and English
very rarely.

Robert of Gloucester observes that "low men"
hold to English : he thinks it well to know both
English and French, "for the more a man can, the
more worth he is." Robert of Sempringham, a
Cambridge student, writes in English, he says,
for simple men, not for "disours," sayers and
harpers. For Latin contemporary chronicle we
are still partly indebted to the monasteries :
St. Alban's continued to maintain its historical
school : in the north and the midlands the monastic
chronicler was still important : but the names of Adam
of Murimuth, canon of St. Paul's, and Geoffrey
le Baker, and Robert Avesbury show that the seculars
were sweeping over this field. Murimuth writes
that he fails to find in the cathedral libraries any

chronicle running beyond 1302, save one at Exeter to 1305, and at Westminster also to 1305 ; he therefore decided to make "a book of his days." More numerous was the party of writers of works of "vulgarisation," who wrote partly with an eye to the minstrel-reciters, and found romance and miraculous wonders gave the best chance of popularity. The minstrels who thronged the court were many of them foreigners : 93 are named in a roll of Edward I.'s time, receiving £114 distributed to them in fees.

10. At the close of the thirteenth century, in London, a brotherhood was formed, after the model of a French gild, associated with the cult of a statue of the Virgin at Le Puy en Velay ; the London statutes record that it was founded to maintain jollity, peace, honesty, sweetness, gaiety and love. The "amorous company" agreed to pay certain fees towards the feast or to provide a song. A "prince"—at the court this chief minstrel was called the "king"—was to act as steward, and there was a grand ceremony with singing at the "crowning" of the prince, who was selected annually. The old and new prince were to judge the merits of the songs composed to be sung at the crowning. When a member married or died or became a priest, the others were to attend and make offerings. For "good love, jolly disport, courteous solace, joy and sweetness," "to destroy anger, rancour, felonies and all manner of vice," the company agreed to mutually support, comfort and counsel one another, and to help each other in sickness. But the principal cause of the gild's

existence was the "royal" feast, when the "royal"
singer was crowned. The royal song was to be
copied and hung under the "prince's" blazon of
arms. "And although it be so that the honest
pleasing of good ladies is proper matter and principal
occasion of royal song," no woman should be present,
in order that "thereby ensample may be taken to
honour, cherish and praise all ladies, at all times and
in all places, as much in their absence as in their
presence." The prince might not spend lavishly of
his own, for the expenses should be borne in common.
But the "prince" and others might wear "cointises," scarves, and fancy dress, at their own
charge. Coat and surcoat, without sleeves, a mantle
of the same suit, of what arms he chose, would
suffice for the "prince," and the room should *not* be
hung with cloth of gold or silk or curtains. But
there might be flowers, fresh reeds, and "bankers"
(tapestry at the backs of benches), and the prize
winner's seat might be draped in gold. The feast
was to consist of bread, good beer and wine, pottage,
one course of large fish, a double roast in a single
dish, cheese and nothing more.

The winner of the prize rode in procession
through the streets between the two "princes," and
before the departure there might be dancing, with
drinks, but no supper. What was over from the
dinners went to the prisoners at Newgate and to the
poor at the hospitals. Due arrangements were also
made for the gild chapel, which was by the Guildhall.

Such a fraternity for well-ordered gaiety shows
that some at least of the minstrels had lifted their

order out of its low associations : the minstrels who played to the king while he was bled, who sang, at the enthroning of bishops and abbots, the good old tales of Colbrand, or Queen Emma and the hot ploughshares, were no doubt not of the same condition as the vagabonds who claimed the same dignity at fairs, and were put under the charge of officers answerable for the control of loose women.

11. Time was when the religious play had been considered eminently a matter in which clerks might be concerned without impropriety. It is generally believed indeed that the origin of the religious play is to be found in a slight dramatising of certain liturgical phrases, the dramatisation having originally formed part of the religious service ; it was only when the laity were brought in to increase the dramatis personæ, when Latin gave way to French and English, and when the churchyard rather than the church became the stage, that a feeling grew up among the stricter sort that the clergy ought not to be mixed up in such performances, least of all in masked performances. William of Waddington, in his " Manuel de Pechiez," written in Edward I.'s time, says that " foolish clerks" have invented the " Miracle," and disguise themselves in visers contrary to law, causing crowds to assemble in the streets and churchyards after dinner. Such a scene is minutely described, about the same time, by a Beverley writer, who says that the Resurrection was played in the churchyard of St. John's by masked players. A crowd assembled ; some came to enjoy the fun, some to admire; but others there were who came prompted

by a spirit of devotion.   The crush was so great that
the boys sought a post of vantage in the upper parts
of the church.   An accident happened which resulted
in the playing of a real " drama of the resurrection "
inside the church, a miracle being worked by the
grace of the Confessor John, which was more exciting
than the imaginary play outside.

A manuscript of the period shows plainly the
mechanical arrangement for a " pageant," very much
after the pattern of our Punch and Judy show, as
regards at least the box and curtain.

None of the extant plays can with safety be
ascribed to a date between 1250 and 1350, though a
doubtful tradition attributes the Chester plays to
1268–1276, and the Scriveners' play at York, on the
incredulity of the Apostle Thomas, bears signs of
great antiquity.   If all the plays were as pious in tone
as the Scriveners', only very puritanical people would
see in it any rock of clerkly offence.   But no doubt
there was a tendency to gross buffoonery, on occasions such as the Feast of Fools, from which Grosseteste recommended the vicars choral of Lincoln to
abstain.

12. The subtleties of mediæval humour still have a
naïve charm of their own, though a jaded palate may
deem their savour vapid.   Certain " cautelae verbales "
have been handed down to us in Latin, which may
serve as an example of fourtenth century " tit-bits."

1. I will make you make a cross, and then will not
touch you, and you will not be able to leave the
house without breaking that cross.   *Answer.* Stand
before a post in your house, with your arms extended.

2. What you do not know, and I do not know, and no one can know after I have told you. *Answer.* I will take a *straw* from the floor of the room, measure its inches, tell you the length, and break the straw.

3. A pear tree bears all the fruit a pear tree can bear and did not bear pears. *Answer.* It bore only *one* pear.

LICHFIELD.

DOGS DRAWING CART WITH HUCKSTER.

XVII

FARMING

1. Improved methods — 2. Manorial extents — 3. Breakdown of the
old system—4. Books on husbandry—5. The bailiffs and the
bondmen—6. Local government.

1. THE accounts of the farms of the Hospitallers,
and of the Lacy estates in the North of England, with
many monastic balance-sheets and manorial court-
rolls, show that from 1250–1350, while the old system
of agriculture was beginning to break down, there
was a movement of advance in farming methods,
especially in the direction of stock-breeding, and
garden cultivation. In the Hospitallers' accounts,
rendered in 1338, every "mansio" is described as
having a "gardinum" which "cum herbagio" is
worth some 10s. a year. The royal accounts with
their purchases of St. Réole (Touraine) pears, Caillon
(Burgundy) pears, the pears "pucelle de Saintonge"

and "pucelle de Flandres," costard and pearmain apples, give evidence of the care to obtain good stocks. The Lacys' Holborn garden account of 1296 shows sales of fruit and of roses. The Cistercians of Wardon, Bedfordshire, at a later time displayed in their arms their famous stewing-pear.

The need for meadow-lands increased with the value of the stock, and with the need some care was taken to increase the supply. Meadow was worth 2s. an acre, in many of the less well-watered parts, where arable was worth only 6d. Next, the mention of such accessories as gravel- and marl-pits becomes more frequent, of water-, wind-, horse-, and fulling-mills, especially in the north of England. The values affixed to these are high. The management of fish-ponds was excellent, and pigeons were bred on a great scale. A dovecote which bears date 1326, and still exists, contains 600 holes. Poultry and pigeons were the same regular items in English mediæval diet that they are nowadays in Italy and France.

From the accounts of stock-profits (staurum), of the "remainder" and the "addition" old and new, rendered on a well-managed estate like that of Henry de Lacy 1295–6, 1304–5, from the care given to the "vaccaria" or cattle-stock-farm, from the good prices obtained, one might draw a very favourable picture. The Templars managing a Northumbrian farm spent £33 10s. as against receipts of over £94, leaving a goodly balance. Such accounts may be exceptional, but both come from backward parts of the country. The Lancashire accountant notes how many of his cows have been strangled by wolves. It was a county where the "unassarted," "unapproved" lands were still extensive.

Stewards, parkers, farm-bailiffs, the "instauratores" or stock breeders, rendered annual account; the average price of an ox was 9s., a heifer or cow 7s., a hide 2s. 6d., a cart-horse £2 or £3, prices that show a great rise on those of a century back. There are

WATER-MILL, FROM THE ALEXANDER ROMANCE, 1338–1344.

attempts to contend with disease : the Templars pay for grease to protect the sheeps' heads from fly ; the Dunstable canons commend their unguent (grease, quick-silver and verdegris) for scab, while they admit that they are powerless to contend against it in a wet season. Their flock of sheep at the Peak numbered 1440, twelve "long" hundreds. The mention of butter in the accounts becomes more frequent : the

sales are not confined to cheese, grain and hay.   On
the other hand the expenditure on spreading and
carrying manure remains very small ; ditching and
draining are scarcely mentioned.   In the Lancashire
accounts charges on lead and coal mining are included
in the accounts of the farmers.

The St. Paul's farm buildings in the fourteenth
century must have still kept their reputation for
excellence and comfort.   In 1335 canon Adam of
Murimuth, the historian, was farming Navestock,
where he had under one roof a bakery, a dairy, a

BARROW, 1338–1344.

kitchen with an oven and two boilers, a hen-house, a
hall with buttery and dispensary, several " chambers,"
a chapel, lined with plaster of Paris and covered
with tiles, not to speak of the granaries, byre, smithy,
and windmill, out of doors.   In his furniture he
reckoned four tables, four tripods, an axe, a chess-
board, a backgammon-board with dice, a mazer set
in silver, 60 cups, 100 " scuttles " or dishes, 22 pans,
10 sauce pots, a tin saucepot, a number of measures,
a roasting-iron, a bread-peel for the baking oven, a
ladder and other items named.

2. The Gloucester abbey extent, 1265–6, takes each manor and gives the number of arable acres in each of the three open fields (see above, p. 109) with their value: a third is then deducted for the fallowing: the values of garden, curtilage, pastures, pig-runs, and various small customary payments of "silver" follow. A virgater's services are then named: besides paying his rent in money, he ought to plough twice a year for his lord, and that ploughing is worth 4d. On the ploughing days he eats at the lord's table: he gives certain bushels of wheat as church-scot: he harrows the lord's land in Lent till all the lord's land is sown, and that harrowing is worth 4½d. He hoes the lord's grain for three days, and that is worth 2½d. Similar prices are named for the lifting and carrying of hay, planting beans for one day, washing and shearing the lord's sheep, making the hayrick in the lord's court, doing pack-carrying between two villages. Finally he reaps 2½ acres weekly for the lord in autumn. These "bederips" or lord's boon reapings he does with two assistants, and food must be provided at the lord's table. He helps further to carry the lord's grain in autumn, or, as an alternative, in the thrashing; he collects nuts for half a day. Such are the services, amounting in all to the value of 12s. 2½d., that complete the virgater's year's labour due for his thirty acres. The survey then proceeds to name all those who hold on similar terms. The values affixed to the "works" in such a statement as the above, may be taken to mean that a payment of the amount named would discharge the tenant from his obligation.

REEVE DIRECTING THE LABOURS OF REAPERS.

If we would compare the eastern with the western
counties, this Gloucester survey may be set against
the Ramsey abbey extent of 1271. In this latter
account a bondsman of Barnwell holds a messuage
and a half virgate, rent 6s. 8d. From Michaelmas to
the mowing of the lord's meadow, he does a whole
day's work in every week for his lord. On the first
day's mowing, he mows for the lord, who gives a
shilling's worth of beer to his men, and so on every
other day : on the off-days he may mow his own
meadow, but he must not cease to mow till, with the
aid of the other cottiers, the whole of the lord's
meadow is mown. From August 1 to September 8
he puts in three half-days a week, so that he reaps
three rood-strips, one on each half-day. Every other
week he must provide a man for a " bederip " without
food, and in the off-week he provides a " bederip "
with all the men and women belonging to his household, exclusive of himself and his wife : for the first
of these bederips the lord gives bread, herrings and
water ; for the second, bread, meat and beer, but the
tenant must find the cup and be content with a
gallon. The boon rendered without food is a
" hunger bederip," boons without beer are " precariæ
siccæ."

In the same way binding and carting is arranged ;
so too the lord's Martinmas brewing. Every seignorial
need is satisfied : indeed the Ramsey house of religious
seems to have shown a special aptitude for fastening
permanent " love-boons " on the soil, or more directly
speaking, on the tenants. The terms of these quaint
contracts are often curiously minute, the result one

may suspect, of some old conflict, some old effort of the renderer of love-boons to seek his own, to cease to suffer all things. Sometimes the vague reasonableness of the early understanding has had to be changed to a precise compromise. The reaper must bring a powerful man, no stripling ; there must be an immediate return to work after dinner ; at evening-tide the mower of grass may carry away a " fasciculus " of grass, as much as he can carry on the handle of his scythe, so that the scythe is not broken, and does not touch the ground, or the mower loses his perquisite. In another example the tenant collects rods, carries them to St. Ives (fair), and, as one " work," must make a hurdle 9 feet long, or close a party-wall between two booths as two " works " : should he act as watchman at the fair or be put in charge of thieves, on the morrow he will be quit of work. A " reeve " or foreman whose business it is to increase the lord's profits by driving others to their works, is excused from all other services. His responsibility is already heavy enough. The widow must take over her husband's services. Gunnilda, presumably the widow of a smith, has a virgate, pays rent and finds four ploughs for the lord, both steel and iron ; she provides all the plough-shares, and shoes eight horses. One labourer is suffered to be ill for a year and a day, quit of all works but ploughing : if his illness lasts he must render then all that his land is bound to render. The widow may have 30 days free from the lord's work. Such contracts securing considerate treatment, in the case of one individual, will be likely to attach to all tenants holding virgates on a similar tenure.

3. But although the framework of the agricultural economy showed no change, the old idea that a lord's best policy was to work his demesne by the labour of tenants, in such a way that the whole estate was self-sufficient, showed signs occasionally of breaking down. The old services did not suffice for the new needs. Labour for the unallotted new services must be hired. Many large demesne farms were being leased to "socage" tenants, to freeholders who would become the "yeomen" of a later generation. By means of grazing it was easier than it had been to make farming pay, and the class of farmer lords grew as the class of feudal lords decayed. The fourteenth century "knight of the shire," secure in his tenure, working his land for profit, taking his share in national and local government, was a different person from his lineal ancestor, the feudal tenant by knight's service, enfeoffed by a great lord upon his land in return for his provision of a mail-coat. Hitherto farming had not been regarded as a profession; the object of owning lands of old had not been to make a profit in money but to provide food and drink enough to live upon, the year through. Nothing that could possibly be provided by villagers was to be bought, but likewise it had not been expected that much of the year's produce would be sold. As soon as the demesne farms of the lord began to produce wool, livestock or grain, in excess of the manorial household's demand, as soon as the trading element came in, the old relation of the acres in the " demesne " or home-farm to the tenants' acres in the " furlongs " or unenclosed fields was bound to change. Free

tenants who will pay rents in proportion to their
speculative expectations of success were becoming
more profitable, in spite of their independence, than
the flock of "tenants at will" holding by ancient
customary tenures and kept in a state of subjection.
The manor was passing out of a "seignory" into a
farm.

4. The multiplication of books intended to teach
estate management and the science of husbandry
shows clearly enough the new tendency to some
specialisation ; the old light of nature was no longer
enough.   The steward at least should be taught his
business.   But though some of the monasteries were
letting large home-farms, having more in hand than
they could till, such treatises as Walter of Henley's,
written before the great sheep-rot of 1283, is a work
(from a reformer's pen) for an estate of the old school.
To the old school, "custom" was worth as much as
rent ; a well-stocked park, fishpond, warren, coney-
garth, and dovecotes should be kept, but grazing on a
large scale was not contemplated.   Concerning the
shepherd it is written that he must not leave his
sheep to go to fairs, markets, wrestling-matches,
wakes or taverns without leave, and in any case he
must find a substitute.   Walter treats a two-field
system as a possibility but recommends that the
two fields be treated on the lines of the three-field
system.   If half lies fallow, the other half should be
divided, under winter- and spring-sown corn.   His
teaching is advanced, in so far as he talks of ditching
and draining, of putting manure on the stubbles and
of marling the sheepcotes.   He appreciates the

26

importance of breeding from good stock.   All superfluous stock should be sent to the lord's other manors.

If a cow has not calved or a ewe has not lambed,
the steward must find out whose fault it is, and charge
the negligent attendant for the issue or its value : and
the same if any should die.   Sheep that die suddenly
should be salted and used as meat for servants and
labourers.   Walter is a believer in oxen as preferable
to horses, though the ideal plough team will combine

MILKING EWES.
From the Louttrel Psalter.

two horses with a team of (probably four) oxen.   A
ploughing horse consumes a halfpennyworth of oats
nightly, *i.e.*, a sixth of a bushel, and a shilling's worth
of grass in summer : shoeing averages 1d. a week if
he be shod on all four feet, and then there is fodder
and chaff besides ; and an old horse is worth only his
skin.   An ox on the other hand costs only a quarter
of this amount, and with tenpennyworth of grass is
fit for the larder.   Walter is an ardent believer in
ploughing and would keep the ploughman at work

all the year through save for two months, which must
be cancelled as holy days or as otherwise unsuitable.
He would plough the land three times between every
two crops. Working till noon, a plough ought to
turn 180 acres in the year : it is due to the malice of
ploughmen, who will not plough beyond their pace,
if less than this be done.

Walter preaches likewise the doctrine of cleanliness : cattle and oxen should be curried : dairymaids

WOMAN WITH DISTAFF FEEDING CHICKENS.
From the Louttrel Psalter.

should be clean.   To the dairymaid he allots, according to the custom of the time, the superintendence of
the poultry, of the farrowing of pigs, and requires
of her half the winnowing of corn, with the help of
another woman.

He tells of apples and pears, what quantity of
cider and perry they should yield ; of nuts, what
quantity of oil. Wild honey is the lord's perquisite
and should be gathered every two years.   One may

expect two gallons from each hive; eight hives can
be fed through the winter on one gallon.

5. He recommends that the customary tenants
should be allowed to choose their own officers, answerable for their services. It was not the villain-reeves but
the bailiffs and "firmarii" superior to these "prepo-
siti," haywards and foremen, from whom both lords
and men had most to fear. The proverb ran "if the
lord bids slay, the steward bids flay," and it is against
the harsh exactions of these officials, not against the
old accustomed order of things, as touching services
and lands, that most of the popular murmuring was
directed.

> "Master beadle, as rough as a boar,
> Says he will strip my lodgings bear,"

sings one politician, and others detail the claims set
forward by the bailiffs to roast chicken, lampreys,
salmon on fish-days; to provide silver they will sell
a man's corn whilst it is green, and those who do not
give all they ask have cattle and goods distrained.
The weapons in the lord's hand were indeed for-
midable. All accountants, in their turn, were liable
to be imprisoned if in arrears; to remain in prison
at their own cost until the debt be paid.

Examples of a general resistance to a lord's exactions are not wholly wanting: they are exceptional,
but they tell of what will happen when a social
cataclysm takes place. In an Exeter bishop's register,
for instance, the bishop's account of an attempted
resistance at Paignton is given. Sixty men refused
to bind the cut corn: the bishop hired labourers, and

at night the rebellious sixty scattered the sheaves
over the field, because they had been made to pay
the labourers' hire. They protested that this binding
of sheaves was not part of their duty. The bishop
reminded the villagers that they held their chattels
and their land *at his will:* they received them back
on his own terms, paying a fine of £10. In 1283 the
Dunstable chronicler enters :—" At this time we sold
W. Pyke our native with his 'sequela' (his brood),
and we received one mark (13s. 4d.) from the buyer."
Such an entry however has become by this time
something of a rarity.

In 1290 the St. Paul's officials were directed to
enquire whether the "nativi" marry their daughters
within the manor or without, without due payment ;
whether they sell, without leave, calf, foal or ox, or
damage the trees in the hedges ; whether the "nativi"
or their "nati" are manumitted, sold, or made clerks
or apprentices ; wherein are they rebellious to their
lord ; who are fugitive ; who die? The convent of
St. Alban's drew up about the same time some rules
for the more conservative management of their
property. The warnings are these :—Be very careful
that no freeman enters on a villain's services, for we
lose service thereby : No serf must sell or let his land
except to us : No serf must be pledge for a freeman,
or let him be punished " acriter pecunialiter " : Mind
how villains buy lands of freemen with our chattels :
enter upon such purchases at once : They must not
sell even to other villains "quia plurima destructio
est." Villains may breed pigs and have a single
bercary or sheep-fold, and a pig-stye, as of old

custom, but they may not rear plough-beasts or horses without risk of forfeiting them.

If the political song tells much of the harshness of officials, it tells also of the uppishness of serfs. "Now-a-days one can not find a boy to bear a letter but he asks for the best meat, beef and bacon." The preachers were for ever urging the serf to remain where God (or man) had placed him : the lowborn, who go to school to learn courtesy, are like the worm who thought it had wings, or the rat who wished to marry the sun's daughter. But against the clergy the lords complained that they encouraged serfs to make wills, contrary to all reason—for their chattels are the lord's. On the Templars' fiefs the agreement was that all should pay a third of their chattels at death, and the serfs were got to do the same.

6. Most abundant are the records which show how real was the share taken by country. folks of all classes in the departments of local government as it was then understood. Assize rolls, coroners' rolls, frank-pledge rolls, manorial rolls, may all be adduced to prove that at least some of the men of the shire and of the villages had education enough to grapple with the formalities of legal business, even though it be always under the guidance of a trained and lettered clerk who could pen his roll in Latin. The law was an instrument for the civilisation of the people not less powerful than the ecclesiastical machinery.

The local "moots" in the course of time had greatly changed their character, but they remained all-important features in English country life.

Attendance at periodical court-meetings, sometimes at a considerable distance from home, must be constantly arranged for.   In 1314–5, the men of Berkshire petitioned that their gaol be not at Windsor.   Some of the Berkshire vills which send their freemen to the "gaol delivery" find it takes a week to get there, yet absence renders a man liable to amercement.   In 1258 and later it was a common grievance that men suffered from unlimited fining, if absent from the judicial eyre or from the sheriff's "tourn" when the frank-pledges were grouped.   If the four vills nearest to the spot where a sudden death had occurred did not appear by their representatives, all persons over the age of twelve (and therefore in frank-pledge) might suffer fine.   Many coming to the courts from divers parts died of famine, and if the inquest ventured to report that this was the cause of death and that they knew no other, then fines would be levied because the hue and cry had not been raised against the phantom offender, or because there had been no presentment of Englishry, proving that the dead man was not a foreigner.   But heavy as the burden might be, the system of "presentments," by a jury of persons likely to know the facts, at the periodic "tourns," had great merits which were duly appreciated.   At the sheriff's visitation not only were the accusations made against persons suspected of crime, but here likewise all nuisances could be "presented," all encroachments upon highways or commons, all stopping of footpaths, and the like.   The jury was a jury of freeholders, but the villains who must be grouped in tens and dozens under a chief pledge at the "tourn" are in that respect under the same system as freemen. The Normans had not scrupled to put themselves under the English system of "frithborh" which they construed as "frank-pledge" and took to be an institution fitted for the freeborn.

Some civil actions required a jury of knights, who might on occasion have to travel up to attend the courts at Westminster from the ends of the kingdom.

It is a jury of the neighbourhood that decides questions of villenage, of disputed succession, and brings its evidence to prove a man's age. It is difficult to realise that such passionate lovers of order and system as the mediæval lawyers overlooked the necessity for a register of births and deaths and marriages. The only proof was the sworn testimony of the witness-jurors. Christening, wedding and funeral feasts were useful institutions inasmuch as they provided witnesses in the event of legal difficulties. Such an one remembers the baptism because he held the candle, another by a great rain and flood. Many curious customs seem to have been kept up as a means of securing publicity, and so informing the people of the county. When a man offered the excuse for his late appearance in court that he was delayed by a flood, he was asked did he raise the hue and cry? "for otherwise the country would have no knowledge of your hindrance." "No, Sir," was the reply, "I did not know so much law, but I shouted and yelled" (criay et brayay).

The neighbourhood, the "visnetum," was continually summoned to give its sworn judgment on questions civil and criminal. The older methods, compurgation, ordeal, trial by battle, had all given place more or less completely to a jury system. Rarely save in the ecclesiastical and the borough courts was it possible to resort to the simple method which allowed a man to defend himself by an oath, more or less supported by the oaths of his friends. The Church had withdrawn its support from the ordeal, which, if it had not the sanctions of religion, had little indeed to commend it. Even the appeal to battle failed to hold its own when men could hire prize-fighters to champion their suits. For the innocent it was wise policy to choose the judgment of their " country." He who refused to put himself upon an inquest, to clear himself of the suspicion of ill-fame, was rendered the more suspect. He must be put in hard and strong imprisonment, lie on bare ground, eat bread of bran or barley one day, drink stagnant water the next, and be laden with as much iron as he can bear.

TAVERN WITH BUSH, AND BEGGAR DRINKING,

BLIND BEGGAR, WITH CHILD ON HIS BACK AND BEGGING-BOWL
ASKS FOR BUTTER-MILK.

XVIII

TOWN LIFE

1. Self-government in towns—2. Unpaid service—3. Bye-laws—4. Organisation of crafts—5. Foreign trade—6. Sphere of municipal government—7. Tallage rolls—8. Social intercourse—9. Expulsion of the Jews—10. Population—11. Summary.

1. THE readiness of the lord of a flourishing village to lift his tenants-at-will by a stroke of his pen to the estate of the burgess is shown by several charters creating boroughs in this period, and nothing witnesses more clearly to the elasticity and adaptability of mediæval society.   The gulf between an ancient and a modern social system is easily leapt ; a few words on parchment, a " quick pass change " that seems like sleight of hand, and the status of a whole group of men is changed.   The mediæval answer to " What's in a name ? " might well be an unhesitating " everything."   The bondman and the free burgess were divided by sharp specific differ-

ences, the handiwork of human creators : yet a group
of men could be lifted from a lower to a higher
order, if it should seem desirable to the lord and
his men that this should happen. To the group of
tenants-at-will the central condition of their being
was their relation to the lord's demesne : lifted to
burgherhood, the lord's interference is bought out
more or less completely and the essential " freedom "
of the burgage tenure is, that it is free of seignorial
exploitation in certain stipulated directions ; it is of
privileged condition. The relation to the lord in the
burgesses' case became as a rule one of finance
merely, and even the fiscal relation grew less and less
important as the contracts fell out of date. What
was a hard price to pay for privileged condition in one
century was an easy one in the next. In these contracts there is every gradation from a subjection only
very slightly modified by privilege to a complete
system of burghal self-government. The lord may
name the borough's head officer, may choose between
certain nominees selected by the burgesses, or he may
leave the selection wholly to the burgesses. He may
or may not require the burgesses' aid in his agricultural works ; he may require real or nominal evidences
of his seignorial right. Many village groups, boroughs
in little else but name, showed no commercial vitality
and became manors again both in fact and in name
when villainage had lost its onerous character.
Manchester is a case in point. But the days of
servile tenancy at will were numbered ; no village
group ever fell back to the servile estate once
it had escaped, not even when, later, the privi-

leged condition of burgherhood involved a man in heavy burdens, burdens heavy enough to make the once envied privileged condition an undesirable possession. For new tests of burgherhood were evolved within this period, and just at the time when the condition of the villager was improving, the burgess was being asked not only to pay a larger fraction of the national taxation, but to incur the expense of sending a representative to parliament to agree to it. Not all the boroughs showed the public spirit and advanced political judgment of the burgesses of St. Alban's, who, to prove that they were not villains, as the abbey insisted, claimed their parliamentary representation as a test of their order. A test by which perhaps they really set more store was the sending of a jury of twelve burgesses to answer for the borough before the Justices in eyre, a jury on which no " foreigner," no non-burgesses might sit, none, that is, who was not inclined to take a lenient view of burgesses in trouble and a severe view of non-burgesses in like case.

2. London, of whose barons Henry III. had said that they were so rich they could buy the fabulous " treasures of Octavian," is scarcely to be spoken of as of one family with the struggling inconspicuous blossoms of the same order : in everything municipal London was half a century or more in advance of her nearest competitor. With its two dozen wards, each with a police organisation, its well-armed gates, its " bretasched " quays, its busy courts of law and active council, it stands as an example of a mediæval city at its highest point of

development.   The business of local government here
as everywhere was carried on for the most part
by men who received no pay : not even the clergy-
man's 5-mark stipend fell to the share of those who
spent a large part of their time in the public service :
in this one department the doctrine was not taught
that the labourer is worthy of his hire.   In the watch
alone was there hired professionalism : in the higher
offices there was a fine for refusal to serve, but there
is no indication of a general unwillingness to take up
duties which gave power, position and patronage.
Only the actual out-of-pocket expenses of authorised
officials were defrayed by the common chest, and
there might often be a difficulty in obtaining even
these.   The Mayor of London received a large grant
for the maintenance of hospitality, £40, but in small
towns 20s. sufficed.   A town-clerk and town-sergeant
received small salaries, but the list of paid officials is
always very short.   Aldermen and councillors were
unpaid, like their ancestors the elders of the portmanmoot or borough court.   The interest of the work
centred in certain very practical issues, not in the
study of political or economic principles or even
in party struggles.   The principal concern of the
governing body of the town, the principal concern
indeed of the whole community, which that body was
supposed, by a more or less tacit understanding, to
represent in some sort, was to " run " the borough in
such a way that its inhabitants should incur as few
pecuniary mulcts for public purposes as possible.
The council is there to defend the town in all
its franchises, or to " amend " them, if it be possible,

by some immediate outlay, that thus expense in the
future may be saved.   The borough, for all its
seeming independence, must be ever watchful in its
dealings with exterior powers, above all with the
king.   The towns, except London, steered clear of
politics ; they could not afford to be carried away on
any tide of national conflict ; the risk of incurring
some crushing amercement, the expression of the
royal displeasure, was too great to allow of any but
a waiting policy.   The kings had realised the value of
the boroughs and the ease with which a big " miseri-
cordia" could be distributed in the form of a rate.
Every borough lived under a permanent cloud which
was big with " mercy " of a finite sort and might
break very destructively over mercantile heads.   How
fully the value of the boroughs had been realised
in the royal scheme of economy is seen by the
frequency with which borough " farms " were being
used as royal grants to queen-mothers, queen-consorts,
and other needy persons, where in old days a corrody
would have been provided.

In the management of municipal affairs the records
tell us more of " unanimity," real or supposed, than of
divisions of opinion.   If there were serious division of
opinion, as there was in questions of finance, such
divisions almost of necessity entailed a revolution, for
no one had as yet conceived the convenient doctrine
of the duty of the minority to submit to the rule of
the majority.   But revolution meant the interference
of the central government, and risks which neither the
majority nor the minority would lightly incur.   As a
rule borough legislation is drawn to pattern and

rarely is a new departure taken. What has been
handed down to us, however, is the final decision,

CROSS FOR A TEMPORARY MARKET ERECTED NEAR HEREFORD
AT THE TIME OF THE BLACK DEATH.
From a photograph by Miss Cunningham.

such as the town-clerk would permanently preserve,
not the discussion or the rejected proposals.

3. Much legislation had to be continually reissued,

with fresh attempts to enforce it, for the local executive often broke down. The aim of it all was to
secure the keeping of the peace, to control competition in favour of the burgesses, to check dishonest
dealings on the part of traders and craftsmen. But
in London in the thirteenth century the scope of
legislation was considerably wider ; there were
elaborate building "assizes," not only to protect the
city from the risk of fire, but to prevent encroachments on the street. The overhanging "solars" had to
be of such a height that a man mounted on a large
horse could ride underneath. From the fixing of
prices for bread and ale, the list was gradually
extended to many other articles of food, especially in
times of scarcity or crowding. A London parliament
made a law in 1315, a time of dearth, which fixed
very high town prices, and laid down maximum
charges for grain and salt, for the fat ox, fed with
grain, or otherwise, pigs, sheep, geese, capons, hens
and eggs. The chronicler of Bridlington observed
at the time the futility of these regulations, saying
that prices are the result of a divine dispensation, and
vary with the fertility of the season. A rise in prices
might likewise be due to causes more under man's
control. For instance, when Edward summoned
Scotch commissioners to London in 1305 to consider
the government of the conquered country, he ordered
that none be so bold as to enhance the price of
victuals by reason of this parliament.

London was the first to invent a sumptuary law
(1281), perhaps in imitation of some French rule ;
women-hucksters, nurses, servants and loose women

were forbidden to dress in the guise of their betters ;
they had been wearing hoods lined with furs too good
for persons of such humble estate ; only those who
could afford furred capes might wear hoods trimmed
with such fur as they liked.

4. At the close of the thirteenth century, in London
particularly, evidence is forthcoming to show that
among the craftsmen there was a tendency to more

BEAR-BAITING.
From the Louttrel Psalter.

organisation.   Master-workers began to form a
separate hierarchy from the journey-men, apprentices,
or servers as they had been called.   The young man
who would take up a trade must go through definite
stages of service, like the youth who sought knighthood : he must submit to a curriculum as definite as
that prescribed for the university degree.   Elaborate
"ordinals" containing the rules of a craft now began
to be drafted.   In addition to the old rules for the

processes used by dyers, weavers and fullers, pre-
scribing particular dyes, particular qualities of wool,
regulating wages, or requiring the fuller to full with
his feet, and not to use instruments that might injure
the cloth, the London records now register the bye-
laws of other crafts, drafted by the craftsmen themselves, and accepted by the city council. From 1261
come the rules of the London lorimers or makers of
the metal ornaments of harness. The lorimers
suggest the rules, "for the abating of guile and
trickery"; the Mayor and barons of the city accept
them and record them. There is to be no night-work,
no re-furbishing of old horse-bits to sell as new, but a
rich man might if he liked have an old bit mended.
The terms of apprenticeship and the fees, the
feasts and half-holidays customary in the trade, are all
set out at length. Those who take up the trade pay
an entrance-fee to the city and a fee to the alms-box
in aid of poor lorimers. In token of the city's
superiority the Mayor was to receive a new bit at
Easter.

   5. By the rule of the cappers (1269) all caps were to
be of wool and old caps might not be sold for new.
None might be dyed in black, for they are apt to
" run " in the rain and lose colour. No night-work
was allowed, a rule made less in the interest of good
workmanship than in the interest of the workmen,
who are said to be poor and numerous. Later on
these ordinances were revised to prevent the use of
flock and to shut out foreign caps. The stream of
mediæval legislation was steadily poured out against
the admission of all foreign goods that could compete

with native produce, against the introduction of any novel process that could injure those who used an older process. Marvellous and overwhelming, howsoever hidden, are the forces that set against permanence in vested interest. Proscription, penalties, disfranchisement, all the machinery of law, seem ever and anon to be time's playthings. He uses them as the enemy's pieces to effect "stale mate."

Within the boroughs there was no power capable of sufficient political insight to detect any way to stimulate industry, and to promote that common weal for which even the municipal politician was genuinely anxious, so far as his own locality represented it. But a higher authority, Edward III.'s council, more than once showed a disposition to attack the problem from a new point of view. Magna Carta had secured and Henry III. had confirmed to the foreign merchant safe-conduct, protection from new exactions and liberty to buy and sell, but Edward III.'s act of 1335 was more explicit. By this law all merchants, stranger or denizen, might buy or sell corn, wines, wool, cloth, flesh, fish, both "avoirdupois," that is bulky goods sold by the large scale or trone, and "merceries" or small wares, at this time chiefly spices, sold by the troy or small scale—in fact "all things vendible"—at any place, and of and to whomsoever they would. Wine alone might not be carried from the realm. This law is expressly stated to supersede all borough privileges, and had it been carried out, it would have proved the death-blow to the "merchant gild," and would have made "the franchise of the borough" a commodity no longer vendible, in as

much as it would have ceased to be of value. But
an act of 1378 acknowledged the nullity of the
earlier law, and the franchise of the borough remained
a necessity, to those plying certain trades, till 1835.

The act of 1337 which declared it to be felony
to carry wool out of England, and forbade any but
members of the royal family to wear woollen cloth
made out of England, seems equally original and
important, but it was merely a step in securing the
alliance of the Flemish people, an act of reprisal
against their count, and was not intended to be
permanent. But Edward III.'s council, at a time
when all the superior woollen cloths were being made
out of England, began a policy of fostering cloth-
making which ultimately had great results. Foreign
cloth-workers were placed under the king's protection,
encouraged to settle and enfranchised by the king.
At the same time the act sought to encourage an
English fur-trade, forbidding the use of foreign furs
to any who had not £100 a year. But human nature
is stronger than human law and Murimuth the contemporary chronicler observes how ineffectual the
rule was. Even the council felt no desire to forbid
the import of canvas, linen or silk goods, for which
England was wholly dependent on the continent.

The transport of stores, whether for Edward I.'s
Welsh or Scotch wars, or the wars of his successors,
effectually stimulated shipping and trade, especially
with Ireland, which was regarded as a great storehouse for provisions in times of sudden emergency.
Men's ideas of the possibilities of English trade became
larger, and commercially the Black Death found

England prosperous. The fair, with its special law and special arrangements for the recovery of debts, afforded a useful outlet to the forces which burghal monopoly had attempted to control too closely. For a few days in the year, the borough threw open its

BURY ST. EDMUND'S WATERGATE.
From a photograph by Miss Cunningham.

gates to all and sundry, and supplied its own needs for the year. The " foreign " merchant might pass a large part of the year in moving from one fair to another, free of toll. The largest fairs were held at St. Bartholomew's, Smithfield, at Winchester, under a

charter of Rufus, at Boston, St. Ives, Stourbridge
(Cambridge), Bury, Stamford, and Beverley, but every
centre was served by a fair of more or less notoriety.
Most of the fairs were under the control of the
municipal officers, either by definite grant or by
usurpation.

6. It is scarcely possible to exaggerate the multi-
farious character of the municipal duties.   Mayors,
bailiffs and sergeants were the maids of all work on
the scanty staff of the mediæval executive.   From an
early time the borough rulers who had displaced a
lord were guardians of orphans ; a feudal borough
must see " wardship " answered for somewhere, and
accordingly by charter or tacitly, the community
made itself guardian ; that is to say, the mayor or
bailiff with the council where there was one, or where
none was yet evolved, then the officers of the
borough court, appointed certain guardians, answerable to them for the property of the minor.   In
London in 1299 men were saying that the aldermen
took the money of the common chest, under pretext
of wardship of orphans, and spent it on themselves.
The aldermen, acting as judges in their own cause,
sent the libeller to prison.

Again, it is through its governing body that the
community protected its burghal chase or warren, and
to the same body it entrusted the election of the
church-wardens of the borough's parish church and
the audit of the church-wardens' account.   The
hospitals were in many cases under borough control.
The borough as well as the Church provided for the
needs of the lepers, the sick, and the poor.

The town not merely looked to its mayor and his brother jurats to levy and assess the taxes, to judge the offences done within the limits of the community, including in some cases the felonies, but found in the borough court also a convenient repository for every record. Here were arranged all matters of surety, contract, specification, obligatory notes, arbitrations in disputes, bonds of apprenticeship and, from old time, all " bookings " of land. The borough officers registered not only all conveyances but also all wills made by burgesses, and thus secured a valuable weapon against ecclesiastical interference.

To the borough officers was left the arrangement of the muster-roll, the equipment of the town's quota of men with bows, arrows, wadded-leather-coats, knives, caparisoned horses and the rest, when the royal summons for a military levy had been issued. Not only must provision be made for those whom the borough, of its grace, must send to the host, but for the guarding of the town itself. This duty was of old the burgess's prime duty ; his chartered franchise repeatedly protected him from all military calls that took him away for more than the daylight hours of a single day. " With the sun out, and with the sun in ; " to do more military service was made matter of special bargain.

Besides impressing soldiers to meet the royal " commission of array," the borough officers might have to impress labourers to meet any royal demand for labour : in return for " reasonable " pay, the king was in the habit of requiring masons and builders for his palaces and castles, even parchment-makers to prepare skins for his rolls, and the mayor and bailiffs might have to despatch such people from the borough ; they must also settle the housing of visitors to the borough, and see to it that no one take lodgers without giving the required police guarantees.

On all the great festal occasions the community looked to its ever useful organ : the council arranged the play, the pageant, the procession, the minstrelsy. The mayor and aldermen of London in 1312, when a prince was born, led the " carols " or " ring dances " in the church of St. Paul's, went in " carols " through the city, all the rest of the day and for a great part of the night ; they dined in the Guildhall, excellently well tapestried and arrayed, and saw to it that the conduit in Cheap ran wine.

That same conduit, with all the water-works therewith connected, was of the council's making (1237). It was, the council that assessed the brewers, cooks and fishmongers for the " easement " they enjoyed of the said conduit, and spent the levy in repairing and maintaining it. Theirs was the duty, in London, already in the early years of Edward I., to abate the coal-smoke nuisance, and repress the Southwark lime-kilns. The " assizes " of ale and bread, wine and other victuals, gave them control of prices, weights and measures, and sanitary inspection. In 1309 the taverners of London numbered 354, the professed ale-brewers 1,334 ;[1] the council's work of " abling " and

---

[1] The population of London in 1350 has been estimated at 90,000 but this is perhaps too low. Paris in 1328 has been given a total of 300,000.

testing every cask broached for sale must have engaged the attention of a large staff.

Chief of the council's duties should be the organisation of local police, but here London failed, as she failed more than once in later times. The London records are full of weary complaints of " roarers " and bullies, in the time of Edward I. and Edward II. ; London has ever been prolific of names to describe its human pests. But parliament itself found a like difficulty in keeping control within a much smaller area, the very " palice " of Westminster. A statute was petitioned for, to prevent children playing in Westminster yard at " bars" or "snatch-hood," so as to disturb people desirous of going about their business in peace.

7. From the tallage rolls, which in several cases name in detail every item of furniture or property charged to the fraction on moveables, a good idea of the burgesses' comfort, or want of comfort, can be obtained. But it must always be remembered that just the articles which, to modern notions, might have been taxed most heavily, were those which a mediæval parliament of knights and burgesses exempted—for instance, several kinds of jewellery, armour, riding horses, and sometimes the provisions of all who were not merchants.

The injustice of the system of taxation which allowed of no graduation was observed by the political song-writers of the period. A man of £40 worth of goods " is laid to twelve pence round."

> And also much payeth another that poverty hath brought
>   to ground,
> And hath a heap of girls sittend about the flet (hearth).

Of the printed tallage inventories, that of Colchester is a fine example, showing what each has in "camera," in " domus," in kitchen, in brewhouse, and the like.   Beds, clothes, kitchen pots, cattle, pigs, firewood, and so forth, are all set down in minute detail with the valuation of each item ; the extremely slender lists of some household stock-takers may be due less to poverty than to judicious concealments or private arrangement with the collector.   But the very limited vocabulary of such lists is the most certain proof of the absence of household comforts.

8. The best evidence as to the nature and amount of organised social intercourse in towns and villages is derived from the records of fraternities, clubs or gilds.   The mediæval impulse towards organised association of every kind was no less strong, perhaps stronger, than that of later times.   Wherever a common interest bound together a handful of men and women, the idea of levying some little tax to serve a common object was seized upon by a few influential people, and a gild was formed with a code of written rules.   The common interest was very often an interest of occupation ; craftsmen were united by the interests of their craft, and palmers, pilgrims, kalendars, the rectors of London churches, the worshippers at a particular church, devotees of a particular saint's altar, traced back their association as a fraternity either " beyond memory " or to a given date, when certain named persons " founded " the gild.   Where no trade interest united the brethren and sisters (for in many cases sisters—usually wives of brethren only—were admitted), interest in certain

altar lights, desire for the insurance of funeral
expenses with proper "hearse" and tapers and masses
to release from purgatory, were common initial
motives : an annual dinner, a procession, in all the
glory of a " livery," the social position of the fellowship, would make the gild-roll of members long or
short, according as success or failure crowned the
founders' efforts. Rules of membership, of election,
an oath of submission to rules of a more or less
elaborate kind, were generally regarded as essentials :
and few indeed were the mediæval associations which
attached themselves to no special patron in the
Company of Heaven. Although a Pope had laid it
down that corporations are soulless, it were as
dangerous an oversight for an earthly corporation as
for an individual to omit to seek the spiritual favour of
either the head or a member of the divine Company.

The idea of attaching some charitable purpose to
the gild was sometimes, it would seem, rather the
result of its religious character than the result
of a deliberate purpose to insure men against
temporal dangers. Some gilds may have been rich
enough to propose to maintain all members who
had fallen into poverty, through no fault of their
own, but often in a poor gild the charitable purpose
was deemed sufficiently represented if it were agreed
to maintain *one* poor member at 1d. a day, or two at
½d. each. A rich gild maintained a chaplain of its
own in the church to which it was attached, and kept
up the church-books and vessels in a good state. The
government of these clubs gave the members a useful
education in account-keeping and constitutional forms,

for the rules and system of elections were often elaborate. In some cases the gilds were the means no doubt of enforcing a good deal of social and ecclesiastical tyranny, of dividing the sheep from the goats, as the London rectors put it. Many gilds were willing, where their own authority broke down, to invoke the episcopal power against an unruly member, handing him over to a summary conviction for perjury "absque strepitu et figura judicii," as the phrase ran. The church had no reason to look askance at the gilds; they were the best security for large "oblations" in the churches, for the presence of members at certain services, and a regular offering at a fixed tariff, were always required by rule. In return the bishop might see fit to offer an indulgence.

The fullers of Lincoln, founding their gild in 1297, combined, with trade rules on the processes of the craft and on the hours of labour, rules for a light before the Holy Cross, and church processions, and a clause on pilgrimages to St. Peter and St. Paul; if the pilgrims' start was made on a festival day all brethren and sisters went to the Eleanor Cross and gave them ½d. each. The palmers of Ludlow, twenty-seven men, founded their gild in 1284, with three chaplains, one to celebrate for the dead, one for the living, one for the honour of the Holy Cross. The assurance to members of help in trouble was in this case a first motive; dowries were provided for good girls of the gild, or means to enter a nunnery; members (men only) might attend wakes, but were forbidden to wear masks or to masquerade during the death-watch.

The gild in its various guises covered all the mediæval forms of locally organised association. Our vast modern associations in which the organisation is centralised and not identified with a single locality had no mediæval counterpart, unless we except perhaps some incipient beginnings of free-masonry. The gild in its various forms supplied to the people of the fourteenth century local clubs, local trade unions, and local friendly societies.

9. The expulsion of the Jews in Edward I.'s reign changed considerably the character of English town-life. The number of those who left the country was estimated by a contemporary at 16,511. The expulsion had been gradually led up to by a number of circumstances. The hold the Jews had got on English land by means of mortgages was so strong that a mediæval government could scarcely continue to tolerate it : the royal needs had for some time been supplied from other sources, and the odium attached to dealings with the Jews did not attach to dealings with Italian bankers, Christians who lent on the credit of the national taxes and customs duties. To relieve the landowners of mortgages, largely made in the De Montfort wars, all rent-charges held by Jews on landed estates were made invalid by a law of 1269. Next they were forbidden to hold real property in any form ; interest was made irrecoverable by law, and heavy amercements were taken. All these measures reduced the importance of the Jews, as they robbed them of the power to do business. Edward I.'s religious queen, and his mother

too, prompted by the friars, urged on the expulsion. The country paid a tenth to be rid of the poverty-stricken band, who had long ceased to be the great capitalists of Henry II.'s time. With customary mediæval barbarity a shipload of them was left to perish on a sandbank by a cruel shipmaster, who was, however, punished with death for this offence.

10. Little work of a satisfactory kind has yet been done to secure statistics for the population of England 1066–1350. Professor Maitland suggests 1,375,000 as a possible answer for 1086. Historians are still at issue as to whether the population in 1346 was five millions or two and a half.[1] The statistics of town populations rest in a like obscurity. Dr. Gross considers that 500 to 1,000 persons was a fair average in a prosperous borough : very few numbered 5,000.

11. Here this account of English mediævalism from the twelfth to the fourteenth centuries must close. Enough has been said perhaps to show that the mediæval spirit of religion and law, politics and commerce, is represented by nothing exactly parallel in modern times, although it has graven with a firm hand the lines that may be read like palimpsest.

It is idle to attempt to sum in a few words the final contribution. The ages of faith, art, chivalry, romance, of the foundations of modern law, language, commerce, the vigour and strength of that time are

[1] In 1328 France is believed to have had a population of about twenty millions.

known to us by reason of the permanence of its work. Wholly unlike the modern age in its social discomfort, it was nevertheless like ours, business-like, methodical and formal in ways that we are apt to ignore because its order is another than our own. Mediæval records prove often to be only too systematic, once the reader has apprehended what the system is. An age of religious devotion, even into faith business was permitted to enter : clerk and lay share equally the blame of the financial element which was allowed to corrupt religion. Corruption, competent judges will tell us, had eaten very deeply into mediæval society, yet the springs of life were not destroyed. We scarcely have the materials for a judgment on the measure of moral progress that may be traced to this period of history, but intellectual progress is well marked by the measure of constitutional growth. Yet no sun of new convictions making plainer the rule of life had risen above the horizon : the social changes working through the Black Death were soon to bring a faint glimmering.

Egoism was not then a prevalent vice : one can think of few who may keep Gerald of Wales company among the mediæval examples of that failing. The invaluable works of " Anon " are the product of old time for the most part : anonymity was fashionable then. Into the great crowd of the anonymous were content to fall most of the architects, artists, builders, benefactors, writers. And this perhaps because most mediæval works were the result of co-operation. A scribe who penned the whole of a great work might ask a prayer for his soul, or utter a desire for a cup

of wine for his thirsty body, at the end of his tedious
task, but too many hands were at work on the
volume for one man to be often able to put forward
a claim to it in his own name. This is also an
excuse for mediæval plagiarism. No one was greatly
concerned to know which part of a chronicle was
copy or epitome, which part original work.

Courage, and its occasional accompaniment,
cruelty, are thought of, not without reason, as the
typically mediæval virtue and countervailing vice.
But if the old courage was the courage of hot blood,
so also was the cruelty. The refinements of cold-
blooded cruelty belong to a later age. Torture had
scarcely yet been conceived as part of any legal
process. It was even ruled that a man should not
be fettered in court lest his chains should destroy his
self-possession.

The old respect for the oath was gone, as the
Statute of Winchester shows, and whether the respect
for truth (which, as has been aptly said, generally
stands in inverse ratio to respect for the oath) had
proportionately increased, is not yet clear. Historic
truth had become hopelessly overlaid by the romanticists, but in the more elaborate international
diplomacy of the fourteenth century, and in the law,
new ways were discovered for pinning men's imagina-
tion down to the prose of veracity.

An intensely artificial society, it had the qualities
and the defects of human artifice. It would fix for
ever the generations of men in unalterable relations :
but in this fixity there might be some security.
" Whosoever hath not, from him shall be taken even

that which he seemeth to have " was a doctrine less true of mediæval than of modern society. In the Middle Ages the idea of allowing free competition, whether in society or commerce, could not be formulated ; geographical conditions put it outside men's ken even as a possible generalisation ; and the local units, which had built up all that men knew of prosperity out of monopoly, could think in no terms save those of monopoly. But the mediæval monopolies had this merit—they were shared by locally organised groups and were not the property of an individual. The principle of association,—association on certain particular lines,—was strongly developed in these men : to hold apart from the fellowship, which had been formed to supply weak individuals with strength, was to court destruction. The principle of individualism had no attractions to offer. Not that disinterestedness and self-sacrifice were at all in vogue as favourite virtues ; far from it ; but in a society where the weak had so much to fear, even the comparatively strong found it well to pay the required fee and receive in return a certain amount of organised protection.

Besides the organised co-operation of those group units, formed for the purpose of defending an interest, of which I have spoken, there is evidence too of a certain spirit of genuine fraternity and fellowship among those prompted by interest to the creation of such unions, a fellow-feeling that was more than a fellow-hate ; and in this there lay something to sweeten the age, to dignify the humblest village and town life, to control the impulses of brute force.

With the past ages it is not as with individual men that the good is oft interred with their bones. What was sordid in them is forgotten, may rightly be forgotten, when we stand in the presence of the monuments which they have raised for themselves in all that is left to tell of their greatness.

CARDING HEMP AND ROPE-MAKING *C.* 1340.

CHRONOLOGICAL TABLE

WILLIAM I. 1066–1087

b. 1027, m. 1053 Matilda of Flanders, by whom he had Robert, William II., Henry I., Adela.

1066. Dec. 25th. William crowned at Westminster.

1067. Odo Bishop of Bayeux and William fitz Osbern left as viceroys while William went to Normandy.

1068. William I. crushes the insurrection in the west and besieges Exeter.

1069. William I. crushes the insurrection in the north and fortifies York.

1070. Lanfranc made archbishop : brings Gundulf from Rouen. The Tower begun about this time. Chester reduced.

1071. Hereward's rebellion crushed. Hugh the Wolf made Earl of Chester. Wars with the Welsh begin.

1072. William invades Scotland.

1073. William conquers Maine.

1074–5. Conspiracy of William fitz Osbern's son Roger Earl of Hereford with Ralph Guader Earl of Norfolk and Waltheof Earl of Northumberland.

1075. Danish fleet in the Humber.

c. 1076. William I. refused the oath of fealty requested by Pope Gregory VII. (Hildebrand).

1077–8. Rebellion of Robert against his father.

1079. Roger Earl of Shrewsbury obtains pardon for his son Robert Bellême who had joined Robert.

1081. William I.'s expedition to Wales.

1082. Arrest of Bishop Odo of Bayeux ; tried as Earl of Kent.

1083. Death of Matilda : a " mickle geld," 6s. on every hide.

1085. Domesday inquiry ordered.   Danish invasion threatened.
1086. All the landowners of England, whosesoever men they were, swore fealty to William I. on Salisbury Plain.
1087. Sept. 9th.   Death of William.

WILLIAM II.   1087–1100

b. 1060.

1087. Sept. 26th.   Crowned by Lanfranc at Westminster. William of St. Calais, Bishop of Durham, the King's private adviser.
1088. Rebellion of Odo of Bayeux and Roger Earl of Shrewsbury.   Siege of Rochester.   William II. aided by the English "fyrd."
Nov. Trial of William of St. Calais : his appeal to Rome.
1089. Death of Lanfranc : archbishopric kept vacant.
1090. War in Normandy.   Colonising of Wales.
1091. William II.'s expedition against Malcolm III. of Scotland.
1092. Carlisle colonised by William II.
1093. Anselm made archbishop after William's illness.
1094. War in Normandy.   Ralph Flambard, Bishop of Durham, is justiciar.
1095. Council of Rockingham.   Dispute with Anselm on the choice of a pope.   Rebellion of Robert de Mowbray, Earl of Northumberland.   Siege of Bamborough by William II.
William II.'s expedition to North Wales.
1096. Duchy of Normandy pawned to William II. while Robert went on crusade.   A geld exacted.   William's two expeditions to Wales.
1097. Quarrels with Anselm terminate in his departure.
1098. Robert of Bellême carries on William II.'s war in Maine.
1099. First court in the Westminster new hall.   William's march upon Le Mans.
1100. Aug. 1st.   William II. died in the New Forest.

HENRY I.   1100–1135.

b. 1068, m. 1100 Matilda of Scotland, by whom he had William, and
    Matilda : m. 1121, Adela of Louvain. Among his illegitimate children,
    Robert, Earl of Gloucester ; Richard and Matilda, both drowned with
    William ; Reginald of Dunstanville, Earl of Cornwall ; Juliana, wife
    of the Lord of Breteuil ; Sybilla m. Alexander King of Scots.

1100.   Aug. 2nd.   Henry hastens from the New Forest to
        Winchester and gains command of the treasury.
        Aug. 3rd.   The Witan choose him king.
        Aug. 5th.   Crowned at Westminster.   Issue of a
        charter, later the model of Magna Carta.   Henry the
        " Lion of Justice " prophesied by Merlin.
        Ralph Flambard imprisoned in the Tower.
        Anselm's return and refusal of homage.   Discussion
        postponed.   Henry's English marriage.
        Dec.   Escape of Flambard to Normandy.   Robert of
        Normandy's conspiracy.
1101.   Invasion of England.   Henry teaches the English
        "fyrd" how to fight.   Ivo of Grantmesnil's private
        war.   Escheat of his lands, given to Robert of
        Meulan, made lord of Leicester.
1102.   Rebellion of Robert of Bellême helped by the Welsh :
        he fortifies Bridgenorth : is expelled from England.
1103.   Anselm goes to Rome to push forward the investiture
        dispute.
1104.   Robert of Bellême, Robert of Normandy and William
        of Mortain make war in Normandy.
1105.   Caen and Bayeux won by Henry.   Heavy taxation.
1106.   Battle of Tenchebrai made Normandy a dependency
        of the English crown.   Flight of Bellême ; Duke
        Robert imprisoned and William of Mortain blinded.
1107.   Terms of the investiture compromise settled.   Roger
        Bishop of Salisbury becomes justiciar.   Flambard
        reinstated at Durham.   Carlisle and district or-
        ganised.
1108.   Death of Gerard Archbishop of York.   Monetary
        reform.
1109.   William " Clito " son of Robert of Normandy made
        the centre of trouble in Normandy.   Border warfare

with the king of France.   Death of Anselm, and the
archbishopric kept vacant.

1110.   Expulsion of rebellious barons from England.

1111.   Cardigan subdued by Gilbert of Clare.   Pembroke
colonised with Flemings.   War in Maine.

1112.   Capture of Bellême.

1113.   Homage done to Henry for Maine.

1114.   Matilda, Henry's daughter, marries the Emperor
Henry V.   Henry's Welsh expedition ; castles built.

1115.   Thurstan Archbishop of York refuses the oath of
obedience to Canterbury.

1116.   Great Council of Salisbury Plain, and oath of fealty
taken.   Dedication of St. Alban's.

1117.   Wars with the King of France, and the Counts of
Anjou and Flanders.   Defection of many lords.
Death of Queen Matilda.   Plot to assassinate Henry I.

1118.   The Templars' order begins to increase.

1119.   Henry besieges Breteuil, and Juliana discharges shot
at her father.   The tournament, in manner of battle,
at Brenneville, resulting in a success for Henry.
His interview with Pope Calixtus II. at Gisors.   The
sons of Robert Earl of Leicester dispute with the
cardinals.

1120.   Peace with Louis and the Count of Flanders.   Loss of
the *White Ship* with Henry's son and heir.

1121.   Marriage with Adela of Louvain.   Welsh expedition.

1122.   Henry visited Durham.

1123.   Rebellion in Normandy in support of William " Clito."
" Strong gelds and strong moots."
Canon William of Corbeuil made archbishop of Canterbury.   Alexander nephew of Roger of Salisbury
made bishop of Lincoln.

1125.   Coinage re-modelled.   Return of the widowed Empress Matilda.

1126.   The Council sworn to receive her as lady of England
and Normandy, in the event of Henry's death
without a male heir.   Louis again supports William
" Clito."

1127.   Count of Flanders supports Louis, but Henry detaches
Fulk of Anjou.

1128. Matilda the ex-Empress married Fulk's son Geoffrey. Death of William " Clito."
1129. Henry takes fines from the married clergy. Henry of Blois abbot of Glastonbury made bishop of Winchester.
1130. Consecration of the rebuilt Christchurch, Canterbury, and of Rochester. Henry receives Innocent II. at Rouen.
1131. Renewal of the oath of fealty to Matilda. Charter to London about this time.
1132. Austin canons put at Carlisle cathedral. Birth of an heir to Matilda. Renewed oath of fealty.
1133. Nigel made bishop of Ely, and Geoffrey the Chancellor bishop of Durham.
1134. Death of Robert of Normandy in prison.
1135. Death of Henry Dec. 1st. The "Constitutio Domus Regis" written.

STEPHEN. 1135–1154

Son of William I.'s d. Adela by Henry Count of Blois. b. 1097 ? m. 1124 Matilda of Boulogne, by whom he had William, Earl of Warrenne, d. 1140, Mary a nun, m. Matthew of Flanders, Eustace d. 1153, and others dying young.

1135. Dec. Repulsed in Kent, Stephen chosen king by the "aldermen and wise folk" of London. His brother Bishop Henry secures for him the Winchester treasury with the crown.
1136. Innocent II. recognises his sovereignty. David I. of Scots invades Northumberland on Matilda's behalf : is bought off. Great charter to the church. Exeter blockaded.
1137. Stephen received in Normandy.
1138. Stephen harries south-west Scotland. Robert of Gloucester rebels. Scotch invasion : Battle of the Standard : David defeated.
1139. Stephen arrests the Justiciar Roger of Salisbury and his son the Chancellor, and his nephews Nigel the Treasurer and Alexander Bishop of Lincoln ; their

castles besieged. The papal legate, Henry, cites his brother to answer the outrage at a church council.

The Empress lands near Arundel, and is given safe-conduct to Bristol (Earl of Gloucester).

1140. Siege of Ely (Nigel). Court held in the Tower, and only one bishop attends.

1141. Siege of Lincoln (Alexander). Stephen caught and sent to prison at Bristol. Church council declares him deposed by God's judgment. Robert of Gloucester caught and confined at Rochester. Exchange of Stephen for Robert. Matilda is acknowledged Lady at a church council at Winchester. Goes to London, and offends the citizens. Driven out, she flees to Oxford. Attacks Wolvesey Castle (Henry of Winchester) but is in turn blockaded. Stephen re-crowned.

1142. Tournament in Yorkshire. Matilda is besieged by Stephen in Oxford, and escapes.

1143. Stephen arrests Geoffrey de Mandeville, Earl of Essex.

1144. Campaign against Robert Earl of Gloucester.

1145. Death of Mandeville. Ralph Earl of Chester joins the king.

1146. Ralph gives up Lincoln castle.

1147. Death of Robert of Gloucester. Geoffrey of Anjou secures Normandy for Matilda.

1148. Matilda goes to Normandy.

1149. Young Henry lands in England. Earl of Chester's revolt. Vacarius forbidden to teach at Oxford.

1151. Earl of Leicester helps Henry. Death of Geoffrey of Anjou and succession of Henry to Normandy and Anjou.

1152. Stephen attempts to get papal recognition for Eustace his heir. Henry gets the duchy of Aquitaine by marriage.

1153. Henry's invasion and war. Death of Stephen's queen and of his son Eustace. Treaty of Wallingford secures Henry's succession.

1154. Oct. 25th. Death of Stephen.

HENRY II.   1154–1189

b. 1133, m. 1152 Eleanor of Guienne, by whom he had Henry, Richard I.,
     Geoffrey Count of Brittany, John, Matilda m. Henry of Saxony,
     Eleanor, m. Alphonso of Castile, and Joan m. 1. William II. of Sicily
     and 2. Raymond of Toulouse. Among his illegitimate children,
     Geoffrey, Archbishop of York, and William Longsword.

1154.   Dec. 19th. Coronation at Westminster. Charter, to
              church and state, reverting to Henry I.'s position.
              Demolition of castles. An English Pope elected.
1155.   Restoration of order.
1156.   Possession of Aquitaine secured.
1157.   Malcolm King of Scots made to give up Northumber-
              land, Cumberland and Westmoreland. Homage of
              Welsh princes.
1158.   Overlordship of Brittany secured. New coinage.
1159.   Overlordship of Toulouse claimed. Scutage for the
              Toulouse war ; and John of Salisbury dedicates his
              Polycraticus to the Chancellor Becket.
1160.   Normandy border strengthened by marriage of young
              Henry to Margaret of France.
1161.   Death of Theobald of Canterbury.
1162.   Becket made archbishop of Canterbury. He resigns
              the Chancellorship.
1163.   Council of Woodstock : disputes with Becket.
1164.   Constitutions of Clarendon on relations of church and
              state. Council of Northampton, to try Becket : his
              flight.
1165.   Welsh expedition.
1166.   Assize of Clarendon reorganises judicial arrange-
              ments : jury inquests : new assizes protecting free-
              holders, and curtailing powers of feudal courts.
1167.   Louis VII. shelters Becket. Brittany campaigns.
1168.   Revolt in Aquitaine. Politic marriages arranged.
              Death of the Justiciar Earl Robert of Leicester.
1169.   Treaty of Montmirail with Louis VII.
1170.   Inquest of Sheriffs : 7 only reinstated. Coronation of
              young Henry. Becket excommunicates the arch-
              bishop of York. Reconciliation and return of

Becket. Murder of Becket. Welsh knights' expedition to Ireland.

1171. Henry's Irish expedition. Court at Dublin.

1172. Henry's humiliation before the legates at Avranches, and absolution.

1173. Homage from Count of Toulouse. Young Henry's conspiracy, and grand league against Henry II. Civil war in England. Scotch invasion.

1174. Henry II. does penance at Becket's tomb. William the Lion caught and risings suppressed. Queen Eleanor imprisoned.

1175. May. Henry returns to England. Richard prior of Dover made archbishop of Canterbury. Young Richard sent to reduce Aquitaine.

1176. Assize of Northampton carries on the work of the Assize of Clarendon : oath of fealty required of all men, including villains.

1176–7. Dialogus de Scaccario written.

1177. Great inquest and tallage. John made lord of Ireland. Henry arbitrates in dispute between Castile and Navarre.

1178. Reorganisation of the Curia Regis.

1179. Retirement of Richard de Lucy : Richard of Ilchester and Geoffrey Ridel replace him. Council of Windsor and the Grand Assize, giving proprietary action in King's Court, to be determined by a jury, not by trial by battle.

1180. Ralph Glanville made Chief Justiciar. New coinage.

1181. Assize of Arms, reorganising militia or "fyrd."

1182. Disturbances in Aquitaine.

1183. Young Henry and Geoffrey of Brittany rebel against Henry II. and Richard. Death of young Henry.

1184. Assize of the Forest (Woodstock).

1185. John sent to Ireland. Queen Eleanor released.

1186. Death of Geoffrey of Brittany. Richard invades Toulouse. Henry II. takes homage at Carlisle.

1187. Saladin conquers Jerusalem.

1188. A tax on moveables, called the Saladin tithe, for a crusade of Henry II. and Philip. Richard transfers his homage to Philip.

1189. Philip, aided by Richard and John, expels Henry II.
from Touraine.
July 6th.   Death of Henry II.

RICHARD I.   1189–1199

b. 1157, m. 1191 Berengaria of Navarre.

1189. Sept. 3rd.   Coronation at Westminster.   Preparation
for the third crusade, against Saladin.   William Longchamp Chancellor.   Geoffrey made archbishop of
York.   Hugh de Puiset Bishop of Durham left in
charge of England.
1190. Longchamp made Chief Justiciar, and Bishop Hugh is
given jurisdiction in the North.   Hugh arrested by
Longchamp, who is both Justiciar and Chancellor
and papal legate.
1191. Walter of Coutances, archbishop of Rouen, sent to
England by Richard, to act for him.   Geoffrey of
York arrested by Longchamp's order.   The "communa" of London recognised.   Revolution, and flight
of Longchamp.   Walter of Coutances succeeds as
Justiciar.
1192. Return of Queen Eleanor.   Richard I. captured and
imprisoned.
1193. Richard's ransom raised.   John's plot with Philip of
France.   Return of Hubert Walter bishop of Salisbury from Richard I.   Made archbishop of Canterbury.   Truce with John.   Hubert Walter succeeds
Walter of Coutances as Justiciar.   John's homage.
1194. Release of Richard I.   Second coronation.   Reconciliation with John.   Tournaments licensed.
1195. General oath to keep the peace.
1196. William Fitzosbert's rising in London.   His death.
Unpopularity of Hubert Walter.   Richard begins
Château Gaillard.
1197. Assize of Measures.
Dec.   Bishop Hugh of Lincoln refuses a military
service.
1198. Richard I. retracts sentence against him.   Resignation

of Hubert Walter. Geoffrey fitz Peter succeeds him.
Tallage on non-military tenants.

1199. April 6. Death of Richard.

JOHN. 1199-1216

b. 1167, m. 1189 Isabel of Gloucester, 1200 Isabel of Angoulême, by
whom he had Henry III., Richard Earl of Cornwall, Joan queen of
Scotland, Isabella wife of the Emperor Frederic II., and Eleanor m.
1. William Marshal and 2. Simon de Montfort. Many illegitimate
children.

1199. Hubert Walter and William Marshal and fitz Peter
       govern in England while John secures his position
       in France.
       May 27th. Coronation. Hubert Walter Chancellor.
1200. Scutage, and carucage on every plough. Peace with
       France. John's progress.
       Oct. 8th. John and his new wife crowned. Progress
       to the North of England.
1201. Hubert de Burgh made warden of the Welsh Marches.
1202. John cited to appear before Philip in Paris. Raids on
       Normandy. John summons Arthur of Brittany to
       him. Arthur captured.
1203. Disappearance of Arthur. Invasion of Normandy.
1204. Death of Queen Eleanor. Loss of Normandy, Maine,
       Anjou, and Touraine.
1205. Oath of fealty required in England. Death of Hubert
       Walter. Disputed election at Canterbury.
1206. John's expedition to Aquitaine : Poitou regained.
1207. Innocent consecrates Stephen Langton archbishop.
1208. Interdict. Confiscation of clerical property.
1209. Papal order to excommunicate John not executed.
       No bishop in England except Peter des Roches.
       Llewelyn does homage at Woodstock.
1210. Persecution of the Jews. John goes to Ireland. Death
       of Maud de Braose by starvation. Cistercians
       heavily taxed.
1211. Pope excommunicates and threatens to depose John.
       North and South Wales unite to make war.
1212. Eustace de Vesci and Robert fitz Walter, baronial
       leaders, go to France, to join Philip.

1213. John forms alliance with enemies of Philip, *i.e.*, the Emperor, and the Counts of Boulogne and Flanders.

William Longsword's naval victory at Damme (May).

The Pope having charged Philip to expel John, in May John surrendered his crown to the Pope, was reconciled, did homage, and paid tribute. Langton received.

Assembly at St. Alban's ; Henry I.'s charter brought out by Langton at St. Paul's. Death of Geoffrey fitz Peter, succession of Peter des Roches.

1214. Defeat of John's allies at Bouvines and John's fiasco in Aquitaine and Poitou.

1215. John takes the cross. Barons collect an army and hold London. Magna Carta.

Legate excommunicates baronial leaders, and Innocent disallows the Charter. Barons offer the crown to Louis, son of Philip of France.

1216. John defeats the Northern barons. Louis lands, and takes Winchester.

Oct. 19th. Death of John.

HENRY III. 1219–1272

b. 1207, m. 1236 Eleanor of Provence by whom he had Edward I. Edmund Earl of Lancaster, Margaret m. Alexander III. of Scotland, Beatrice m. Duke of Brittany, and others.

1216. Oct. 28th. Coronation at Gloucester. Homage to the legate.

William Marshal made regent and governs with the legate, as guardian, and Peter des Roches.

Reissue of the Great Charter with modifications.

1217. Defence of Lincoln by Nicolaia. Hubert de Burgh destroys the French fleet. Departure of Louis.

Reissue of a modified Charter.

1219. Death of Marshal. Pandulph, Peter des Roches and Hubert de Burgh govern.

1220. Second crowning, at Westminster. Queen Isabella marries Hugh of Lusignan.

1221. William de Fors made to give up castles. Rebels

helped by the Earl of Chester. Langton gets rid of the legate. War on the Welsh border.

1222. Rising in London. Faukes de Breauté and barons oppose Hubert de Burgh's government.

1224. Louis VIII. invades Poitou and Gascony. Faukes besieged at Bedford and banished. Franciscans arrive.

Confirmation of the Charter preparatory to French war.

1225. Richard Earl of Cornwall sent to Gascony, which is recovered. Papal claim to " provisions."

1227. Henry declares himself of age. Continues Hubert as Justiciar. Peter des Roches on crusade. Charters ·renewed for fines. Earl of Chester and others rise in favour of Richard of Cornwall.

1228. English failure in Wales. Death of Langton.

1229. Papal demand of a tenth.

1230. Henry allies with feudatories hostile to Louis IX. and goes to Poitou.

1231. Death of William Marshal, and fresh Welsh war.

Return of P. des Roches.

1232. Fall of Hubert. Influx of Poitevin officials. Death of the Earl of Chester : break up of a great baronial power.

1233. Richard Marshal leads the barons hostile to the king : they attempt to remove Peter.

1234. Civil war and death of Marshal. Archbishop Edmund Rich gets rid of Peter and the Poitevins. Henry attempts to do without great state officials.

1235. Marriage of Henry's sister Isabella to the Emperor. Grosseteste made Bishop of Lincoln.

1236. Marriage of Henry and influx of Provençals.

Council of Merton. Henry recalls ministers.

1237. Attempt of the council to control expenditure. Influence of William of Valence the Queen's uncle.

1238. Secret marriage of Simon de Montfort with the king's sister. Death of Peter des Roches. Henry's attempt to make Valence bishop of Winchester. Valence dies.

1239. Flight of Simon de Montfort.

1240. Heavy papal exactions from the clergy : 300 English benefices given to Romans. Death of Archbishop Edmund.

1241. Boniface of Savoy uncle of the Queen made Archbishop : Savoyards and Provençals fill the court. Submission of David of Wales. Louis gives Poitou away. Death of Gilbert Marshal.

1242. Aid for the recovery of French possessions given conditionally.

1243. Return of Simon de Montfort. Fiasco in France, and king returns in triumphal progress.

1244. King applies for money to the council and a ministry is demanded ; Grosseteste stands by the opposition.

1245. Expedition against Wales.

1246. Grosseteste's remonstrance against the papacy. Henry pillages the Londoners. Death of Queen Isabella, Henry's mother. Her sons by her second marriage come to England.

1247. Further protests against papal exactions. Provençal brides given to English wards.

1248. De Montfort sent to govern Gascony. Money refused by the council.

1249. Henry sells his plate to the Londoners.

1250. Henry takes the cross and attempts economy.

1251. Simon asks for help in Gascony and is not properly supported.

1252. Henry asks for a tenth of the Church revenues, by papal mandate, for his crusade, and the bishops led by Grosseteste refuse. Asks for an aid (voluntary) instead. The Great Charter being mentioned, "he swore horribly." Renewal of the Assize of Arms.

1253. In return for money Henry confirms the Charter. King goes to Gascony. Death of Grosseteste.

1254. Under the Queen and Richard Earl of Cornwall, the knights of the shire represented in parliament, to report the amount of an aid. Crown of Sicily accepted for Henry's son Edmund. Pope in Henry's name makes war in Sicily. Edward made Earl of Chester and lord of Welsh lands and Ireland.

1255. Attempt to secure election of ministers.

Union of North and South Wales against the policy of young Edward.

1256. All persons owning property worth £20 a year forced to take knightly orders.

Pope claims annates and presses for his Sicilian money.

1257. Immense royal debt confessed.

Richard of Cornwall elected King of the Romans.

Discreditable Welsh peace. Pope threatens excommunication to recover his debts. Simon de Montfort leads the opposition.

1258. "Mad" parliament of armed barons at Oxford. Provisions drawn up and accepted. Government put in commission. Strong union of Welsh princes against the Marcher lords of the Council.

1259. Disputes among the baronial party. Provisions of Westminster to redress grievances. Henry at Paris relinquishes his claim to Normandy.

1260. Queen pelted with filth by the Londoners.

1261. Henry issues a proclamation against Simon's alien friends. At the queen's suggestion he gets absolved by the Pope from his oath to the Provisions. Earl Simon and Earl Richard of Gloucester summon representative knights of the shire to St. Alban's and the king summons them to Windsor.

1262. Death of the Earl of Gloucester : his successor Gilbert more friendly to Simon.

1263. Henry tries to keep the appointment of his household, contrary to the Provisions. Arbitration of Louis IX. invoked. Marcher lords come round to the king, because of Welsh interests and Edward schemes to protect the Marches.

1264. Louis's verdict is for Henry. War begins. King defeated at Lewes and taken prisoner with Edward. Council appointed to rule. Gloucester gets Pembroke and de Montfort Chester, with Edward's position. De Montfort allies with Llewelyn.

1265. Boroughs represented in parliament for the first time. De Montfort and Gloucester quarrel over Welsh

interests.   Escape of young Edward.   Battle of Evesham.   Death of Simon de Montfort.
1266. Siege of Kenilworth ; an amnesty to rebels.   Great forfeiture of baronial estates to the Crown.
1267. Gloucester seizes London but submits.   Provisions of Westminster enacted as the Statute of Marlborough.
1268. Edward goes on Crusade.
1269. Translation of St. Edward.   Great assembly at Westminster attended by burgesses.
1270. Londoners recover forfeited charters.
1272. Nov. 16th.   Death of Henry.

EDWARD I.   1272–1307

b. 1239, m. 1254 Eleanor of Castile by whom he had, of thirteen children, many of whom died young, Edward II., Eleanor m. Henry III. count of Bar, Joanna m. 1. Gilbert Earl of Gloucester and 2. Ralph of Monthermer, Margaret m. John Duke of Brabant, Mary a nun, Elizabeth m. 1. John count of Holland and 2. Humphrey Bohun Earl of Hereford.   Edward I. m. 2 Margaret of France, 1299, by whom he had Thomas of Brotherton Earl of Norfolk and Edmund Earl of Kent.

1272 Nov. 20th.   Fealty sworn to Edward in his absence.   Walter Giffard Archbishop of York and Robert Burnell rule.
1273. Edward lingers in Italy and Gascony.   Robert Kilwardby made archbishop of Canterbury.
1274. Aug. 19th.   Coronation.
1275. Statute of Westminster I., a code of fifty-one laws.   Customs on wools, wool-fells and leather granted.   Jews to live by merchandise.
1276. Legislation, supplementary to the Statute of Westminster.   Session attended by Francesco Accursi.   Castles of Flint and Rhuddlan built.
1277. Welsh war.   Llewelyn planning to marry Simon de Montfort's daughter.   His defeat and confinement to the Snowdon district : he keeps Anglesea.
1278. Visit to Glastonbury : Edward carries Arthur's bones.   Eleanor, those of Guinevere.   Distraint of knight-

hood.   Hundred Rolls drawn up.   Quo Warranto
inquiry to stop claims to jurisdictional franchise.
Resignation of Kilwardby.   The Pope selects
Peckham as archbishop.

1279. 267 Jews hanged in London.   Peckham offends
Edward.   Statute De Religiosis or of Mortmain.

1280. Further action against the Jews.

1281. Peckham struggles for ecclesiastical privilege unsuc-
cessfully.

1282. Renewal of Welsh war.   King's treasurer negotiates
with shires and boroughs for a grant.   Menai Straits
bridged.   Llewelyn killed.

1283. Capture of David of Wales.   His trial.   Statute of
Acton Burnell or of Merchants, facilitating recovery
of commercial debts.

1284. Conway castle built.   Statute of Rhuddlan : settlement of Wales.
A Round Table.

1285. Second Statute of Westminster, a code of fifty laws.
Ecclesiastical jurisdiction confined within limits.
Statute of Winchester re-enacts the Assize of Arms
and regulates the militia and police organisation.

1286. Edward goes to Gascony for three years.   Edmund
of Cornwall, Edward's cousin, left in charge.   Chancellor Burnell and the Great Seal with Edward.

1287. Edward expels the Jews from Gascony.

1289. The lords refuse a grant unless the king comes back.
Complaint against the judges and inquiry.   All but
two dismissed.

1290. Statute forbidding sub-infeudation.   Jews expelled.
Large grant.   Death of Eleanor, the king's wife.

1291. Overlordship of Scotland acknowledged.   Death of
Eleanor, the king's mother.

1292. Court at Berwick.   Baliol does homage.   Winchelsey
made archbishop but lingers abroad.

1293. Cinque Ports' fleet defeats the Normandy fleet.   Welsh
troubles.

1294. Edward's French fiefs declared forfeit to the French
crown.   War with France agreed on.   Seizure of
wool and coin.   Welsh troubles.   Continental alli-

ance bought.   Clergy try to get Statute of Mortmain withdrawn.   Separate negotiations with towns for money.   Shires represented in parliament.   Edward in Wales.   Beaumaris castle built.

1295.   French attacks on the Cinque Ports.   Model Parliament ; " that which touches all shall be approved by all." Representation of clergy, and commons. Large contributions of aid.

1296.   Scotch attack Carlisle.   Edward assaults Berwick. Baliol renounces fealty.   Conquest of Scotland in twenty-one weeks.   English clergy refuse a grant, because the Pope has made his licence necessary.

1297.   Outlawry of the clergy.   They make individual submission.   Defeat in Gascony.   The lords refuse to serve.   Risk of civil war.   Seizure of merchants' wool, and Edward goes to Flanders to attack Philip as planned, having issued a manifesto to the nation. The Regent, young Edward, confirms the Charter : no aids without consent of the realm : no extra tax on wool beyond the custom of 1275.   Meanwhile Wallace victorious in Scotland.

1298.   Truce with France.   Edward wastes the south of Scotland.   French marriage arranged.

1299.   The Scotch make Comyn regent for Baliol.   Disputes with the Council about Forest rights.

1300.   Articles added to the Charter, reforming judicial administration.   Forest reforms.   Edward in Scotland.   Death of Edmund Earl of Cornwall without heir.

1301.   Parliament of Lincoln.   Bill of twelve articles presented, bringing pressure on Edward.   Young Edward made prince of Wales.   Resistance to the demands of Boniface VIII. claiming Scotland as a fief of Rome.   Barons' letter to the Pope.   Historical statement of Edward's claim.

1302.   Large baronial estates lapse to the crown.   Edward in Scotland.

1303.   Victory for Comyn.   Edward again conquers Scotland and reaches Caithness.   Wallace executed.   Gascony formally restored to Edward.

1304.   Edward tallages his demesne lands without consent.
        Siege of Stirling, which surrenders.   Arrangements
        for the government of Scotland.
1305.   Young Edward in disgrace.   The Pope absolves
        Edward I. from his Confirmation of Charters, but
        advantage is not taken of it.   Scotch commission in
        London schemes a Scotch administration.
1306.   Departure of Winchelsey, after long disputes.   Rebel-
        lion of Bruce.   Distraint of knighthood.   Young
        Edward knighted.   Bruce defeated.   Earldom of
        Norfolk lapses to the Crown.
1307.   Statute of Carlisle.   Taxes on monasteries not to be
        levied by the Pope.   Petition for legislation against
        papal provisions.
        July 7th.   Death of Edward.

EDWARD II.   1307-1327

b. 1284, m. 1308 Isabella of France by whom he had Edward III.,
   Isabella m. Reginald Count of Guelderland, Joan m. David, King of
   Scotland ; and others.

1307.   July 31st.   Edward receives homage of some Scotch
        lords at Dumfries and turns south.
        Makes Gaveston Earl of Cornwall and betrothes him to
        his niece.
1308.   Feb.   Coronation of Edward and Isabella.   Banish-
        ment of Gaveston at the request of Lancaster,
        Edward's cousin ; but he is made regent of Ireland.
1309.   Intrigues for Gaveston's return.   The Pope absolves
        him from oaths : he returns.   Articles of grievance
        accepted.   Templars' lands confiscated.
1310.   Lords Ordainers appointed to control the king.
        Expedition to Scotland, by way of keeping Gaveston
        in safety.
1311.   Long list of reforms demanded and banishment of
        Gaveston.   He goes to Flanders.   The king's house-
        hold managed by a council.
1312.   Gaveston returns and war results.   Edward offers to
        recognise Bruce as king or to cede Gascony if he

can find allies for Gaveston. Gaveston caught and killed by Lancaster and Warwick. A party formed against Lancaster.

1313. Walter Reynolds, Edward's ally, made archbishop. Edward goes to Paris. Apparent reconciliation on his return.

1314. Bruce takes Edinburgh and Stirling, which alone had remained to England. Edward defeated at Bannockburn. Edward agrees to change his ministers. Lancaster leads.

1315. Edward's friend Despenser removed. Royal household reorganised. Ireland, Wales, Lancashire, in rebellion. Great famine. Scotch ravages.

1316. Lancaster in disrepute and his party broken. Private war between Warenne and Lancaster. Edward assembles an army nominally for Scotland.

1317. Papal "reservation" of bishoprics.

1318. Bruce takes Berwick and wastes northern England. New council formed. Ordinances confirmed.

1319. Edward and Lancaster besiege Berwick. Scots nearly capture the Queen at York. Truce.

1320. Hugh Despenser and his son are favourites : owing to their Glamorgan lordship disputes begin on the Welsh march with the Mortimers, strong in North Wales.

1321. Despensers banished by parliament. Defeat of their opponents the Mortimers on the Marches.

1322. Edward recalls the Despensers and wins at Boroughbridge. Thomas of Lancaster is caught and beheaded. The Mortimers imprisoned. Ordinances revoked and new ones issued in a great parliament with Welsh representatives.

1323. Truce for thirteen years with Scotland.

1324. Escape of Roger Mortimer to France : he makes friends with Charles IV., and rouses attack on Gascony.

1325. Isabella goes to represent Edward at the French court. An enemy of the younger Despenser, she allies with Roger. Young Edward sent to France.

1326. Hainault match arranged for young Edward, and men

and money provided there for Isabella. She and Mortimer (now her paramour) and Edward land in England. Edward II. retreats.

The Lancastrian connection joins Mortimer.

The elder Despenser hanged. Edward II. caught.

The younger Despenser hanged.

1327. Jan. 27th. Parliament in London. Articles drawn up against Edward. He is made to confess their truth and resign. Parliament renounces allegiance and chooses Edward the son.

EDWARD III.   1327-1377

B. 1312, m. 1328 Philippa of Hainault, by whom he had twelve children.

1327. Jan. 29th. Coronation. Henry Earl of Lancaster his guardian, but Mortimer and Isabella rule. Scotch ravages. Murder of Edward II.

1328. Claim to Scotland abandoned and truce made. Claim to the French throne entered during vacancy and Philip VI. chosen. Lancaster and the king's uncles oppose Mortimer.

1329. Edward, summoned to France to do homage, raises question as to its nature, reserving the point for discussion : Philip reserves the question of restitution of certain lands.

1330. Mortimer executes one of the king's uncles. Birth of an heir to Edward : supported by Lancaster he arrests Mortimer who is hanged.

1331. Edward acknowledges duty of liege homage for Guienne and Ponthieu but does not do it. Philip promises a partial restitution. Parliament favours negotiation, not war.

1332. Flemish weavers invited to settle. The knights of the shire begin to sit with the burgesses, and the lords by themselves. Edward tallages his demesne, but a subsidy is granted to prevent this.

Edward Baliol is crowned, and at Roxburgh meets Edward III. and acknowledges him lord of Scotland. Douglas leads the opposition.

1333.   Scotch defeated by Edward III. at Hallidon Hill.

1334.   Berwick annexed : plans to colonise it. Baliol gives Lothian to Edward and does homage : a party forms again round David II., a Bruce and a minor. Baliol driven out.

Edward reinstates him. Robert of Artois, Philip's enemy, received by Edward.

1335.   Edward rules Scotland and makes a chain of forts. The Scotch secretly helped by France. French invasion expected in England. Edward's seneschals in Guienne aggrieved.

1336.   Henry Earl of Lancaster appointed to command the army in Scotland.

Edward's seneschals expelled from the Agenois. Philip openly declares his intention to help the Scots. Fits a fleet with David Bruce and plunders the Channel Islands. Parliament grants money. Wool heavily taxed. Count of Flanders arrests English merchants in Flanders.

1337.   As a reprisal export of wool and import of cloth forbidden ; the Flemish people ally with Edward against their Count. Portsmouth burnt by the French. Alliances formed against Philip. May. Seizure of Guienne proclaimed. Edward takes the title of King of France (Oct. 7th), and names vicars-general, after issuing to the English the terms of peace he had offered to Philip. Cadsand taken by the English.

1338.   July. Edward sails for Antwerp. Allies not ready. Meets the Emperor, his brother-in-law, and is made his Vicar Imperial in provinces west of the Rhine. Philip buys off some allies.

1339.   Edward enters France but encounter avoided.

1340.   Edward quarters the French arms. No tallage may be levied without consent : large supplies granted. Naval victory at Sluys. Siege of Tournai. Philip challenged to single combat. Truce between England, France, and Scotland.

1341.   Attack on archbishop Stratford for mismanaging supplies. Scotch successes against Edward. Edward supports a claimant to the Duchy of Brittany.

1342.   Edward lands at Brest.   Encounter with him avoided.
1343.   Jan.   Truce for three years.   Pressure on Edward to
          yield constitutional points.   Attack on papal pro-
          visions.
1344.   Round Table.
1345.   Earl of Derby to command in Gascony.   Homage of
          the Brittany claimant.   Edward charges Philip with
          breaking the truce and declares war.
1346.   Invasion of Normandy.   To effect junction with
          Flemish allies, battle of Crecy.
          Defeat of the Scots at Nevill's Cross.   Capture of
          David II.
1347.   Surrender of Calais.   Compulsory loans.
1348.   Commons begin to decline responsibility for the war :
          petitions for redress of grievances.   Grant made
          conditionally.
1349.   Plague begins.   Ordinance fixing wages of labourers.
          Public business at a standstill.

INDEX

INDEX